Between Arab and White

AMERICAN CROSSROADS

Edited by Earl Lewis, George Lipsitz, Peggy Pascoe, George Sánchez, and Dana Takagi

Between Arab and White

*Race and Ethnicity in the Early Syrian
American Diaspora*

Sarah M. A. Gualtieri

UNIVERSITY OF CALIFORNIA PRESS
Berkeley · Los Angeles · London

University of California Press, one of the most distinguished university presses in the United States, enriches lives around the world by advancing scholarship in the humanities, social sciences, and natural sciences. Its activities are supported by the UC Press Foundation and by philanthropic contributions from individuals and institutions. For more information, visit www.ucpress.edu.

University of California Press
Berkeley and Los Angeles, California

University of California Press, Ltd.
London, England

Library of Congress Cataloging-in-Publication Data

Gualtieri, Sarah M. A.
    Between Arab and White : race and ethnicity in the early Syrian American diaspora / Sarah M.A. Gualtieri.
        p. cm.
    Includes bibliographical references and index.
    ISBN: 978-0-520-25532-6 (cloth : alk. paper) —
ISBN: 978-0-520-25534-0 (pbk. : alk. paper)
    1. Syrian Americans—Race identity—History.
2. Syrian Americans—Ethnic identity—History.
3. Syrian Americans—History.   4. United States—
Race relations.   I. Title.

E184.S98G835   2009
305.892'75691073—dc22   2009003364

Manufactured in the United States of America

18   17   16   15   14   13   12   11   10   09
10   9   8   7   6   5   4   3   2   1

The paper used in this publication meets the minimum requirements of ANSI/NISO Z39.48–1992 (R 1997) (*Permanence of Paper*).

For my brother Mark, 1963–2007
and our precious mother, Peggy, 1924–2008
"Go well, stay well"

Contents

Illustrations

Acknowledgments

This book has traveled with me to several different homes, and I am indebted to many people along the way. I thank my mentors at the University of Chicago for their support of the project in its earliest stages: Rashid Khalidi, Kathleen Niels Conzen, and Leora Auslander. To Rashid I owe special thanks for introducing me to the richness of modern Middle Eastern history and for instilling in me an appreciation for transnational perspectives. Michael Suleiman of Kansas State University provided advice that helped strengthen my argument. More generally, I am grateful for his pioneering work in Arab American studies.

I have been fortunate to teach in supportive environments where I benefited from the insights of colleagues and friends. Nancy Fix Anderson welcomed me to Loyola University New Orleans and helped me find my moorings there. In New Orleans I found friendship among a small group of people whose love for the "city that time forgot" moved and inspired me. I am still plotting adventures with Hana Safah and Susanne Dietzel, the pillars of that group. In Los Angeles, Eva Kanso, Clementine Oliver, Gil Hochberg, and Augie Robles have helped me work through challenges in my research while reminding me that it is sometimes more important to go to the beach. I thank them for their care and hospitality. Farika McCarron, my friend since childhood in Ottawa, has graced my life with her love and humor.

My move to the University of Southern California was a smooth one thanks to the warm reception of colleagues in the Department of History.

George Sánchez and Lois Banner have been exceedingly generous with their time. They both read drafts of the manuscript and gave me feedback that made it a better book. Ramzi Rouighi offered important suggestions at a crucial stage of revision. I am grateful for his input and for his irreverence. Lon Kurashige and Jason Glenn commented on different parts of the manuscript and gave me sound advice. I am grateful to Lori Rogers, Joe Styles, La Verne Hughes, and Brenda Johnson for helping me get over administrative hurdles. I thank Steve Ross for his encouragement and leadership as chair of the History Department. My colleagues, students, and the staff in the Department of American Studies and Ethnicity have been a wonderful source of intellectual comradeship. I always walked out of my chair Ruth Wilson Gilmore's office feeling fortified and ready to take on the next challenge.

I am also grateful for the financial support I received from the University of Southern California in the form of a Zumberge Research and Innovation Fund Award. Earlier fellowships from the Fulbright-Hays Commission of the Department of Education supported my research in Syria.

While research and writing can be a solitary enterprise, I am blessed to have found comrades in archives, universities, and conferences. I met Eliane Fersan in Lebanon in 2003 while she was writing her thesis on Lebanese emigration using French consular reports. We have, since then, shared documents, stories, and a passion for uncovering the history of the *mahjar*. I thank her for her friendship and enthusiasm for my project. I also thank Mona Khalidi, Carole Shammas, Maher Barakat, Guita Hourani, Akram Khater, Paul Tabar, Jeff Lesser, Michelle Hartman, Nadine Naber, Joseph Haiek, Sue Braovac, Tatjana Pavlovic, and Paul Ortiz for their support of my work. Kelly Aide opened his home to me and provided contacts for my research on Syrians and Lebanese in the South. Norman Lahood of Valdosta, Georgia, was gracious and helpful. George Lipsitz and Barbara Aswad wrote detailed readers' reports on the manuscript that were extremely useful and encouraging. Mary Severance, Elizabeth Berg, and Elisabeth Magnus guided me through the revisions with tremendous skill. It has been a pleasure to work with my editor Niels Hooper at the University of California Press.

This project could not have been finished without the assistance of the staffs at the numerous archives and libraries that I visited. I extend my thanks to the personnel at the Institut français d'études arabes de Damas, Maktabat al-Asad, the Ministère des affaires étrangères in Paris, the Immigration History Research Center, the Center for Migration Studies, the Smithsonian Institution, the State Archives of Florida, and Eastern Michigan University.

My greatest debt is to María Elena Martínez, whose brilliance continues to humble me. I thank her for her engagement with my work and for her love and support throughout this long journey. I am particularly grateful for her grace and kindness during the completion of this book, which corresponded to a very painful time for my family.

Finally, I would not have started on the scholarly path without the loving encouragement of my father, Nino, and mother, Peggy. They are my original mentors and faithful guides. No words can adequately convey the depth of my gratitude for their sacrifices, their intellectual curiosity, and their courage. My sisters Joanna and Julia have sustained me with their love and generosity. In addition, Julia's keen editorial eye saved me from many embarrassing errors. I dedicate this book to my dear brother Mark and to our precious mother, Peggy. My mother's gift of her luminous presence will forever radiate in my heart. Mark's own path in the academic world was a difficult one. He nonetheless always supported me and took pride in my endeavors. His winsome humor and sharp wit made me laugh when I needed it most. I hope he knew how much this meant to me.

Ottawa, summer 2008

Note on Terms
and Transliterations

I have used the term *Syria* in its late-Ottoman sense of *bilad al-Sham,* or geographical Syria: that is, the territory that now consists of the states of Lebanon, Syria, Jordan, and Israel/Palestine. Although the majority of persons who immigrated to the United States during the period covered in this book came from what is now Lebanon, they most often referred to themselves as "Syrians." I have therefore used this term instead of hyphenated terms like *Syro-Lebanese* or *Syrian-Lebanese. Mount Lebanon* refers to the territory comprising the northern and southern districts of the Lebanon range, which became an autonomous administrative unit (called *mutasarrifiyya*) in 1861. I use *Lebanon* to designate the French-mandated territory and the independent Lebanese Republic.

Arabic words are transliterated according to the system found in the *International Journal of Middle East Studies,* with certain modifications. Aside from *ayn* (ʿ) and *hamza* (ʾ), all other diacritical marks have been omitted. In cases where another spelling is commonly found in Western literature, I have followed that usage: thus "Beirut," not "Bayrut," and "Homs," not "Hims." I have transliterated individual and family names as the individuals themselves chose to do so; thus "Mokarzel," not "Mukarzal." Finally, names of newspapers and journals are transliterated and translated according to their mastheads. Translations of other materials are my own.

Introduction

Without being able to define a white person, the average man
in the street understands distinctly what it means, and would
find no difficulty in assigning to the yellow race a Turk or
Syrian with as much ease as he would bestow that designation on a Chinaman or a Korean.

James Farell, Assistant U.S. Attorney,
In re Halladjian (1909)

In December 1909, a twenty-three-year-old Syrian immigrant named
Costa George Najour appeared in Atlanta's circuit court to hear arguments related to his petition to become an American citizen. He had already filed his first papers and fulfilled the five-year residency and English
proficiency requirements of the U.S. Naturalization Law. The question
to be decided was whether Najour met the *racial* requirement of the law,
which dictated that, to acquire citizenship, persons not born in the
United States—that is, "aliens"—had to be either "free white persons"
or of "African nativity or descent."[1] Ignoring the possibility that Najour
was the latter, the lawyer for the government argued that he was not a
white person but "Asiatic" and that he could not, therefore, be accepted
into the American citizenry. Najour, with the help of his lawyer and a
Syrian voluntary association that mobilized to assist him in his case,
mounted a strong defense in support of his whiteness. The presiding
judge supported Najour's claim that Syrians were Caucasian and therefore white and admitted him to citizenship. Najour thus became the first
applicant for citizenship, among all ethnic groups, to successfully litigate
his status as a white person in a U.S. federal court. When the *Atlanta
Journal*'s reporter learned of the decision, the paper announced, "Najour
Is Now a Real Citizen," underscoring the link between whiteness and
full-fledged citizenship in the United States. Costa Najour later re-
counted how his victory in court helped establish that the Syrians were

"different from the Yellow race."[2] The debate on Syrian racial classification, however, was not over.

This book argues that questions about race were central to the construction of Syrian ethnicity in the United States in the first half of the twentieth century. It examines how Syrian immigrants were racialized by American politics, culture, and law and, as a result, came to view themselves in racial terms and position themselves within racial hierarchies. My analysis thus places Syrians, and Arabs more generally, at the center of discussions of race and racial formation, from which they have for too long been marginalized or ignored. Specifically, Syrians provide an important window through which to explore the problem of whiteness in the United States and in the broader Syrian diaspora in which racial claims were made.

To be sure, Syrians were not the only non-European immigrants to litigate their racial status in federal courts in order to gain American citizenship. Between 1878 and 1944, Chinese, Burmese, Armenian, Japanese, South Asian, Hawaiian, Mexican, and Filipino applicants all had their racial eligibility to naturalize challenged in the courts. Thirteen of these cases were heard before *Najour* and thirty-eight after. In all but one of these racial prerequisite cases (aimed at determining whether the applicant met the race requirement of the naturalization law), applicants petitioned for citizenship on the basis of membership in the white race. What constituted decisive proof of whiteness, however, was a difficult question to answer. Lawyers and applicants marshaled evidence that ranged from skin color to national origin, culture, scientific studies, and popular opinion—or some combination of these factors—to claim whiteness. It was up to the courts to decide which elements should be the basis for determining race and, by extension, eligibility to participate in the privileges of citizenship.[3]

Left unexplained in the literature on these cases is why Syrians were disproportionately represented (just under one-third) in the racial prerequisite cases heard in U.S. federal courts between 1909 and 1923. Why were members of this small immigrant community so heavily represented in cases that would have far-reaching consequences for delimiting the racial boundaries of American citizenship and national belonging? The answer to this question lies in how Syrians embodied, and then attempted to resolve, the tension between "scientific" and "common-knowledge" rationales for determining racial difference. Scientific rationales invoked the work of nineteenth-century ethnologists, notably A. H. Keane, who upheld Linnaeus's (1707–78) fourfold division of the human species, modified to *Homo Aethiopicus, Homo Mongolicus, Homo Americanus,* and *Homo Caucasicus.*[4] In contrast, common-knowledge rationales relied on the nebulous but strangely authoritative understandings of racial difference held by the "average man." When scientific and common-knowledge rationales reinforced each other the courts embraced them, but when they differed the courts jettisoned science in favor of common knowledge.[5] This pattern was evident in the two most important racial prerequisite cases heard by the U.S. Supreme Court, those of Takao Ozawa and Bhagat Singh Thind. In the *Ozawa* case, heard in 1922, the Court ruled that Japanese persons were not Caucasian and thus not eligible for citizenship. In the *Thind* case, heard one year later, the Court revealed its displeasure with the all-too-inclusive category "Caucasian" and argued that although Indians *could* be considered Caucasian they were not white in the understanding of the common man. These decisions had disastrous consequences in the lives of Japanese and Indian immigrants, including the stripping away of citizenship, or denaturalization, of some of them. Syrians avoided this draconian fate. Their successful litigation of their whiteness was due to their ability to fashion themselves as among those thought to be white in the understanding of the common man. The processes of how they did so are at the heart of this book. I trace how Syrians raised money, hired lawyers, and formed associations to lobby for their whiteness. The racial prerequisite cases in fact provided the first major impetus for community mobilization across religious lines and on a national level. "The Syrians of America," wrote Salloum Mokarzel, editor of a Syrian American journal in 1928, "were piqued at this slight to their race and banded together for common defense. That was one of the rare instances in their history when they brushed aside their petty causes of difference and rose in common and with the closest approach to unanimity to engage in the task of self-defense. And they won."[6]

Syrians were able to offer evidence of their economic success, including their acquisition of property, as proof of their ability to perform whiteness—to do what successful white people were expected to do.[7] Finally, in a U.S culture so heavily infused with Christian moral superiority, Syrians effectively used their membership in the Christian fold to make religious and civilizational arguments in favor of their whiteness.[8] In 1909, H. E. Halaby, for example, wrote a letter to the editor of the *New York Times* in which he argued, "The Syrians are very proud of their ancestry, and believe that the Caucasian race had its origin in Syria, that they opened the commerce of the world, and that Christ, our Saviour, was born among them, in which fact the Syrians take high pride."[9] Muslim applicants for citizenship could not make the same connections to Christianity, and their whiteness was therefore harder to prove and historically harder to sustain.

Racial classification was not an affair of the courts only. Legal decisions were influential in producing and disseminating a discourse on race, but they alone cannot explain how and why Syrians generated knowledge about themselves as racial beings. They do not fully answer the question of why Syrians were actors in the production of racial categories. In addition, the naturalization cases suggest a teleology toward whiteness, while a focus on other sites of interaction—such as stores, restaurants, and workshops—reveals patterns of Syrian racial instability and of "inbetweenness."[10] That is, even with their victories in the courts, Syrians continued to be perceived as not fully white but somewhere in between the poles of "Asian" and "black" in American racial schemes. For example, by 1924, when Congress passed the National Origins Act, which severely restricted immigration of non-Europeans into the country, Syrians were considered white "by law" and were accorded the privileges that whiteness conferred, such as the right to become citizens, vote, and to purchase property. However, nativists repeatedly questioned their suitability for assimilation in American society in terms drawn from racist discourse. The North Carolina senator F. M. Simmons, for example, referred to Syrian immigrants as the "degenerate progeny of the Asiatic hoards [sic] . . . the spawn of the Phoenician curse."[11] The white supremacist Ku Klux Klan (KKK) used intimidation and violence to challenge the presence of Syrians in the United States. In 1923, members of the KKK dynamited the home of a Syrian family in Marietta, Georgia, and they were more than likely involved in the lynching of Syrian grocer Nola Romey in Lake City, Florida, in 1929.[12]

This book studies these tensions in the history of Syrian experiences of race during the first phase of their migration and settlement in the United States. It analyzes the ways in which Syrian immigrants (the first Arabs to immigrate to the United States, and the largest group among them until World War II) came to view themselves in racial terms and position themselves within racial hierarchies as part of a broader process of ethnic identity formation. For answering the question "To what race do we belong?" involved not only legal and popular interpretations of race but also immigrant concerns about gender roles and family, fear of violence at the hands of nativist groups, and the interplay of homeland and host country solidarities. It is around this last issue that my examination of Syrian immigrants seeks to push beyond the current paradigm of critical whiteness studies. The tendency in this literature has been to argue that immigrant attachment to whiteness was inextricably connected to desires to become American. In the important formulation of the historians David Roediger and James Barrett, " 'Becoming white' and 'becoming American' were intertwined at every turn."[13]

Yet in the case of Syrians the battle for whiteness, conceived as a battle for citizenship, allowed them to connect to the homeland and to a wider Syrian diaspora. Immigrants used their American citizenship to travel back to Syria and Lebanon and to petition the U.S. government for assistance in securing the independence of these countries. Questions about the racial classification of Syrians were not confined to the United States but occurred in Brazil, South Africa, Australia, New Zealand, Britain, and France—that last of which had especially close ties to Syria and Lebanon and became the colonial power there after World War I. Through family networks, community associations, and the Arabic-language press, Syrians shared information and fine-tuned their arguments about race on the basis of their experiences in different countries. In 1928, for example, Syrians in the United States promised "some of our best legal talent" to help their compatriots in New Zealand secure their right to white citizenship. Salloum Mokarzel warned that "the fight now looming on the horizon in New Zealand should be watched with special interest as it is the latest development in what seems to be a world-wide outburst of antipathy against the Syrians."[14]

It is thus impossible to understand Syrian engagements with race in the United States without situating them in a wider diasporic and transnational framework. Accordingly, I view the Syrian prerequisite cases as a way to explore a wider range of processes that include immigrants' participation in defining their racial identity, the circulation of racial ideas in the context of shifting patterns of world migration, and the impact of diasporic identities on communities of origin. This book aims not only to incorporate Syrians into critical studies of whiteness but to transcend these studies by emphasizing the transnational connections in this particular group's construction of an ethnic identity within a U.S. racial order and racial economy.

RACIALIZATION AND ARAB IMMIGRANTS

Throughout this study, I consider race a historically contingent category that acquires meaning within specific relations of power. Since the early modern era, race has been used to mark groups of people as different on the basis of presumed fixed biological or cultural traits. Yet what constitutes difference, and why, changes over time. Africans, for example, first came to America with specific identities rooted in tribal and linguistic groupings. They were primarily Mande, Ibo, Ovimbundu, and Akan. American law, writings, and social practice extended the term *Negro,* and then *black,* to them, a practice that masked these specific identities in favor of homogenizing categories that served the political and economic demands of chattel slavery. Africans were thus "made into" a race, or racialized.[15] More specifically, as Cheryl Harris argues, because blacks were subjugated as slaves and treated as property, whiteness began to mark those who were "free" or, at a minimum, not subject to enslavement. Thus "the ideological and rhetorical move from 'slave' and 'free' to 'Black' and 'white' as polar constructs marked an important step in the social construction of race."[16]

Just as blackness has a certain historicity, so too does whiteness. Early American colonialists, for example, thought of themselves as Christian, English, and free before they gravitated toward a self-identity as white.[17] W. E. B. Du Bois—scholar and founding member of the National Association for the Advancement of Colored People in 1909—pioneered the historical discussion of modern whiteness when he studied the reasons behind the racism of white workers, a stratum of the population that was itself subordinated and exploited. His argument that their whiteness functioned as a "psychological wage"—a form of compensation rewarded for not being black—has shaped a newer body of scholarship that investigates the dynamics of whiteness. This scholarship has emphasized the invented quality of whiteness by examining how immigrant groups claimed, appropriated, and ultimately defended the status of being white.[18] A central goal of this literature has been to render whiteness visible, to recognize it as a racial construct, to have "it speak its name."[19] Most importantly, scholarship on whiteness argues that white identity is constituted through the exercise of power and the expectation of acquiring material advantages such as property.[20]

Syrian Arabs are an especially appropriate group to study through the lens of whiteness, for they did not have firmly established racial identities prior to migration, yet they gradually began to value whiteness once they settled in the United States. Originally, their primary identities were framed in religious terms. The majority belonged to one of three major Eastern rite churches (the Maronite, Antiochian Orthodox, and Greek Catholic, also known as Melkite), while a minority were Muslim (of the

Sunni, Druze, and Shiʿa branches of Islam). A small number of Syrian Protestants (mainly Presbyterian) and Jews migrated to the United States as well. In addition to religious ties, family and village solidarities were central elements in Syrian self-definition. In the United States, Syrians both amplified and muted these attachments as they adapted to life in different U.S. communities. They did so within a broader American culture that was peculiarly obsessed with race and, in many ways, fascinated by the "Orient."

It is thus not surprising that one of the first sites to generate understandings of Syrian racial classification was the 1893 World's Fair in Chicago. Syrian and other Arab participants performed as part of the exotic displays of Midway Plaisance, a place of imperialist racialized fantasies run amok. Here a contemporary catalog described the "bright-eyed, half-clad, brown boys in dirty little robes" of the "Streets of Cairo" exhibit, where a series of latticed windows "seems to suggest the secrecy of the seraglio . . . and engenders visions of peeping Circassian beauties and black-faced eunuchs."[21] The earliest depiction of the Syrian enclave in New York City, published in 1892 in the *New York Daily Tribune,* also emphasized themes of exoticism and racial otherness. Entitled a "Picturesque Colony," the article's headline announced: "What May be Seen in a Walk through lower Washington St.—A young but growing community with some queer customs."[22] The author of the article began his description with an attempt to classify the Syrians using a mix of phenotypical and behavioral traits: "With their brown complexions, medium stature, lithe, wiry and muscular forms, keen, dark, restless eyes, the people composing this group plainly show their Eastern origin." Relying on the language of mystery, culled from the repertoire of Orientalism, the article asserted that "all through the colony, glimpses of a life foreign to America may be seen, and the veil of mystery which has ever hung over the peoples and countries of the Orient has one little corner lifted in this section of town." To assist the readers in "lifting the veil of mystery," the newspaper provided small illustrations of Syrian life along Washington Street, including a barber at work, an ice cream maker, and the masthead from the first Arabic-language paper published in New York, *Kawkab Amirka* (Star of America). The article ended with a prediction that over time the Syrians would lose their foreignness, "learn American ways and manners, . . . and [become] a factor in the body politic which will make itself felt for good."[23]

As was the case for other immigrant groups, Arab American history began in circumstances that were powerfully shaped by race.[24] The

presence of Syrians in northern cities sparked curiosity about their racial
status, while across the United States Syrians were themselves made aware
of the saliency of race. In the South, in the areas least studied by historians of Arab immigration, Syrian peddlers ventured between segregated
areas to sell buttons, thread, and other household needs to African Americans and native whites. Syrian impressions of these encounters are hard
to access, for many did not leave behind written records that indicate
what they themselves thought about race, but race is there nonetheless in
the early history of Arab immigration and settlement in the United States.
Traces of its importance are revealed in travelogues and in the question-
and-answer sections of Middle Eastern newspapers, where confused immigrants write home asking, "To what race do we belong?" Syrian perceptions of their racial superiority to blacks are exposed in oral histories
with remarks such as "We moved because the coloreds took over the
neighborhood." In other instances, pained silences surrounding threats to
livelihood by native whites suggest how Syrians themselves have endured
racial discrimination. These silences have more recently given way to a
willingness and proud insistence to be heard.[25]

RACE AND ARAB AMERICAN STUDIES

Arab American studies is a small and relatively new field. At this writing, the University of Michigan at Dearborn and Ann Arbor house the
only programs in Arab American studies in the United States, and very
few ethnic studies programs offer courses that deal with the Arab American experience. Since the last writing, the University of Michigan at Ann
Arbor has added a concentration in Arab American studies within its
program in American culture. The field emerged as a response to the
near-erasure of Arabs from narratives of immigration and assimilation
in the United States, and it continues to face constraints related to the political climate in which scholars and practitioners write, research, and
speak. Much of the early scholarship on Arabs in the United States was
published by the Association of Arab American University Graduates
(AAUG), formed in 1967 in the wake of the Arab-Israeli war to mobilize
Arab Americans in the political arena and to combat discrimination and
the proliferation of negative stereotypes in the mainstream media. A sister organization, the American-Arab Anti-Discrimination Committee
(ADC), successfully persuaded the publishers of Roget's *Thesaurus* to remove as synonyms for *Arab* the words "hobo, tramp and vagrant"—an
effort that had to be repeated in 2005 with the release of the online edi-

tion.[26] These organizations were less successful with the Hollywood film industry, which has regularly employed insidious images of Arabs in its movies and seems oblivious to the fact that real Arabs, leading ordinary, productive lives, reside in the United States. Instead, Hollywood relies on the terrorists and harem girls of its imagination.[27]

The first monographs and edited volumes on Arabs in America fell within the celebratory tradition of immigration studies, a tradition that focused on the ability of an ethnic group to maintain a distinctive culture while assimilating into a mainstream American core. This "tactical appeal to sameness" in Arab American studies emphasized the Americanness of Arab immigrants and their children and, in particular, their rapid incorporation into the middle class through English language acquisition, home ownership, and the production of high numbers of educated and successful professionals, including celebrities like Casey Kasem, Paul Anka, and Helen Thomas that non-Arabs admire.[28] This appeal to sameness also aimed to counter the pervasive and deliberate vilification of Arabs in the American media, educational system, and government.[29]

The preoccupation with defending a culture under siege in the United States, however, has constrained Arab American scholars and consumed their time, impeding more thorough explications of Arab culture here and abroad. Writing as a Muslim Arab academic beginning her career in the United States, Leila Ahmed describes feeling "compelled to take that [defensive] stand," in this case to challenge Western feminist assertions that Islam is intrinsically misogynist. No less than Western feminists, she asserts, Arab feminists need to feel free to criticize their societies, but they often refrain from doing so because of pervasive anti-Arab and anti-Muslim sentiment in the United States. She states: "In addition to compelling us to devote much time and energy to pointing out that Western so-called knowledge about the Middle East consists largely of a heritage of malevolently fabricated mythologies, it is also impossible, in an environment already so negatively primed against us, to be freely critical—a task no less urgent for us than for Western feminists—of our own societies. For to be critical in such an environment would be an act of complicity and would make of us collaborators in an exceedingly dishonest and racist process."[30]

The emphasis on assimilation emerged not only from the scholarly observation of empirical data like intermarriage and language of the household but also from a concern that alternative approaches—including studies of internal cleavages within Arab communities—would expose those communities to derision. The emphasis on assimilation, however, led frequently to an uncritical acceptance of whiteness within Arab American studies. For most scholars of Syrian and Lebanese immigration to the United States, the racial prerequisite cases were simply an unfortunate chapter in the otherwise successful history of first-wave immigrant assimilation in the United States. "The events of those few critical years," wrote Alixa Naff, "constituted an aberration," which "hardly dented the spirit of self-esteem of the Syrians."[31] Syrians had, in other words, surmounted an annoying obstacle in the path of full-fledged integration into the American mainstream. While an important response to constructions of Arab Americans as foreign and unassimilable, this celebratory approach avoided discussing the implications of claiming whiteness.

In the 1990s, several scholars moved away from a focus on assimilation and the uncritical acceptance of whiteness to highlight divergent paths of Arab American acculturation and racialization. They used terms such as *honorary whites* and *not quite white* to describe the experience of Arab Americans who are without official minority status yet clearly situated outside the white majority.[32] This scholarship demonstrates, in particular, how the racialization of Arab Muslims in the United States has been accompanied by hate crimes in the form of arson, vandalism, and bombings just as the dehumanization of an Arab "Other" outside U.S. borders has bolstered a policy of aggression and occupation.[33]

There is indeed an urgent need for scholars and activists to study and speak out on patterns of violence, stereotyping, and degradation that vilify a whole class of people. There is also a need to study how anti-Arab racism developed historically and to examine the ways in which different Arab groups have negotiated the politics of race. Doing so reveals how racial constructs are never entirely new but rather are built on the sediment of the past.[34] The arsenal of negative stereotypes deployed against Arabs in the wake of the attacks of September 11, 2001, were not new but had been used for over a century to defame them. Yet it would be a mistake to argue that the blowing up of a Syrian grocery store in 1923 in Marietta, Georgia, and the killing of a store clerk thought to be an Arab (he was Sikh) in the spate of hate crimes after September 11 were manifestations of the same old unchanging anti-Arab racism in the United States. Race and racism are historically contingent, and the conditions that produced anti-Arab sentiment in both these cases are worth exploring not only for their similarities but also for their differences. Recovering this history helps clarify how Syrians confronted and fought exclusionary practices on the part of the state and sectors of American society, but it also demonstrates how first-wave Arab immigrants (the vast majority of whom were Syrian) participated in legal discourse and everyday social practices intended to mark them as different and more suited for national integration in America than nonwhites, specifically blacks and Asians.

The invidiousness of race in the history of Syrian immigrants in the United States is that many were victims of racism and, at the same time, attempted to challenge it by claiming sameness with the peoples and institutions that perpetuated it. Simply arguing that this was a strategic move on the part of Syrians at a moment of crisis, as some scholars have done, minimizes the importance of racial ideology in the construction of early Syrian American identity.[35] Such an argument also minimizes the fact that the process of claiming whiteness was uneven and contested: in certain instances Syrians participated in white supremacy, but in others they resisted it and forged alliances with people of color. My goal is to elucidate these evolutions and contradictions and to demonstrate how Syrian racialization intersected with other dimensions of social identity. Questions about nation, religion, and family were especially salient in this regard.

THE LAND OF SYRIA

This book focuses on the Syrian population because they were the first Arabic-speaking immigrant group to arrive in North America in the late nineteenth and early twentieth centuries. At this time Syria did not exist as an independent nation, and the term was used by local inhabitants and government authorities to describe the area stretching from the Taurus Mountains in the north to the Sinai Peninsula in the south. Its western border was the Mediterranean, while its fluctuating eastern boundary lay in the desert of present-day Syria close to Iraq. This area came under the authority of the Ottoman Empire in 1516 and remained under its control until the empire's demise after World War I. As part of the postwar settlement, Greater Syria was divided up between the victorious powers, Britain and France. Britain assumed the Mandate, or trusteeship, over Palestine and Iraq, while France acquired Syria and Lebanon. Only after World War II did these territories, with the exception of Palestine, acquire their full independence. Today, the area that was once "Greater Syria" consists of the nation-states of Syria, Lebanon, Jordan, Israel, and the Palestinian Authority.[36]

Throughout most of the Ottoman period, Syria was divided into four administrative provinces (called *vilayets*), named after the cities at their center: Aleppo, Tripoli, Damascus, and Sidon. In the second half of the nineteenth century, as part of a broad program of reform, the Ottomans made several important administrative changes in the region. In 1861, the Ottoman central government created the administrative district of Mount Lebanon, or *mutasarrifiyya* of Jabal Lubnan, which encompassed the area lying roughly between the Barid River in the north (above Tripoli) and the Zahrani River in the south, just below Sidon. On the eastern edge of the administrative district of Mount Lebanon ran the Litani River, and on its western edge lay the Mediterranean. In short, the *mutasarrifiyya* included the villages and towns of the coastal plane and the Lebanese mountain range—an area of about two thousand square miles. It did not include the major port cities of Beirut, Acre, and Tripoli, which all became part of the *vilayet* of Syria in 1864.[37] In 1888, Beirut became its own province, incorporating Latakia, Tripoli, southern Lebanon, and northern Palestine. For the next thirty-two years, until the empire's demise, Greater Syria was administratively divided into three provinces (Aleppo, Syria, and Beirut) and three autonomous districts, or *mutasarrifiyyas* (Jerusalem, Dayr al-Zawr in eastern Syria, and Mount Lebanon).[38]

Because of social and economic changes in Mount Lebanon, related in large part to the vicissitudes of the silk industry, this area had a high rate of migration to the Americas. By some estimates, as many as three hundred thousand persons had left Mount Lebanon by 1914, or roughly one-third the total population of the area.[39] However, other towns outside the administrative district—including market towns situated both in modern-day Lebanon and Syria—sent large numbers of emigrants abroad. I have therefore used the broader term *Syrian* to refer to these migrations, both to respect the contours of geographic Syria and because this term appears most consistently in Arabic, English, and French sources to describe the persons immigrating to the Americas in the period under investigation.

Within the historiography, this period of migration has been described as one of rapid assimilation of the Syrian immigrant community in the United States as it transitioned from an itinerant peddling group to a middle-class minority concentrated in the commercial enterprises of dry goods and groceries. Alixa Naff, for example, argues in her pioneering work *Becoming American* that Syrians arrived as sojourners but quickly discovered America's "entrepreneurial Eden." Rather than return to an un-

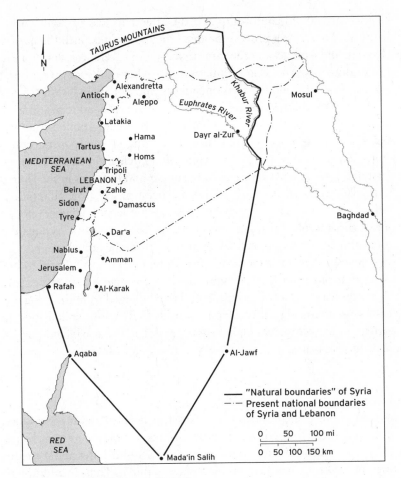

Figure 1. Map of "Greater Syria."

certain future in their homeland, they chose to remain in the United States. Through business acumen and perseverance they achieved middle-class success—an indication of their assimilation into the American mainstream.[40] While Naff and other scholars applauded the initiative and work ethic of the early immigrants and their children, they lamented the loss of a distinctive Syrian Arab identity.[41]

This scholarly emphasis on assimilation, however, obscures the intense debates over what it meant to be Syrian in America in the early period of migration and settlement in the United States. Rather than characterize the history of Syrian immigrants during this period as a gradual slide toward Anglo-conformity and the attendant loss of "old world" identities, I describe a process in which they actively defined themselves as Syrian and American at the same time. A more useful category for understanding this process is "ethnicization"—that is, the construction of a sense of peoplehood vis-à-vis outsiders—and not assimilation.[42]

This book explores two central questions in Syrian ethnicization: To what race did they think they belonged and to what nation? Syrian immigrants posed and answered these questions in newspapers, coffee shops, churches, mosques, courtrooms, and kitchens in an effort to understand how their lives were at once similar and different in the United States. They thus became involved in a process of selection, adaptation, and acculturation, and in each case new self-understandings developed out of the interplay of homeland and migratory identities. Syrians did not simply transplant a fixed set of customs from the homeland, nor did they quickly "become American" once settled on U.S. soil. Rather, they used what they had brought with them to become Syrian American. Their ethnicity was a collective identity that emerged from their engagement with distinct, yet overlapping worlds.[43] Religious solidarities, in particular, helped Syrians make sense of racial and national belonging in the United States.

THE NATION IN THE *MAHJAR* (DIASPORA)

Syrians in the United States participated in debates about their racial identity in order to become American citizens, yet they were also, sometimes simultaneously, drawn into a broader set of debates about the future of the Ottoman polity and their place within it. Thus, in addition to the question of race, the second problem around which Syrian ethnicity articulated was the status of the "Arab nation" and emigrants' connection to a homeland national community.

The issue of diasporic nationalism is surprisingly underinvestigated in both Middle Eastern and Arab American studies. Historians of the Middle East have long been consumed with the development of Arab nationalism (in its multiple forms), and many have acknowledged that nationalist thinkers lived, wrote, and organized from the *mahjar* (the diaspora).[44] However, there is no developed historiography on how the experience of migration, or even exile, influenced specific trends within national movements. Lebanese national myths, for example, incorporate ideas of migration and of the diaspora's role in building a modern merchant republic, while Palestinian nationalism evolved under conditions of exile, of forced migration. These are but two examples of the conceptual connections between the emergence of Middle Eastern nationalism and the practice of, and discourse around, migration.

Scholarship on Arab Americans has likewise avoided the relationship between migration and national identity formation, perhaps an unintended consequence of the commitment to an assimilation paradigm, which has emphasized how immigrants became American, not Syrian, Lebanese, or Palestinian. A few scholars have noted immigrant support of homeland causes and elite involvement in national politics, but in every case they assume that the nation and the diaspora are two distinct entities. The homeland, in other words, is conceived as bounded by a territory and historicity away from its emigrants, who reside "over there" in other nations.

Yet migration and ideas about the nation are very much connected.[45] During Europe's great age of nineteenth-century nationalism, migration was a demographic fact of life, and the new nation-states of Italy, Germany, and Poland sought to claim and "nationalize" their emigrants.[46] Under a new law passed in 1913, for example, Germany extended citizenship to the descendants of Germans living abroad, while it restricted citizenship to the children of alien workers born on German soil. In contrast, Italy embraced the principle of *ius soli* in its first census after unification in 1861 by counting all those born in Italy as citizens whether they lived there or not. In both the German and Italian cases, the central government viewed emigration as part of empire building, and emigrants were thus potential conduits of influence abroad.[47]

High rates of mobility also help explain why exile was often the main place of incubation for new national movements. It was not mere coincidence that the future president of Czechoslovakia signed the agreement uniting the Czechs and Slovaks in a single nation-state in Pittsburgh, not Slovakia, or that the Republic of Cuba was founded in New York, under the leadership of José Martí and the Cuban Revolutionary Party, and that the first Arab Congress was held in Paris.[48]

Migration, mobility, and exile are also important themes in the history of Arab nationalism. ʿAbd al-Hamid al-Zahrawi, Rafiq al-ʿAzm, and Rashid Rida, for example, were members of a large "political migration" of Syrian intellectuals to Cairo, a city that, along with Damascus and Beirut, was bustling with Arabist activity in the pre–World War I period.[49] They became leading figures in the Ottoman Administrative Decentralization Party, formed in 1913 to oppose the centralizing policies of the Ottoman government and to advocate greater administrative independence in the Arab provinces. New York, Paris, and São Paulo were also hubs in the formation and circulation of nationalist ideas, and dozens of Arabist committees were founded in the *mahjar,* away from the homeland. In 1911, for example, Naoum Mokarzel—a key supporter of Syrians in the U.S. racial prerequisite cases—founded the Jam'iyya al-Nahda al-Lubnaniyya (Lebanon League of Progress) in New York. The initial goal of the society was to ensure autonomy for Mount Lebanon within the Ottoman framework, a platform that Mokarzel presented to the Arab Congress held in Paris in 1913.

Acknowledging that exile was an important locus of organization around the idea of an "Arab nation," however, tells only a portion of the story. The geographic dispersal of the members of the putative Arab nation, across the globe and within other nations, influenced the particular kind of nationalism that developed before World War I. The emphasis on culture, language, shared experience, and political rights, and not on a particular piece of the map, made eminent sense for a "nation" whose people, perhaps as many as one in six, lived and worked outside geographical Syria.[50] It was not accidental that Syrians—not Moroccans, Egyptians, Sa'udis, or any other Arabic-speaking people—first articulated ideologies of Arab nationalism and that the development of nationalist thought had much to do with Syrian specificities, including specific histories of migration and specific claims to modernity. Moreover, as this book demonstrates, the early debate on Arab nationalism was racialized and gendered because it relied on assertions of difference between modern and backward, virile and effeminate, civilized and uncivilized, enslaved (to tyranny) and free. Precisely these racial and gendered idioms helped give rise to competing national projects in the post–World War I period. Proponents of a specific Lebanese nationalism, for example, invoked a civilizational discourse that drew on the classic tropes of white supremacy: Christian moral superiority and fear of contamination by other "less developed" people. Significantly, it was in the diaspora that many of these ideas crystallized and were transmitted back to homeland communities.

BRIDGING THE HOMELAND AND DIASPORA

A basic premise of this book is that the term *homeland* describes more than the place from which a people departed. Syria continued to exist as a living, changing reality in the imagination and everyday lives of individual migrants. The subjects of this study are individuals who left and arrived, emigrated and immigrated, who were present in one community yet not entirely absent from another. For them, the homeland was not a distant place but a central part of migrants' "ideological geographies."[51] In the minds of Syrian immigrants, "Syria" and "America" were not fixed and separate entities but were linked together, rather like an imagined community in which they were participants. Yet very little work has been done on how the experience of Syrian immigrants reveals this dynamic relationship—a problem that one scholar argues is "rooted in the false notion that . . . once departed from their homeland [they] are no longer components of the society they left behind: the assumption, as Michel Chiha [framer of the Lebanese constitution] once symbolized it, is that the butterfly does not become a caterpillar again."[52]

I have taken a cue from Chiha and from the Syrian immigrant imagination to conceive of the homeland and host country as one analytical field or, put another way, to treat emigration and immigration as two faces of the same reality.[53] Only this approach would enable me to capture the complexity and richness of the immigrant experience and convey the process of migration as one that moves across space and time in interesting and complicated ways. This book thus brings American and Middle Eastern studies into conversation with each other around the figure of the transnational Syrian immigrant, a person who creates familial, cultural, linguistic, and economic ties across national borders.[54] Toward that end, I have conducted archival work in Syria, Lebanon, France, and the United States, drawn on literature across the disciplines, and incorporated the oral histories of immigrants whose personal stories are part of the architecture of this book. I will cite one such story, that of Ahmed Masud, who encouraged me to think of migration in new ways.

In the spring of my research year in Syria, I traveled to the town of Nebik (situated about fifty miles north of Damascus). There I interrupted Ahmed's evening repose in front of his television to ask him about his experience as an immigrant in Argentina. Over ninety years old, hard of hearing, and a little confused as to why I would be interested in such a thing, he began to answer my questions. His Argentinean wife left the room and began to make Turkish coffee, eventually apologizing for its weakness by pointing to her eyes and twice repeating in broken Arabic, "Ma b'shuf" (I cannot see).

Our conversation was filled with many awkward moments. I asked him something in Arabic. My Syrian friend re-asked the question in the heavy dialect of Nebik, and Ahmed answered him, not me. The only time he directly engaged me was when he found out I spoke a bit of Spanish. "Well," he exclaimed, "why didn't you speak to me in Castilian?" I could

have, but that would have meant translating back into Arabic for my
Syrian host, who had kindly introduced me to Ahmed. If I had learned
anything since beginning this project, it was that something always gets
lost in translation.

The evening with Ahmed, and our sometimes bungled attempt to settle on a comfortable language of communication, revealed more than
just the quirkiness of the interviewing process. What became clear to me
was that he existed in a set of overlapping worlds. He spoke Spanish flu-
ently because he had immigrated to Argentina as a young man and
worked there his entire adult life. He had married a "Castiliana" (as he
called her) and had naturalized and become an Argentinean. Like hundreds of thousands of Syrians who had left in the first great wave of
transatlantic migration (including the parents of former Argentinean
president Carlos Menem, from nearby Yabroud), Ahmed considered Argentina his home. Yet he was incontrovertibly Syrian, from the Qalamoun region, and had returned there in what I could only interpret as a
yearning to die in the place of his earliest childhood memories. As I left,
Ahmed gave me his carefully organized scrapbook to review. In it were
letters from family and business associates who kept him informed of developments in Argentina. One, dated October 7, 1981, and written in
Spanish on the letterhead of Abdo Ale Hiho, "abastecedores de carne"
(suppliers of meat), informed him of the death of his cousin Abdo. It was
written by Abdo's wife, Josefina, who told him how much his cousin had
loved him and how he had wanted to return to Syria also. She concluded
by expressing her hope that her son could one day get to know his father's "beloved Nebek and complete the dream of his father."[55]

I encountered the melding of allegiances and solidarities as I spoke
with other Syrian emigrants who had returned to the "other side," but I
also read it in the diaries, newspapers, oral histories, letters, and travel
accounts of those who remained in the *mahjar,* the diaspora. When, for
example, M. Sarkis learned in 1900 that his brother was going to sell his
share of land in the northern Lebanese village of Bishmizeen, he quickly
sent a letter from Cleveland, Ohio, to his mother. "Let me know how
much is the amount, and I shall send it to you," he wrote. "Then you will
transfer his share to my name." Two years later, his mother wrote to him
from the village to tell him the good news: "We have bought for you the
olive orchard. If you have an extra amount now, send it, and we shall
buy more land for you." She added that M. Sarkis should continue
to take good care of his sisters who had traveled to the United States
with him. One of the sisters, Deebeh, had left her children behind in the

care of her mother. "Tell [her] that her children are doing very well," her mother wrote, and, in a gesture that conveys the emotional significance of the little bits and pieces sent across the ocean, she enclosed a lock of hair from each child.[56] This exchange between M. Sarkis and his mother typifies the ways in which emigrants constructed an imaginary bridge between Syria and *Amirka,* between the place they had left and the place where they had arrived, between the person they had been and the person they had become. Conceptually, I have tried to account for the ways in which first-generation migrants moved back and forth between places, often physically but more often in the realm of their imaginations.

The stages of this movement are reflected in the organization of this book. I have not broken with the scholarly practice of starting the story of migration to the United States in the homeland, although I have tried, in chapter 1, to bring a fresh perspective to the premigratory context. Specifically, I situate the Syrian migration to the United States in relation to other migratory movements within the Ottoman Empire. The large-scale movement of peoples out of Syria was only one of many nineteenth-century Ottoman migrations linked to profound socioeconomic changes in the empire.[57] The chapter makes these linkages, paying particular attention to the way Syria became integrated into the capitalist world economy in the second half of the nineteenth century. My concern, however, is not only with the structural context that shaped specific migratory patterns but also with the generation of narratives about emigration from Syria. Among these is the still popular story that Syrian transatlantic migration in the late nineteenth century was the resurrection of a practice originated by the ancient Phoenicians.

Chapter 2 focuses on Syrian naturalization cases heard in federal courts between 1909 and 1915 and analyzes their impact on the legal construction of whiteness. I examine how Syrians from California to New York mobilized around the cases, and I discuss the evolution of their argument in support of a racial classification as white. Chapter 3 explores connections between emergent national and diasporic identities in the pre–World War I and early Mandate periods. I focus on Syrian American participation at the 1913 Arab Congress in Paris, where the discourses of nationalism, migration, race, and modernity came together in new ways. In chapter 4, I examine the lynching of the Syrian grocer Nola Romey in Lake City, Florida, in 1929. This incident demonstrates how, despite the legal rulings that Syrians were to be classed as "white persons" for the purpose of naturalization, their whiteness remained unstable, or "probationary," particularly in the color-conscious South.

Chapter 5 explores questions of gender and sexuality in the debates on marriage in the Syrian immigrant community as it transitioned from a sojourner status to a settler one. I link the concern with racial misidentification and immigration restriction to first-generation immigrants' desire to police the marriages of their children, principally by avoiding outmarriage. The chapter ends with a discussion of how the Syrian desire to assimilate carried with it a certain price: the celebration of ethnic identity moved more and more to the private sphere and lost its earlier political dynamism.

In sum, this book is an excavation of the principal sites of Syrian ethnicization before World War II, during the first wave of Arab immigration and settlement in the United States. Shards and fragments of past practices of exclusion are showing through in newer forms of racism directed at Arabs, notably in the area of immigration law and "homeland security." Strategies of resistance to these practices, both organized and informal, are not wholly disconnected from earlier choices, although there are also important divergences that I address in the epilogue. In this "prolegomena to the present" I explore changing patterns of Arab migration to the United States since 1945. Energized by Arab nationalism and Third World politics, a more diverse Arab American community organized to protect their civil rights and to forge solidarities with people of color. Segments of the community challenged their official classification as white and lobbied for a separate category for Arabs in the U.S. Census. I examine the political bases of this challenge and the different arguments made for official minority status. In the wake of September 11, 2001, with increased profiling and scrutiny of the Arab and Muslim communities in the United States, the campaign to change the category in the census has been muted. This poses interesting questions about Arab racial and ethnic definitions, and their relationship to citizenship, in a new period of heightened American nativism and global reconfigurations of power.

CHAPTER I

From Internal to International Migration

This chapter places Syrian immigration to the United States within a larger Ottoman framework and traces both continuities and discontinuities in patterns of migration into and out of the Arab provinces of the empire. In doing so, I counter the romanticized theory that Syrians immigrated to the Americas because they had a predisposition, or a migratory "trait," to pursue opportunities beyond Mediterranean shores.[1] For example, in his 1999 open letter from the Lebanese Ministry of Emigrants, El Emir Talal Majid Arslan linked Lebanese emigration to a heroic Phoenician precedent: "Our ancestors the Phoenicians were the first pioneers to venture the seas. They exchanged science with nations, spread the alphabet from Byblos with Cadmus, geometry from Tyre with Pythagoras, not to mention but two. As good merchants they introduced the market system of bargain trade. A few millennia later, *Lebanese reinitiated the same process of migration.*"[2]

For proponents of this theory, the Phoenicians of the first millennium BC were the pioneering emigrants from the land of Syria, the transmitters of a great tradition of movement, migration, and commerce.[3] They bequeathed their love of adventure, commercial skills, and mercantile "mind" to their nineteenth-century descendants. Georges Moanack, writing in French about the Lebanese emigration to Colombia, South America, made the connection more explicit: "This call [to emigrate,] is it not the voice of the past, a residue of the Phoenician soul that continues to inhabit our souls?"[4] The promotion of an ancient point of origin is common in narratives of migration. Spanish Galician immigrants to Buenos Aires, for example, asserted that their impulse to migrate lay in their Celtic warrior roots, and Italians in New York City cast their arrival there as a legacy of the voyages of Christopher Columbus.[5] Linking Lebanese emigration to the ancient Phoenicians also served nationalist purposes, and like much nationalist mythology—Egyptian orientations around the Pharaohs, for example—"Phoenicianism" had its roots in the field of archeology.[6] A series of French archeological digs in the mid–nineteenth century unearthed remnants of old Phoenicia, whose seafaring communities, according to Greek texts, had stretched along the Syrian coast of the Mediterranean from Latakia in the north to Acre in the south. Phoenicia was thus added to the list of interests held by the roving band of Orientalists in Syria who were already busy digging up, categorizing, and collecting other pieces of Syria's past.[7] Debates on the significance of the French finds were at first limited and mostly antiquarian. Increasingly, however, archeological evidence was put at the service of politics, and in the heady days of World War I a group of Lebanese intellectuals began to conceive of a modern Lebanon independent of Syria and of Arabism.[8] This Lebanon, they argued, was none other than Phoenicia resurrected. By the interwar period, "Phoenicianism" had become an important ideological tool in the construction of a specifically "Lebanese" (as opposed to Syrian) nationality. Its most avid proponents were found in a pro-French Christian milieu, and the Phoenicians represented to them the ancient mold for the westward-looking Lebanese.[9] The symbols of Phoenicianism, "the first boat and the first oar," for example (employed by Michel Chiha), were especially useful to the financial-mercantile bourgeoisie, who were intent on implementing a political and economic program for a modern merchant republic.[10]

While still popular among some segments of Lebanese society, the idea that a distinct Lebanese history and nationality is rooted in an ancient Phoenician past has been criticized by many writers as ahistorical and exclusivist. Historian Kamal Salibi argues that "not a single institution or tradition of medieval or modern Lebanon can be legitimately traced back to ancient Phoenicia" and that "Phoenicianism in Christian Lebanese circles developed more as a cult than as a reasoned political theory."[11] What mattered for Phoenicianists, however, was the power of symbols, not evidence, and the westward migration of Syrians to the Americas fit nicely into their vision of a Lebanon that was a natural bridge between East and West. It was the Phoenicians, they argued, who had first harnessed the desire for adventure and set sail from the rocky Mediterranean coast; centuries later, Syrians embarked on a similar journey across the ocean in search of economic opportunity. According to this interpretation, the legendary success of the Phoenician trader foreshadowed the story of the Syrian immigrant who became a comfortable store owner in the *mahjar*. Writing on Syrian business in New York, Salloum Mokarzel noted that "it thrives today in the age of steel and steam and under the shadows of towering Manhattan skyscrapers as it ever did when the first Phoenician ventured across the billowy main in his wind-driven galleon. . . . Curiously enough, the men supplying this element of romance in American business are the direct descendents of the Phoenicians."[12] In short, the Syrian linen and dry goods traders of New York City were the modern incarnation of the Phoenician soap and olive oil merchants of Carthage. The history of Syrian migration to the United States began to be written as a classic "rags to riches" story, and Phoenicianism became a kind of "Mayflowerism"—a mythology of noble and ancient immigrant origins and exaggeration of the successes and contributions to the host societies.[13] Some Syrian writers of the early twentieth century argued that the Phoenicians were in fact the first to "discover" America. Significantly, and presaging an argument that would be crucial to the construction of Syrian ethnicity in the United States, Mulhim Halim 'Abduh wrote to the Cairo-based Arabic journal *al-Hilal* from Greenfield, North Carolina, in 1901 claiming that the Phoenicians were the "first Caucasians to land in America."[14] These arguments would later be used by Lebanese immigrants to claim a non-Arab, non-Turkish identity during periods of heightened twentieth-century nativism, when government officials in Latin America and the United States debated their suitability for assimilation. And they would continue to be used in the twenty-first century to bolster Lebanese pride. In 2006, the Southern Federation of Syrian Lebanese American Clubs held its annual convention in San Antonio, Texas. The most popular presentation was entitled "The Phoenician Discovery of America." Here audience members learned that Phoenician sailors had landed in present-day Mexico, taught the ancient Maya how to build pyramids, and then returned to their Mediterranean homes. A thrilled listener thanked the presenters and urged them to disseminate the findings widely so that other Americans could learn of the historic achievements of the Lebanese.[15]

As a theory of migration, however, Phoenicianism minimizes the historically specific and changing realities of late-Ottoman Syria. It also obscures the fact that the end-of-the-century transatlantic migration broke with what had been the dominant pattern of migration in the nineteenth century, indeed for most of the Ottoman period: that is, internal migration within and *between* provinces of the empire. These internal migrations included seasonal laborers, itinerant merchants, religious pilgrims, and, especially in the Syrian interior, nomadic camel and sheep herders. The wars of the mid–nineteenth century produced another class of persons on the move: refugees. Thus one of the interesting, but often overlooked, developments in the history of nineteenth-century Syrian migration is the transition from internal to international migration. Like European migratory patterns of the nineteenth century, Syrian internal migration is important for the study of transatlantic migration, for it helped establish a grid onto which the latter migration was placed.[16] Immigrants making their way to the Americas, for example, traveled on sea routes that originally linked commercial hubs within the Ottoman Empire, such as Beirut and Alexandria. These routes then expanded to include ports within a wider Atlantic world, notably Marseilles and New York City. In addition, emigrants often had family members who had left the village to find work in the port of Beirut, bringing back with them stories that demystified the city and boasted of the opportunities that it offered. For other workers, moving to Beirut to work in the silk industry allowed them to make enough money to then purchase a ticket for steamship travel overseas. In what follows, I examine internal migration trends in late-Ottoman Syria and assess their impact on the political and economic context out of which migration to the Americas sprang.

OTTOMAN SUBJECTS ON THE MOVE

Prior to the great wave of transatlantic migration in the late nineteenth century, migratory movements in Syria were connected either to Ottoman imperial policies to boost economic output through demographic means or to the dislocation of war. While the central government in Istanbul experimented with forced migration (sürgün) to the Syrian interior,[17] a much more common Ottoman policy was to encourage migration by offering incentives, such as free land or exemption from taxation and military conscription to prospective migrants. The latter was a strategy used for the settlement of frontier areas in Syria situated near the eastern desert line. The groups targeted for these incentives were often embroiled in local disputes, and the Ottoman government viewed relocation as both a strategy for settlement and a means to avoid further conflict. In 1849, for example, a small band of Ismailis, under the leadership of a dissident tribal chief, were enticed to settle in the abandoned fort town of Salamiyya, situated approximately nineteen miles east of the Syrian town of Hama.[18]

Throughout the nineteenth century, the Ottoman central government linked the policy of relocating Ottoman subjects to areas that were underpopulated and in need of cultivation to its goal of increasing the empire's agricultural output. The revitalization of agriculture was part of a much larger project of military, administrative, and economic reform known as the Tanzimat, or "reorganization." The problem, however, was one of manpower, and government officials deemed migration (both forced and voluntary) necessary to populate and cultivate unsettled or thinly settled land. In 1857, a new policy on migration and settlement was given imperial sanction, and the high council of the Tanzimat issued a decree that circulated throughout the empire and abroad. The decree promised settlers excellent land, exemption from taxation and military service for six years, and protection under the law.[19] According to historian Kemal Karpat's analysis of the records of the Turkish Foreign Ministry, foreign interest in the Ottoman government's offer was significant. Italian, Irish, and American families queried Ottoman consuls about the settlement policies,[20] and representatives of two thousand families of German origin living in Bessarabia on the Black Sea (then under Russian control) expressed their interest in moving to Ottoman lands and promised that if their demands were received favorably many thousand German families would follow. From New York, the Ottoman consul, J. Oxford Smith, relayed questions asked by Americans who expressed interest in immigration to the empire. He wrote that "there are many industrious, steady men who would like to take up residence in that land, especially Syria and Palestine, if they can obtain land and be protected in the cultivation of it." He inquired further "whether persons of color who are natives to this country or others are included in these conditions [put forth in the decree]." The foreign minister in Istanbul, Fuat Pasha, replied "yes," because "the imperial government does not establish any difference of color or other [sic] in this respect."[21]

Despite the favorable terms of the decree, the empire did not receive a deluge of European or American immigrants, and settlement of agricultural lands was accomplished largely through internal migration of Ottoman subjects. What turned out to be rather small movements of people were soon overshadowed by larger internal migrations connected in 1860 to the civil war in Lebanon and in 1878 to expulsion policies implemented by European governments in the wake of "recapturing" Ottoman-controlled territory. Most importantly, the civil war in Lebanon shaped the social, economic, and political context in which Syrian transatlantic migration began.

This war is remembered chiefly as a sectarian conflict that pitted Christian against Druze. Beginning in Mount Lebanon in May 1860, the conflict left thousands dead or exiled from their burned and looted villages. A few weeks later, riots broke out in Damascus, and Muslims ransacked the Christian quarters of a city hitherto accustomed to a high degree of religious cooperation between these two communities. Estimates of the casualties in Damascus vary widely (from five hundred to ten thousand), but it is likely that the devastation matched what had occurred in the battles in Mount Lebanon.[22]

While early scholarship on Syrian migration argued that the civil war created a climate of insecurity among Christians that precipitated transatlantic migration, more recent scholarship has revised this thesis.[23] The violence did indeed produce a migration that was hugely uprooting and disorienting for the families involved, but the connection to the transatlantic migration of thirty and forty years later was based, not on sectarian violence and fear, but on economic and political developments in the wake of the conflict.

Those who fled the Mountain and Damascus in 1860 were first and foremost refugees, not migrants. They flocked to Beirut, where they hoped to receive shelter and assistance from one of the many relief organizations authorized to help victims of the conflict.[24] The speed at which towns like Zahle and Dayr al-Qamar were rebuilt, however, suggests that refugees returned to their villages in large numbers not only to rebuild but also to collect indemnities promised by the Ottoman central government.[25] Others, less connected to the land, did resettle permanently in Beirut and became part of the town's growing commercial and educational sectors in the second half of the nineteenth century. Another principal area of resettlement for refugees was the hilly area east of the Hauran plain in the south of present-day Syria. By some accounts, seven thousand Druze families originally from the Shuf immigrated into this area, which, not surprisingly, came to be known as Jabal al-Duruz (Mountain of the Druze).[26]

The migration to Beirut, and its connection to other transformations in the Syrian economy, would prove to be an especially important development. In the second half of the nineteenth century, this once sleepy Ottoman town was fast becoming a bustling commercial port city and a nexus of foreign missionary and consular activity. The new educational institutions in Beirut, for example, were a symbol of the city's growth, which was fueled by foreign investment, local entrepreneurship, and migration from the Mountain. Every year, thousands of people from the surrounding areas poured into Beirut, rapidly changing the physical and demographic character of the town. Between 1830 and 1850, Beirut's population quadrupled, and it doubled again immediately after 1860.[27] Many of the migrants had relocated to the city in the wake of civil strife in the 1850s and 1860, but the size and scope of this migration could not be attributed solely to the episodic outbreaks of factional violence. The composition and pace of this migration were rooted in processes that ran deeper than sectarian differences, and population growth was among the most important. Ottoman Lebanon had one of the highest rates of increase, especially in the two decades after 1860, when peace and security were restored in the area. Charles Issawi estimates a growth rate of between 0.7 and 0.8 percent between 1878 and 1895, meaning that by the close of the nineteenth century the population of Mount Lebanon had reached nearly a quarter-million.[28]

For the Ottoman government population growth was a sign of a healthy subject population, but for the Syrian peasantry it meant increased pressures on the land and an uncertain future. Migration to urban areas was one solution to looming indebtedness and possible displacement due to creditors calling in loans. Like so many other large towns in the Middle East in the second half of the nineteenth century, Beirut began to attract migrants from the countryside. Louis Charles Lortet traveled throughout greater Syria between 1875 and 1880 and published his impressions in a book *Syria of Today: Voyages in Phoenicia, Lebanon and Judea*. Lortet's account (written in French) is replete with Orientalist tropes and racist epithets. When describing the women in the port city of Latakia, for example, he wrote that "they carefully cover the face with awful cotton scarves. . . . The effect is horrible!"[29] On other matters he was more measured. He noticed the transformations under way in Beirut and remarked that "a constant emigration from the neighboring areas has continually increased the importance of the city."[30]

The choice of Beirut over other Syrian towns was made on the basis of proximity and ease of travel. Workers could descend from the Mountain fairly easily, and those from the Damascus area could make the journey in one day, thanks to the newly opened Beirut-Damascus road in 1863.[31] The building of the road "guaranteed Beirut's place as the leading trading and economic center of the region," and thousands of travelers and tons of goods moved along it each year.[32] Thus the move to Beirut was about opportunity, not only for peasants who found work in the port or in construction, but for skilled artisans and traders who were attracted to the cosmopolitan character and growing prosperity of

Beirut. In terms of internal migration trends, then, the decades following the events of 1860, a period described by historian Engin Akarli as
"the long peace," witnessed a new pattern of migration consisting primarily of Christians, linking the Lebanese hinterland to the growing port
of Beirut.

Less studied is the overwhelmingly Muslim migration connected to
another nineteenth-century war between the Ottoman Empire and its
formidable enemy Russia. The latter resulted in the migration of tens of
thousands of refugees from the Caucasus into the northern and southern portions of Syria.[33] While Christian and Druze families were relocating within a hundred-mile radius of their villages after the events of
1860, for example, a much larger number of people were immigrating
into Syria as part of the chaotic resettlement efforts established in the
wake of the Russian-Ottoman wars of 1853–56 and 1877–78. This migration consisted of Muslims from the Crimea, Caucasus, and Balkans—
the casualties of Ottoman defeat and a Russian-styled *reconquista*.

Having refused the Russian offer of immigration into the Russian interior (and conversion to Orthodox Christianity), over one million Muslims left the Caucasus between 1856 and 1864, most of them en route
to Black Sea ports, where they began the journey of resettlement into the
Ottoman Empire.[34] Thousands were dumped at the first Ottoman port
of call, Trabzon (on the Eastern Black Sea, in modern-day Turkey),
where the authorities were ill prepared to deal with a deluge of people in
need of food, lodging, and water.[35] Sickness ran rampant through the
makeshift camps, claiming the lives of migrants at an astonishing rate,
five hundred a day by some estimates. Nearly thirty thousand Circassians
died in Trabzon alone.[36] Those who lived were resettled in Anatolia, Bulgaria, and Syria, straining slim village resources and inspiring fear among
local inhabitants, who were swayed by stories of Circassian banditry.[37]
In 1878, the cycle of migration began again as tens of thousands of resettled Circassians were forced to leave Bulgaria during the province's
bid for independence.[38] Twenty-five thousand reached southern Syria,
where they revived agriculture in areas like Qunaytra and the Jaulan. Others moved further east to occupy and cultivate land along Syria's desert
fringe, effectively becoming a buffer against the marauding Bedouin.
There was also considerable Circassian settlement in the north in the
province of Aleppo and along the desert line stretching from the northern
frontier all the way to Amman, where Circassians had first found shelter
in the ruins of the deserted Roman theater.[39]

In terms of large-scale Ottoman population movements, the Circassian immigration into different provinces of the Ottoman Empire in the
1860s and 1870s preceded Syrian transatlantic emigration. Moreover,
the movement of peoples associated with the Lebanese civil war of 1860
and the Russian Ottoman wars of the next two decades established the
mechanisms of travel that facilitated the Syrian migration to the Americas at the end of the century.

Both the Circassian and Mount Lebanon migrations were initially in-
stigated by violence and warfare, and while it is tempting to focus on
these events because they generated a disproportionate amount of doc-
umentation we should remember that thousands of Syrians migrated for
more prosaic reasons. Damascus, for example, received periodic waves
of seasonal laborers who moved back and forth between their villages
and the city regularly.[40] Syrian émigré writer Abraham Rihbany recalled
in his memoirs how the majority of male inhabitants from his village of
al-Shwayr left each year between spring and late autumn to ply their
trade as stonemasons.[41] Internal migration also represented an opportunity for upward mobility within the empire, which, despite a Byzantine
complexity, was unified, particularly in the urban areas, by a shared Ottoman culture. The Syrian migration to Egypt, for example, represented
a "career migration" in which educated Syrians relocated to pursue work
opportunities in the more dynamic and open environments of Cairo and
Alexandria.[42] Underlying the migration from the countryside to the city
was a deeper transformation in the economy of Lebanon that would ultimately link what had been an internal migration system to an international one: the incorporation of Lebanon into a capitalist world economy. This precipitated changes in village life and ultimately shaped a
new pattern of migration at the end of the nineteenth century consisting
of peasant cultivators and small-scale traders. Nowhere was this incorporation more clear, and nowhere were the effects on migration more
stark, than in the silk industry.

SILK AND THE REORIENTATION OF THE ECONOMY
IN SYRIA

Changes in the methods and rates of production of silk in Syria were directly related to the growth of the industry in France. By the 1830s, demand for silk in Europe was extraordinarily high and the French silk industry was booming. French sericulturalists were eager to expand their

base of operation, yet they were not so eager to pay the wages their
workers were demanding.[43] A few enterprising investors, making use of
their connections to Levantine merchants, began to build filatures (the
factories where cocoons are rendered into silk thread) in Syria in areas
where a local culture of silk production existed. The intervention was
tentative at first, but within a decade new filatures with basins heated by
steam instead of wood were springing up on the Mountain.[44] A decisive
shift in levels of Syrian silk production occurred in the 1850s, when disease devastated the silkworms in France. Foreign cocoons were urgently
needed, and investment in Syrian-produced cocoons doubled, then
quickly tripled. Syrian peasants turned increasingly to the cultivation of
mulberry trees, the staple of the silkworm diet. By the 1890s, 90 percent
of the cultivable land in Mount Lebanon was taken over for the plant-
ing of this hardy, broad-leafed tree, and cocoons became a cash crop in an
industry oriented toward the demand of France.[45] In fact, at every level—
from production to distribution—the Syrian silk industry depended on
France. In 1911, Gaston Ducousso, attaché of the French consulate general in Beirut, conveyed the extent of this reorientation in his detailed study
of Syrian sericulture. He described the industry as one that, "by the mul-
tiplicity of its connections to ours, has become French [naturalisée], to the
extent that we can now rank Syria right after our own silk-producing
areas."[46]

The dramatic expansion of the Syrian silk industry would have been
hard for a traveler arriving in Beirut in the last quarter of the nineteenth
century to miss. Sacks of raw silk were weighed and then shuttled out to
ships waiting to make the journey to Marseilles or Lyons. In and around
the port itself, merchants bought and sold cocoons as well as silk thread,
which was twisted into huge glistening braids called shilal. Making her
way out of Beirut toward the Mountain, the traveler would have seen one
of the largest silk-reeling factories in Syria, owned by Doumani Habib.[47]
If she got close enough, she might have smelled the foul odor that em-
anated from the site, a particularly potent combination of discarded and
decaying chrysalides and the gluelike substance embedded in the cocoons
by the silkworms. Smaller factories dotted the Mountain, and inside them
young girls worked in oppressive steam and heat for thirteen hours a
day.[48] The ugliness of the work environment paradoxically matched the
intense beauty of the Mountain's fertile terraces, which overflowed with
mulberry trees. And all of this was linked to a less obvious but nonetheless ubiquitous web of exchanges between Beirut, the hinterland of the
city, and Europe.

European investors had pioneered the mechanization of silk reeling in Mount Lebanon, but local entrepreneurs quickly invested in different phases of production and distribution. Beiruti merchants, for example, became the owners of silk-reeling factories financed by creditors in Lyons. Some of them, like the Bassouls (Bassul) and Pharaons (Farʿun), also owned local banks that enabled them to build factories, finance the export of silk, and extend credit to local cultivators.[49] These merchants were the backbone of an emerging bourgeoisie in Beirut. They were men whose everyday world involved the interplay of local premodern custom and cosmopolitan modernity. It was a world forged out of a specific conjuncture of population growth, migration, and foreign investment; but it was also a world made possible by an Ottoman government committed to an ambitious, but ultimately misguided, program of reform.

It was, after all, the reformist zeal of Tanzimat administrators that facilitated the massive European intervention into the affairs of the Ottoman economy. With grand plans to modernize the military, the Ottoman government had quickly turned to foreign advisors, and military and political support came (as is so often the case) with strings attached. In the case of British assistance, this was made abundantly clear in the 1838 Anglo-Turkish Commercial Convention, which reduced internal duties and outlawed the use of monopolies. Other European governments demanded similar arrangements, and between 1838 and 1841 the Ottomans signed free-trade treaties with France and Russia. The Ottoman government then introduced a new commercial code based on French practice, which was designed to ensure that commercial transactions in the empire, and especially those involving foreign interests, would be conducted according to French law. The enactment of the code was accompanied by the establishment of commercial courts for the settlement of business-related disputes between Ottoman and European subjects.[50] Finally, the Ottoman government's stupendous debt gave British and French entrepreneurs a field of opportunity that made earlier favorable trading agreements granted by the Ottomans (known as the Capitulations) look positively protectionist. European merchants would have thought twice about investing in Syria had their governments not secured important commercial concessions from the Ottomans, although, as the landing of a French military force in Beirut in August 1860 (ostensibly to help, as Napoleon III instructed the troops, "the Sultan bring back to obedience subjects blinded by a fanaticism from another century") would clearly show, the use of military might did much to boost their confidence.[51]

The administrative reorganization of Mount Lebanon in the wake of
the 1860 civil war was a clear example of the interplay of Ottoman reformist principles, foreign intervention, and local interests. The central
government agreed to the implementation of a new political framework
that effectively granted the Mountain a semiautonomous status. Called
the *mutasarrifiyya*, this new Ottoman governorate was to be headed by
a Christian, appointed by and responsible to the central government in
Istanbul.[52] The details of the Mountain's physical and political remapping were enshrined in a constitutional document called the "Règlement
et protocole relatifs à la réorganisation du Mont-Liban," signed in 1861
and guaranteed by five European powers. The basic aim of the document, which was issued in the form of an imperial decree expressing the
sultan's sadness "over the recurrence of troubles in Mount Lebanon,"[53]
was to outline a set of changes that would guarantee peace and prosperity to the people of the *mutasarrifiyya*. Chief among these changes
was the attack on "feudal" privileges, which were blamed for the unrest
of 1860. In this regard, the Règlement was quite effective, as Mount
Lebanon became the only place within the empire where tax farming was
abolished.

The success of the Ottoman reform policy was mixed. The judicial
and political reorganization of the Mountain, for example, facilitated
the rapid expansion of the silk industry, but in ways that were ultimately precarious for peasant cultivators. The 1860s had seemed like
good years for the people who planted the mulberry trees, fed the silkworms, harvested eggs, and cared for the cocoons. International silk
prices were high, as was the demand for Syrian silk. During this phase
of expansion peasants used the extensive financial network associated
with the silk industry and borrowed heavily to expand their areas of cultivation. The boom was short-lived, however. In the 1870s, disease rav-
aged the silkworms and the mulberry trees, and the Syrian silk industry
faced the first of many crises since its incorporation into the world economy. The industry around Beirut was dealt a devastating blow, and observers wondered whether it could ever recover.[54] Prices paid for Syrian
cocoons dropped from 42 piasters per *oka* in 1865 to 15.5 in 1876, and
despite fluctuations over the next two decades prices never again reached
the highs of the 1860s.[55] The importation of cocoons from abroad briefly
remedied the situation, but the Syrian industry had a harder time competing with silks from the Far East, which became, after the opening
of the Suez Canal in 1869, more readily available on the international
market.[56]

The Syrian silk industry was turning out to be far more fragile than its enthusiastic supporters had envisioned at its beginning. The hardest hit by the falling international prices were the cultivators who had borrowed money to purchase silkworm eggs at exorbitant interest rates, only to sell the developed cocoons six months later at a loss, still owing the original creditor.[57] Others, like the inhabitants of Zahle, who were not directly involved in silk production but whose market town depended on the surplus generated by the industry, were also affected. They were among the first to pursue a new opportunity to make money: overseas migration.[58]

CROSSING THE WATERS: THE BEGINNINGS OF A DIASPORA

The changing character of the port of Beirut played a major role in the dramatic increase in Syrian transatlantic migration. Newly rebuilt in 1894, it was made more accessible to steamships and the operations associated with steamship travel, such as ticket agents and telegraph services.[59] The use of advertising in a flourishing local press was also an important tool for those engaged in the immigrant trade. Syrian, Egyptian, and *mahjar* papers carried ads announcing fares, travel times, and cargo services. The Pharaon brothers, Mikhail and Taufail, representatives of the French company Frasinet, took out huge ads announcing the advantages of traveling on their steamboats, including the fact that those steamboats took only six days to reach Marseilles.[60] The Pharaon family was, as noted above, a banking family that had prospered during the height of the silk industry. By the end of the nineteenth century, members of the family had redirected their activities into the business of overseas migration and were fast becoming representatives of a transnational bourgeoisie.

Histories of migration typically begin with the story of pioneers, the first persons to chart a path that others would follow. Narratives of Syrian immigration to the United States are no different. They describe the World's Fairs in Philadelphia (1876), Chicago (1893), and St. Louis (1904) as the magnet that drew the first wave of immigrants across the waters to a new life in the *mahjar*. At the fairs, these pioneers sold wares from the "Holy Land" (such as small crosses, rosaries, and holy water) to thousands of fair-goers intrigued by the "people from the East." They then began to peddle these wares, and other household goods, beyond the fairgrounds. In this way, peddlers acquired savings that they channeled into the purchase of small stores, the economic pillars of the first

Syrian communities in the United States. The success of these early pioneers initiated an "emigration fever" in Syria, and thousands of young
men and women left their villages to pursue their dream of making money
in *Amirka*.[61]

Syrians did indeed participate in the Philadelphia, Chicago, and St.
Louis fairs, but the significance of the fairs as a major "pull" factor in
their immigration to the United States has been exaggerated. It is not
clear, for example, that the Syrian participants at the Chicago fair became immigrants or worked beyond the venue of the fair. They were employed by Ottoman entrepreneurs who organized the Ottoman exhibit
on the Midway Plaisance—the section of the fair reserved for reproductions of the "habitations, manners and customs of remote peoples."[62]
The Ottoman exhibit contained numerous reproductions of "Turkish"
daily life, from the mosque of the Hagia Sofia to the embroideries, carpets, and silverware of the grand bazaar.[63] A *New York Times* article announced the arrival of "247 Syrians, Arabs, and Turks" as a "Living Oriental Exhibit." "One of the features of the Oriental exhibit," the article
continued, "will be a realistic representation of an attack on Bedouins
upon a caravan. The Syrian women who accompany the hippodrome
will allow themselves to be daily abducted by Bedouins and daily rescued
by their dusky friends."[64] The manager of the popular "Turkish Village
and Theatre" was R. J. Levi, a well-known caterer from Istanbul who re-
cruited Syrian actors for the daily shows in the theater.[65] The billing for
the shows was carefully worded to appeal to a Christian audience, promising to represent "all the features of social and domestic life among the
inhabitants of the . . . places and sections famous in sacred and profane
history."[66]

We know of several individual Syrians who took part in the exhibits
of the Midway Plaisance. Milhim Ouardy from the Lebanese town of
Dayr al-Qamar, and a dragoman by profession, participated as a swords-
man, not in the Turkish Theatre, but in the adjacent Moorish Palace.
This display was immensely popular among fair-goers because of its
"dancing girls" (two of whom were Ottoman Jews from Jerusalem and
Beirut respectively). Another Syrian from Mount Lebanon, Prince Mere
Hemcy (probably Mir Homsi), was admired as "a fearless rider" for "his
feats of daring horsemanship at the Wild East Show," qualities, the observer noted, "for which his race is noted."[67] Still another was Mere Alli
Harfush, whose photo is in a published collection of portraits of participants in the exhibits of the Midway Plaisance. The caption under the

Figure 2. Mere Hemcy, participant in the Chicago World's Fair, 1893.

photo reads: "He comes from a spot which is one of the most mysterious places on the globe, where the ruins of the great City of Baalbec still
stand and where the columns of the Temple of the Sun challenge the curiosity and wonder of the world, for they were built at a period which
antedates history."[68]

Given the journalistic interest in the Syrian participants at the fair,
it is possible that their presence had a greater impact on the development of American Orientalism than on patterns of migration. Moreover, viewing these participants as pioneers in the history of Syrian immigration to the United States misses the more complex transnational

Figure 3. Mere Alli Harfush, participant in the Chicago World's Fair, 1893.

dimensions of their lives. As Mae Ngai argues for the Chinese participants at the Chicago fair, the businessmen and migrant artists involved
in presenting aspects of their culture did so with the goal of boosting international trade and cross-country exchanges.[69] They were not merely
quaint curiosities and objects of a "one-way white gaze" but active subjects in an entrepreneurial undertaking that drew on their extensive experience in other contact zones: homeland port cities (like Beirut) and international fairs (such as the Paris Exposition of 1889). These nuances
account for the fact that the "Oriental" exhibits were not always viewed
through the lens of American imperial arrogance. An article in the *Nation* on the "Turkish Restaurant" at the Philadelphia Exposition, for ex-

ample, noted that "perhaps the most singular feeling the place gives you, after contrasting the urbanity and affability of those in charge with the general rudeness and brutality of the crowd[,] is that they are really the civilized people and we the barbarians."[70]

The success of the Chicago fair in particular was certainly one of the many pieces of information that Syrians used to shape their ideas about America, but it was not necessarily the most important. Syrians had already established an enclave on Washington Street in New York City before the Chicago fair began, and new arrivals made greater use of the networks there than in Chicago.[71] There was a Chicago community, but it was sizable enough before 1893 to suggest that the Syrians had been drawn to Chicago for reasons other than the fair.[72] Moreover, by 1891, there were sizable Syrian communities in Boston, Wooster, Cleveland, Detroit, Toledo, Saint Paul, and Minneapolis, to name a few, all cities chosen by Syrians for their economic potential and not because of the fairs.[73]

An overemphasis on the role of the fairs and the depiction of the United States as a beacon to which migrants headed also obscures the fact that there were substantial migrant flows to other parts of the Americas, particularly to Argentina and Brazil. In 1889, for example, Argentina received three times as many emigrants from "Turkey in Asia" (the majority of whom were Syrians) than the United States, and while Syrian immigration to the United States surpassed that of Argentina during the late 1890s and early 1900s, the trend was soon reversed. Indeed, during the peak years of Syrian immigration to the United States, beginning in 1905, arrivals in Argentina were consistently higher, sometimes as much as double—a trend that was due in part to the fact that immigrants to Latin America did not have to undergo the stringent health tests that forced many of them away from the United States.[74] In addition, Syrian immigrants took advantage of incentives offered by the Argentinean government, such as free lodging upon arrival in the port of Buenos Aires.[75]

While official figures for Brazil are spotty for the late nineteenth century, Ottoman sources point to the early and sustained migration of Syrians to this republic. A widely publicized religious pilgrimage to Christian holy places in Syria by Brazilian emperor Dom Pedro II in 1876–77 helped pique initial interest, especially after he touted the work opportunities in his country. Within the next ten years, thousands of Syrians had left to pursue the emperor's promise of employment.[76] Ottoman diplomatic sources estimated that there were twenty thousand Syrians in

Brazil by the end of the nineteenth century.[77] Typical of Syrian migrants throughout the Americas, they sent money home to their families, often remigrated back to Syria, and opened up their villages to a new world of goods, language, and customs.[78] Philip Hitti, for example, described the turn-of-the-century town of Zahle as full of Portuguese speakers whose connection to Brazil would later be inscribed in the town's principal road, "Rua Brasil."[79] Syrians returning from South America introduced the ritual of drinking *mate* (the tealike drink common in Brazil) into the daily life of friends and family. Emigrants also brought with them less tangible items, as was the case in 1896 when scarlet fever appeared for the first time in Mount Lebanon, brought by returnees from America.[80]

The decision to emigrate from Syria could not have been easy for these early migrants. Although intense competition between steamship lines lowered ticket prices over time, purchasing a ticket and other expenses related to travel still made the cost of the voyage prohibitive for prospective emigrants. They were vulnerable at every stage of the journey, especially in the ports, where the services of middlemen were needed to evade the Ottoman authorities, since emigration from the empire was technically illegal. Emigrants routinely circumvented the official ban on emigration by relying on smugglers to get them onto ships bound for western Europe. Elizabeth Beshara remembered hiding out for over a week along the northern Lebanese coast at Batroun, waiting for smugglers to take her family and over fifty others out to a ship. Her exasperated father finally decided to attempt the departure from the port of Beirut, which involved yet another series of expenditures and payoffs. She arrived with her father, stepmother, and sister in Toledo, Ohio, in 1893.[81] Most emigrants saved for years and borrowed or sold their possessions to pay for the journey. While some surely left knowing that they would not return, the vast majority believed that their sojourn abroad would be brief but rewarding.[82] In the hope of ensuring this, emigrants leaving the village of Rashayya tied a strip of their clothing to a tree that was on the footpath leading out of the village as an omen for good fortune abroad and safe return. The tree became so laden with small pieces of cloth that it came to be known as the "Tree of Rags."[83]

For those who had borrowed heavily, especially if they had mortgaged their land, the primary objective in the first few months of their migration was to pay the lender back. Mikha'il Nu'ayma, for example, remembered that in his village of Biskinta relatives of emigrants would routinely answer the question "How is your son/husband doing?" with either "Praise God! He sent the passage money *[al-nawalun]*" or simply "He still hasn't sent it."[84] After this debt was paid, emigrants hoped they would soon return to the homeland with more cash in hand. Yusuf Za-kham, a resident of Lincoln, Nebraska, and a frequent contributor to the Arabic-language press in the United States, argued in 1910 that for this reason Syrians abroad should be called, not immigrants, but "travelers" *(musafirun)*. "If you ask a Syrian in North or South America whether he has emigrated from Syria, he will reply, 'Absolutely not. I am away from her for a while. I left *[nazahtu]* in search of wealth, and when I succeed I will return to my homeland.' "[85] The expectation that earnings would be put to use in communities of origin helped emigrants endure the difficulties associated with the journey to the Americas. No adequate figures for return migration exist for this period, but it is clear from oral histories and written memoirs that many emigrants did make return trips to Syria, often many times over.[86] They certainly bought land, and so rapidly that prices in the *mutasarrifiyya* (governorate of Mount Lebanon) rose exponentially.[87]

Ottoman government officials were aware of this new emigration wave and tried in various ways to control it. In the late 1880s, letters from the governors of Mount Lebanon and Beirut to Istanbul revealed a growing unease at the tide of "Lebanese" emigration.[88] Ottoman officials were not only alarmed by the size of the emigration from Mount Lebanon but also troubled by the clandestine methods of travel. In collaboration with the governors of Mount Lebanon and Beirut, they attempted to deal with the problem of illegal emigration in a variety of ways. They handed down stricter punishments for smugglers and travel agents in the hope of curtailing the illicit traffic of emigrants. The coast was, for a short time, patrolled with greater frequency, and Ottoman government officials appealed to foreign governments to assist in the regulation of travel abroad. None of these measures proved effective, however, because of the ambiguity of the existing laws. While emigration was technically forbidden for political and moral reasons (the government was concerned about opposition movements organizing in the diaspora but also worried over the hardships that Ottoman subjects faced at different stages of their migration), emigrants could acquire an internal travel permit without much difficulty. This permit allowed them to travel to a port of departure within the empire—such as Alexandria, Egypt—from which they would embark for a European port. Ottoman officials realized that the tide of emigration would be stopped only by one of two measures: draconian enforcement of stricter travel laws or a radical improvement of the economic situation in Mount Lebanon. The second was the most attractive but also the most elusive. Emigration actually benefited the Mountain economically through substantial remittances from abroad. By 1900, Noël Verney and George Dambmann estimated that Lebanese emigrants sent between 2.5 and 3.5 million francs home each year.[89] Emigrant earnings often went into the purchase of land, although by the end of the nineteenth century they were more obviously displayed in houses with red-tile roofs and in the consumer goods associated with a bourgeoning middle class.[90] In what would become a pattern throughout Lebanon, emigrants from Zahle contributed to the building of a new hospital in their hometown in 1908.[91]

Lifting restrictions altogether, however, presented another set of concerns. This could encourage Muslim peasants to leave, a strategy that many had already contemplated since the extension of military conscription into areas of Syria previously unaccustomed to service. The large-scale departure of Muslims at a time when the central government in Istanbul needed recruits for the army and was consciously trying to enhance its image as the supreme Islamic power would compromise its legitimacy. Despite these reservations, the government made the decision in 1898 to allow the "Lebanese" to travel freely, provided they pledged to retain Ottoman citizenship. The liberalization of emigration policy, however, did not radically change the methods of travel. The network of middlemen was entrenched in the economy of Beirut, and they continued to dominate the migration trade. Abuse and exploitation of emigrants continued. Ten years after the reform in Ottoman policy, a group of Syrians formally petitioned the Ottoman consul in Washington, D.C., to help protect emigrants from unscrupulous officials and rapacious middlemen in Beirut, as well as in the main ports of call in the journey to the United States.[92]

GENDER AND RELIGION OF FIRST-WAVE IMMIGRANTS

The authors of the petition were especially concerned about the abuse of female travelers and the elderly. By 1908, when the petition was drafted, women had become a significant portion of the Syrian migration flow into the United States. Between 1899 and 1914—corresponding to the peak years of Syrian migration to the United States—women made up 32 percent of the total, a high figure especially in relation to other Mediterranean immigrant groups. Southern Italian women, for example, made up 21 percent of the late nineteenth- and early twentieth-century migration from Italy.[93] Even in the two years preceding the outbreak of World War I, when Syrian men left in greater numbers than in previous years to avoid conscription into the Ottoman army, women were still a significant portion (5,665 out of 18,233) of the total number of arrivals to the United States.[94]

Many of these women arrived as the wives or fiancées of men who had preceded them. Oral histories of Syrian immigrant men and women relate how elder female relatives orchestrated matches and sent daughters, nieces, and cousins of marriageable age off to the United States to meet up with marriage partners. Essa Samara, for example, was preparing to marry an American woman he had met in Manchester, New Hampshire, when his mother intervened and sent him a bride from his village. The young woman arrived in New York in the company of Essa's sister, and although the voyage and the medical inspection at Ellis Island had terrified her, the idea of marrying a man she had seldom, if ever, set eyes on may not have troubled her. Essa was doing well. He had a house, knew a fair amount of English, and could promise a degree of comfort that was above what the young woman had known in Syria.[95] For Sultana Alkazin, however, the reunion with her husband was a bitter one. She arrived in Philadelphia in 1901 with her three children, only to find that he had a mistress and expected them all to live together with him. Sultana refused, left her husband, and eventually moved to Atlantic City, where she sold linens on the boardwalk.[96]

While the literature on Syrian migration views marriage to a male emigrant as the most logical explanation for the arrival of Syrian women in the United States in the three decades before World War I, there is considerable evidence to support other explanations and to suggest that the chain migration thesis, in which the first link is a young, unmarried male, needs significant revision.[97] The 1930 U.S. Census, for example, shows that 16.1 percent of the Syrian female population over fifteen years old were widowed and 9.9 percent were single.[98] These widows could have been the wives of men who came during the peak years of Syrian immigration to the United States, but this would assume an abnormally high mortality rate among their husbands. The relatively large number of widows in the census might more accurately reflect the lives of women like Martha Cammel, who arrived in the United States *as* a widow operating outside the traditional chain migration paradigm. Martha, a widow from Beirut, was preceded not by a husband or son but by several daughters whom she had sent ahead of her to the *mahjar*.[99] When she had saved

Figure 4. Sultana Alkazin, her unnamed husband, and her son Fred in Beirut,
ca. 1887. Photo courtesy of Faris and Yamna Naff Arab-American Collection,
Archives Center, National Museum of American History, Behring Center,
Smithsonian Institution.

Figure 5. Sultana Alkazin, Atlantic City, early to mid-1900s. Photo courtesy of Faris and Yamna Naff Arab-American Collection.

enough money, she too made the journey. On the way over, she met twenty-year-old Amen Soffa from Douma, Syria, who had left his five-acre vineyard in the care of his sister. The travelers must have kept in touch because in 1902 Amen married Martha's oldest daughter Nazera, and they settled on a ten-acre parcel of land bought with Amen's earnings from ten years of peddling between Lacrosse, Wisconsin, and Greenleafton, Minnesota.

Annie Midlige (née Tabsharani), also a widow from Beirut, emigrated two years after Martha in 1894. Annie had made her first big move at the age of eighteen when she left her village of Dhour al-Shwayr to work in Beirut's largest silk factory. Twelve years later, a widow with four children, she sailed to New York City. She then pushed on to Ottawa, Canada, made contact with suppliers there, and moved northeast to establish herself as one of the most successful independent traders in the Quebec interior. She reached beyond existing outposts to trade with Indian populations and became a fierce competitor to the powerful Hudson's Bay Company. Alarmed at her encroachment into the Hudson Bay Company's fur-trading territory, one company inspector wrote in his report that "opposition has been creeping nearer and nearer every year by way of the Gatineau [River] in the shape of a woman, Mrs. Medlege [sic]."[100]

The migration of Syrian women in the first decades of the twentieth century appears to have combined two patterns noticeable in the migration streams studied by Donna Gabaccia in her work on Italian immigrant women: first, a family strategy to preserve subsistence production as a way of life; and, second, a migration of young wage earners drawn simultaneously by the American side of an international market for their labor and by a "marriage market" that offered new prospects for family formation under changing circumstances.[101] The second pattern characterized the migration of Selma Nimee, who worked in a Syrian-owned kimono factory in Chicago, and by Margaret Malooley, who emigrated at the age of twenty to join her father and with the aim of working to pay the passage from Syria for her mother, brother, and sister.[102] Margaret peddled goods in Spring Valley, Illinois, until she married and then continued to supplement her husband's income by selling her tatting, embroidery, and lace. Despite her husband's early death, "with my work" and the money he left her, she noted, "we didn't need anyone's help—not the government's."[103]

As in other migration systems—the Mexican, for example—the decision to emigrate was made in the interest of the family and was characterized by a high degree of flexibility—a necessary quality in a rapidly changing homeland economy.[104] Most often the husband was the first link in the chain, but it was not uncommon for single or widowed women to be pioneers who entered the U.S. labor market as seamstresses and peddlers. Many had been exposed to wage labor in Syria or had already maintained the household in the absence of a spouse or male relative.

Proportionately, Mount Lebanon sent the greatest number of emigrants from Syria, both female and male, abroad. The most reliable statistics estimate that over one-fourth the population left for the Americas and Africa between 1885 and 1914.[105] There were also sizable emigrations from other Syrian areas, particularly the Qalamoun (Yabroud, Nebik, Dayr 'Atiyya), Homs, Safita, and Suweida regions.[106] Karpat estimated that 320,000 Syrians emigrated in the years between 1881 and 1901, a figure that would represent approximately one-sixth the total population of Syria.[107]

The question of how many of these emigrants entered the United States is answered with widely diverging numbers. The U.S. Immigration Commission claimed that 56,909 Syrians had entered the country between 1899 and 1910, while the Thirteenth Census of 1910, under the category of "foreign stock" of Syrian origin, gave a figure of 46,727 persons.[108] Syrian community estimates were much higher, sometimes three times that of the census.[109] Part of the reason for the inaccuracy of U.S. government statistics lies in the fact that Syrians were not distinguished from other Ottoman subjects until 1899. Also, many Syrians, afraid of being turned away at Ellis Island as carriers of the infectious eye disease trachoma, entered the United States via Mexico or Canada, thereby avoiding registration as immigrants. Louise Houghton's 1911 study of Syrian immigrants supplemented U.S. government figures with community estimates to reach a figure of over 100,000. The 1920 U.S. Census counted 51,900 Syrians as part of the "foreign-born white population."[110]

The other important government sources of information on the Syrian community in the United States (and forty-five other countries) are the French consular reports sent to the Ministère des affaires étrangères shortly after France assumed the Mandate over Syria and Lebanon in 1920. These reports consist of population surveys of the Syrian migrants in French consular districts, but like U.S. statistics their quality and accuracy varies. The French were interested primarily in emigrants who registered for French protection. The number of those who did not was often a product of educated guesswork and information furnished by leaders of the community.[111] Moreover, the reports were completed at different dates, making it difficult to "freeze" the number of migrants in one place and at one time. Adding the totals of the reports submitted between 1921 and 1931 yields a figure of 143,980 persons, significantly smaller than the number proposed by Philip Hitti, who argued that the number of Syrians in the United States had reached 200,000 in 1924.[112]

Syrian immigrants of this first wave of migration were overwhelmingly Christian, and the areas of heaviest concentration were in the Northeast and Midwest. New York City was their "mother colony," and the city served as a hub for the Syrian community for several decades.[113] The earliest Syrian immigrants to New York forged an economic niche in the peddling trade, with the more prosperous among them setting up supply shops along Washington Street on the Lower West Side. For many Syrian immigrants, this busy avenue was their first stop after going through the arduous immigration processing at Castle Garden and later, when it was opened in 1892, Ellis Island. They found along Washington Street a network of co-ethnics who facilitated their transition to working life in the United States. Pack peddling drew a steady stream of Syrian immigrants to New York, and they busied themselves selling household items and curios from the "Holy Land" to buyers in the city and elsewhere. Syrian wholesale suppliers were central figures in the peddling circuits, becoming, in many cases, members of a trade diaspora with branches of their businesses in New York City and other points along the transatlantic route to the Americas.[114] By the early twentieth century, the variety of businesses along Washington Street and Broadway Avenue was extensive. A survey of the advertising sections in the early Arabic-language press in New York indicates the presence of stores selling a range of goods including sewing machines, coffee, Arabic music, phonographs, and linens. Syrian silk merchants revived their trade in the city and tapped into a growing consumer interest in silk goods. Washington Street soon housed thirty-five Syrian manufactures of kimonos. Other textile manufacturers focused on the production of woolen knits. In the mid-1920s, one in three sweaters worn in New York was produced by the firm of N. P. and J. Trabulsi.[115]

As the community grew and prospered, many members moved from the Lower West Side to Brooklyn to purchase homes and businesses and to establish religious institutions there. Lucius Miller's comprehensive

1904 study of the Greater New York community found Melkites (Greek Catholics) in the majority, followed by the Maronites, Eastern Orthodox, and a much smaller number of Protestants. Out of a total population of 2,482 persons, there were only seven Muslims and approximately one hundred Syrian Jews.[116] The U.S. Census of 1910 revealed that there were just over 6,000 persons born in "Turkey in Asia" living in New York City, the vast majority of whom would have been Syrian.[117] As the names of some of the "Syrian"-owned businesses indicate (Parkyan and Narian, for example), there were also a good number of Arabic-speaking Armenians in the community, most probably from the cities of Aleppo and Damascus.

The Syrian colony in New York generated the earliest American representations of a Middle Eastern immigrant community. Indeed, despite its relatively small size, the Syrian enclave on the Lower West Side drew a number of journalists, scholars, and tourists to its midst. Given the American fascination with the Orient, this curiosity is hardly surprising. Observers of the Syrian colony appeared to graph their encounters with the Syrian population there onto already formed ideas of Eastern mystery and religiosity. E. Lyell Earle noted in his lengthy article entitled "Foreign Types of New York Life" that the Syrian colony, "while fairly clean," supported a number of "Turkish restaurants," at which a meal would be "an ordeal few Americans can undergo." While Earle suggested that his digestive system rebelled against the seasoning of Syrian food, we are left wondering whether he indulged in what he called the "mysterious hubble-bubble," which produced, at least among the Syrians, a "supremely soothing effect."[118]

One also finds in the early descriptions of the Syrians in New York the idea that they exist along a color continuum. A *New York Times* article on the Syrian enclave around Washington Street noted that "a good many of them are easily distinguishable by a rather dark complexion, and might by some be taken for Italians or Frenchmen from the South of France, but not a few are of quite light complexion, with light-colored hair."[119]

These representations objectified the Syrian community and generally marked it as foreign and Other, but they did not go unchallenged. Cromwell Childe, for example, noted in his 1899 article that these "same colonies are by no means haunts of Asiatic mystery and seductions." He chastised another writer for fabricating a "theatric Syrian quarter [with] red-fezzed heads, and languorous eyes." "It is foreign, quaint, interesting," Childe continued, "but not in the manner the tale-tellers scribble about it." Childe objected to some of the more fanciful depictions of the Syrian quarter, but he did not restrain himself from exaggeration when describing poor immigrants of the colony: "The lower class, men and women alike, have little that is attractive about them. They have been called the dirtiest people in all New York [and] the women here have no beauty of either face or form."[120] In contrast, the "well-off Orientals" impressed Childe greatly. He noted that Michael Kaydouh, owner of Sahadi's wholesale shop, "save for his olive skin and his cast of features, scarcely seems a Syrian at all. His English is pure and he has little foreign accent."[121] Childe had difficulty recognizing Kaydouh's cosmopolitanism as Syrian, but this merchant typified an emerging transnational bourgeoisie who cleverly exploited American's desire to "shop the Orient" by rapidly producing carpets, fine silks, and lace. The purchase of these goods, combined with attendance at wildly popular Oriental-themed plays and films such as The Arab (1915) and The Sheik (1921), starring Rudolph Valentino, allowed Americans to access feelings of reverie, release, and sensual pleasure that they associated with the East and to break with the constraints of nineteenth-century Protestant piety.[122] A 1924 article on the Syrian colony in New York, for example, began in this way: "To one just come from the Occident, a descent upon the Syrian quarters in New York is like a dream travel. . . . Take the Sixth Ave. Elevated at Forty-second Street . . . and in a few minutes you are in Rector Street, walk a block westward to Washington Street, and you are in Syria."[123]

By the turn of the second decade of the twentieth century, Syrians had settled far beyond the New York colony and could be found in every state of the United States. While the prototypical experience of early Syrians was peddling, other niches attracted them as well and help explain their geographical concentrations. Mill owners in Massachusetts, for example, hired Syrian laborers, many of whom participated in the "Bread and Roses" strike in Lawrence in 1912. A Boston Globe article reporting on the strike noted that "people of 51 nationalities, speaking 45 languages could be found. . . . The Irish came first, then the Germans, English and French-Canadians, then the real flood—Italians, Greeks, Syrians, Poles, Lithuanians, Eastern Europeans . . . after almost seventy-five years of submissions—23,000 of those workers stuck against unfair wage cuts and oppressive conditions."[124] Like other working-class immigrants, some Syrians were drawn to Henry Ford's promise of five dollars a day. By 1916, 555 Syrian men were working at the Ford car plants

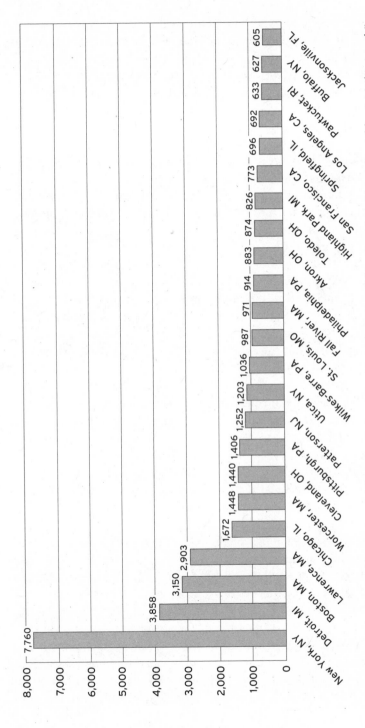

Figure 6. Major Syrian populations in the United States, 1920. Population figures based on "mother tongue of foreign white stock" (Syrian and Arabic), as listed in the Fourteenth Census of the United States, 1920, vol. 2, *Population* (Washington, DC: Government Printing Office, 1922). Cities listed are those with a population of six hundred Syrians or more.

in Dearborn, Michigan.[125] Over time, the Syrian community in metro-
politan Detroit surpassed that of Greater New York in terms of diversity,
concentration, and institutional complexity. In 1920, according to the
U.S. Census, the top five areas of Syrian settlement were New York, Detroit, Boston, Chicago, and Cleveland. While the first wave of Syrian immigrants was predominantly Christian, more research needs to be done
on the sectarian breakdown of this population. In New York Maronites
formed the largest religious sect, but in other communities the situation
was different. In Worcester, Massachusetts, for example, the Antiochian Orthodox constituted the majority, and in Ross, North Dakota,
the Syrian immigrant population was primarily Muslim.[126] Communities in the South tended to be Greek Catholic and Maronite, although
there were sizable numbers of Russian and Antiochian Orthodox as
well.[127]

The Syrian emigration to the Americas was one of several large-scale migrations changing the demographic makeup of greater Syria in the last
quarter of the nineteenth century. As this chapter has argued, transatlantic migration began, not as a flight from the oppression of the Ottoman regime, nor as the expression of an intrinsic migratory trait bequeathed to the Syrians by the Phoenicians, but as a response to the
changing economic organization of the Syrian coast and its immediate
hinterland. Transatlantic migration became a possibility because of the
way that Syria (and especially Mount Lebanon) had become integrated
into a capitalist world economy. Once started, emigration from Syria
produced a dynamic of its own, or, as Elie Safa succinctly summarized
the phenomenon, "L'émigration sollicite l'émigration."[128] But this dynamic must be disentangled from larger transformations in the Syrian
economy, which both encouraged transatlantic emigration and made it
possible.

Situating the beginnings of the Syrian migration to the Americas
within a world economy perspective does not mean that individual migrants lacked agency and were caught in a system over which they had
no control. It took courage to embark on a journey to a place that was
a mysterious, mispronounced place in one's mind, and it required persistence to tolerate the sickening journey in steerage class. And while it is
easy to imagine the excitement of a family receiving its first remittance
from abroad, it is harder to conceive of the anguish upon learning that
others never made it to *Amirka*. Twenty-two Syrian emigrants drowned
on their way to Venezuela in 1898, for example, and many more per-

ished among the over 1,500 persons lost in the *Titanic*'s inaugural voyage.[129] Might not these losses have caused fellow villagers to reconsider their own plans to emigrate? Did they also believe—as an obituary in the New York Arabic newspaper *al-Hoda* claimed—that "there was nothing worse than dying in a strange land"?[130] These are questions that cannot be readily answered by relying on the workings of large economic structures.

For the early migrants to the United States the *mahjar* was "strange" on a number of levels. They were confronted with a new language and unfamiliar food, smells, and faces. Tanyus Tadrus, for example, recalled wandering the streets of Philadelphia after his arrival in 1885, not knowing where to turn or what to do until he heard a voice in Arabic ask, "Where are you from?" The voice belonged to an Ottoman Jew from Jerusalem. "You can't imagine how happy we were when we saw someone speaking to us in our language," Tanyus explained. "We embraced him and said to him, 'We are not leaving you until you show us a place to stay, or take us to others like us *[ibna' jildatina]*."[131] Speakers of Arabic could console newly arrived immigrants and provide them with information about where to eat, sleep, and find work.

Other, less practical considerations made the United States especially different for Syrians: the emphasis on race as a marker of social difference. Where exactly Syrians fit into America's complicated racial taxonomy soon became a question whose answer was far from obvious.

CHAPTER 2

Claiming Whiteness

Syrians and Naturalization Law

Race in the present state of things is an abstract conception,
a notion of continuity in discontinuity, of unity in diversity. It
is the rehabilitation of a real but directly unattainable thing.

Circuit Judge Lowell, In re Halladjian et al. (1909)

No one was white before he/she came to America. It took
generations, and a vast amount of coercion, before this became a white country.

James Baldwin (1984)

As the number of Syrians in the United States increased and people like
Tanyus Tadrus found work, many began to contemplate acquiring American citizenship. Naturalization gave immigrants access to certain privileges. They could vote, travel more easily—including back and forth to
Syria—and purchase property. Essa Samara noted that he chose to naturalize "to be like the people with whom we were doing business, to vote,
and it was useful in case one went to Canada or back home or elsewhere."[1] Although not entirely happy about this development, the French
consul in Seattle argued that "it is natural that all these immigrants pre-
fer to naturalize as Americans because of all sorts of advantages that result [from it]."[2]

Acquiring citizenship, however, was not so straightforward in a country that was increasingly concerned about its "foreign element." In this
context, naturalization law became a key arena for determining who
could and could not become an American. Because the naturalization
law was limited to "aliens being free white persons, and to aliens of
African nativity and to persons of African descent" the contest was, at
its root, a racialized one. For Syrian immigrants, acquiring citizenship

came to hinge on the question of whether they were white. It is this history that Costa Najour alluded to in an interview conducted fifty-two years after Circuit Court Judge Newman deemed him to be a "free white person," eligible for naturalization. Reflecting on the experience, he described the "great furor in some states (and especially North Carolina) that the Syrians were yellow, not white [min asfar laysa abyad]."[3] Najour, whose 1909 case helped secure the Syrian legal status as "white," seemed to understand his whiteness only in relation to a racialized Other, to a group he described as "yellow." He did not so much *affirm* his status as a "white" person as *negate* that he was something else. This chapter examines how and why Syrian immigrants, whose premigratory conceptions of difference were rooted primarily in religion, developed a new racial awareness and became increasingly invested in whiteness.

SYRIANS AND THE NEW NATIVISM

The question of whether Syrians met the racial requirement of the naturalization law did not become controversial until the first decade of the twentieth century. Syrians who had applied for citizenship before 1909 had been granted it without much deliberation.[4] Many had filed their first papers (the so-called declaration of intent to become a citizen) and were waiting the requisite time period before they could complete the application process and be sworn in as citizens. This wait became more difficult as anxieties over the United States' large immigrant population intensified and as nativists sharpened their rhetoric with demands for restriction on immigration and greater surveillance of the foreign born—particularly those born in southern Europe and Asia. The concern with controlling immigration found institutional support in 1906 with the creation of the Bureau of Immigration and Naturalization in the Department of Commerce and Labor. The bureau's responsibilities involved the administration of a new naturalization law aimed at curtailing many of the abuses that had plagued the naturalization process in the nineteenth century. The law of 1906 banned, for example, naturalization hearings held within thirty days of a general election in a court's area of jurisdiction. Such a measure would, its framers hoped, discourage political bosses from rounding up immigrants and herding them to court to secure their naturalization papers and thereafter their votes. An extensive bureaucracy that included three hundred naturalization examiners stationed throughout the country administered the newly codified law.[5]

This reinvigorated nativism produced elaborate theories of the contaminating effect of the "new immigration" from southern and eastern Europe. Members of the northern intelligentsia, for example, churned out literature on Anglo-Saxon "race suicide" and allied themselves with the proponents of eugenics. Southern whites, in contrast, were principally concerned with cracks in the color line. Particularly threatening to white southerners was the "inbetweenness" of the new immigrants.[6] The ambiguous racial status of Italians, East European Jews, and Syrians stemmed from the perception that they possessed cultures and habits that were fundamentally at odds with southern traditions and values and that immigrants would not abide by the "white man's code." Southerners could point, for example, to the close relations that Italian immigrants had with blacks with whom they worked as evidence of interracial alliances that threatened to undermine white supremacy.[7] In the wake of the lynching of three Italians in Hahnville, Louisiana, in 1896, some whites feared that Italian immigrants would bond with blacks (who were regularly the victims of lynch mobs) and seek revenge.[8] Nativists lashed out at the alleged "immigrant menace" in public denunciations and in behind-the-scenes schemes that involved intimidation and violence. It was in this climate of rising nativism that North Carolina senator F. M. Simmons claimed that the new immigrants were "the spawn of the Phoenician curse."[9]

Senator Simmons's use of the biological metaphor "spawn" was in keeping with the most vitriolic nativist language of the day, which linked immigration to contagion and disease. Government health officials helped fuel this prejudice by quarantining entire immigrant neighborhoods, ostensibly to control whatever disease that they believed was spread by immigrant habits.[10] The Chinese and Russian Jews were especially pathologized in this regard, and it was possible that Syrian immigrants would suffer the same fate. Already Syrians were being refused entry into the United States at an increasing rate as carriers of trachoma. Caused by the bacteria *Chlamydia trachomatis,* the disease occurred at high rates in countries with a lack of clean running water and often led to blindness.[11] The U.S. Public Health Service considered trachoma (along with favus, venereal diseases, parasitic infections, and tuberculosis) a "loathsome and dangerous contagious disease" warranting exclusion.[12] In 1909, Ellis Island officials certified 103 Syrians for trachoma, and of the thirty-nine "races" listed according to numbers deported in 1909 for medical reasons, Syrians were ranked sixth at 113 cases, 35 of whom were women.[13] While these documented cases of trachoma did represent a health risk, the perception that Syrians were, as a group, medically unfit for immigration did not correspond to reality, for less than 2 percent of Syrian immigrants received medical rejection certificates at Ellis Island. Still, Dr. Alfred Reed of the U.S. Public Health and Marine Hospital advocated a general exclusion of them because they were "unfit" and "undesirable."[14]

The experience of having trachoma, but also the fear of contracting it, shaped many Syrian journeys to the United States. Tafaha Laham al-Tin, for example, recalled how she was "held up in Paris for three years because of my eyes" while her husband and children went on ahead of her. Alice Abraham remembered being separated from relatives in Marseilles after they did not pass the medical inspection there.[15] Thirteen-year-old Eli A. B.'s father tried to avoid the inspection of his son's eyes by purchasing a ticket for him in first class where they were less likely to be scrutinized, but to no avail. A doctor who boarded at Liverpool to inspect passengers discovered Eli's trachoma and took him off the ship without his parents' knowledge. It was three months before Eli, his eyes treated thanks to the assistance of an Arabic-speaking boardinghouse owner, was reunited with his father in Halifax, Nova Scotia. They then made their way to Worcester, Massachusetts, where the rest of the family was located. Eli's voyage from Mahiethett, Lebanon, to Worcester had taken ten months.[16]

The fear of being excluded because of trachoma prompted many Syrians to attempt entering the United States via Mexico.[17] Alice Abraham sailed on to New York from Marseilles and reached her destination of Cedar Rapids, Iowa, but her relatives went to Mexico and entered the United States from there; the journey took them four months. Some Syrians even "disguised" themselves as Mexicans by learning rudimentary Spanish and crossed into the United States from Mexico at El Paso, Texas.[18] Other Syrians got caught in the extortion ring organized by Dr. Edward D. Sinks, who was acting assistant surgeon of the Public Health and Marine Hospital Service in El Paso. Sinks coordinated with Dr. John W. Coffin, a U.S. physician practicing in El Paso and Juárez, Mexico, and with Kahil Koury, a Syrian boardinghouse manager in Juárez. According to the research of Ann Gabbert, the extortion scheme ran as follows: Koury brought Syrians to the border for inspection by Sinks, who denied them entry on the basis of trachoma, even though most were in perfectly good health. Koury then brought the "diseased" Syrians to Coffin, who, upon payment of twenty dollars in cash, treated them with a silver nitrate solution placed in the eyes every three days for a total of ten treatments.

When this treatment was completed, Coffin issued certificates to each Syrian attesting to the fact that he or she was now cured of trachoma. Koury then took the Syrians back to Sinks, who allowed them entry into the United States. An undercover agent for the Bureau of Immigration discovered the scheme, and Sinks was brought under investigation. He was replaced in January 1907 and spent the next six months treating trachoma in Juárez. Coffin died of meningitis in 1908, but the smuggling and extortion schemes did not. Investigators discovered that Syrian immigrants avoided the scrutiny at El Paso by entering at other border communities such as Piedras Negras and Eagle Pass.[19]

Syrians did, then, find ways to evade authorities, but trachoma separated many of them permanently from members of their family and sent them sailing out of U.S. ports of entry to South America and even as far away as Australia.[20] As Alan Kraut has argued, the "disease status" of a particular immigrant group, whether real or imagined, served as a gauge of the desirability of their entry both into the country and into the polity.[21] In this context of heightened nativism, bureaucratic reform, and concern with disease, Syrian racial identity began to be challenged by politicians, academics, and, eventually, lawyers and federal judges.

One of the pillars of the nativist movement was the literacy test, a test that would restrict entry into the United States to literate persons only. Like much proposed legislation aimed at curtailing immigration, however, its proponents linked illiteracy (in English) to other undesirable traits. Popular Alabama congressman John L. Burnett, for example, proposed the literacy test as a means to control the entry of nonwhite persons into the United States. Of particular concern to him were the Syrians, Jews, Poles, and Russians, who he argued "belonged to a distinct race other than the white race." His comments did not fall on deaf ears, and in response, a leading member of the Syrian community in Birmingham generated the first significant argument in favor of Syrian whiteness. In a carefully worded letter to the editor in the *Birmingham Age-Herald*, H. A. Elkourie, a physician and president of the Syrian Young Men's Society in Birmingham, Alabama, challenged Burnett's views on the literacy test and on racial difference.[22] Elkourie argued that the test was an inadequate measure of a person's qualifications, and he added in good humor that "my experience has shown me that scoundrels exist among the educated in greater proportion than amongst the uneducated."[23] The most important issue for Elkourie was Burnett's claim that Syrians "belonged to a distinct race other than the white race." Elkourie responded by emphasizing Syrian compatibility with Western civilization and by relying on a religious argument that would become key to Syrian understanding of whiteness.

The first step was to argue that the Syrians were Semites. Then, citing "authorities" from Edward Gibbon to *Webster's Dictionary,* Elkourie placed the Semites within a branch of the "white race." But his argument went beyond the purely ethnological, for at the core of his defense of the Semitic peoples was a description of their contribution to Western civilization. From the Phoenicians to Jesus Christ, he wrote, the "Semitic was the original civilizer, developer and intermediator of culture and learning."[24] The power of this argument derived not from a claim to any special racial phenotype but from a reclaiming of a Semitic origin for the Syrians and an emphasis on the Syrian connection to the Holy Land and to Christianity. However, Elkourie's argument was not merely an attempt to emphasize religious affinity with southern whites (a difficult argument to sustain given that southerners were unfamiliar with the Eastern rite churches to which most Syrians belonged); it was an attempt to understand difference—in this case racial difference—the way Syrians had traditionally done so, that is, in religious terms. Thus Elkourie made his argument for inclusion in the "white race" on the basis of membership in the Christian fold. Alone, this argument would not hold up in a court of law as constituting decisive proof of whiteness, but it became a pillar of Syrian legal argumentation and community self-construction. The sense of Christian entitlement to share in whiteness became markedly evident in a series of naturalization cases that soon followed the controversy around Syrian racial identity generated by Congressman Burnett.

LITIGATING WHITENESS

Scholars of the Arab American experience have tended to assume that Syrians encountered difficulty in the naturalization process only in the "color-conscious" South, with its culture of racial segregation and Jim Crow laws. This was not the case. Syrians litigated their racial status in Massachusetts, Oregon, Ohio, Missouri, and California, in addition to South Carolina and Georgia. In fact, the first Syrian racial prerequisite case to provoke a coordinated response by Syrians was that of George Shishim, which was heard in the Los Angeles Superior Court in 1909.

George Shishim immigrated from Zahle, Lebanon, to the United States in 1894. As a young man, he traveled with the "Streets of Cairo" exhibit and later settled in Venice, California, where he became a police

officer. His legal battle to prove his whiteness began after he arrested the
son of a prominent lawyer for disturbing the peace. The arrested man
claimed that Shishim could not charge him with the crime because he
was not, and could not become, an American citizen since he was not of
the white race. This argument echoed the one made by a white defendant
in *People v. Hall* in 1854. Convicted of murder, Hall appealed to the
California Supreme Court on the grounds that the testimony against him
by a Chinese witness was invalid under the provisions of an 1850 statute
stating that "no Black, or Mulatto person, or Indian shall be allowed to
give evidence in favor of, or against a White man."[25] The court ruled in
favor of the defendant, reasoning that *black* was a generic term encom-
passing all nonwhites and that it thus included Chinese persons.

Leading members of the Syrian community in Los Angeles, including
Phares Behannesey, Mike George, Elias Shedoudy, Nick Baida, Saleem
Sawaya, and John Safady, pooled their resources to hire an attorney,
Byron C. Hanna, and defend Shishim. Judge Frank Hutton, who ruled
in the case, based his decision primarily on legal precedent. He argued
that "the courts of this nation, both state and federal, have whenever
called upon for more than a century, construed the term 'white person,'
or members of the white race, to include the Syrians."[26] According to the
Los Angeles Times, the decision in Shishim's favor "made every feature
of his dark, swarthy countenance roseate with pleasure and hope."[27]

Judge Hutton's argument that the courts of the nation had decided
and would continue to decide in favor of Syrian whiteness was quickly
undermined in the case of Costa Najour, heard in Atlanta, Georgia, in
December 1909.[28] Najour was from the coastal town of Batroun, situated north of Beirut in present-day Lebanon. He immigrated to the
United States in 1902, following the lead of his mother, who had come
twice before with her brothers and had returned to Batroun. After working as a clerk in Atlanta (where he had cousins), Costa purchased a dry
goods store.[29] He petitioned for citizenship in the fall of 1909 but was
denied on the basis of the argument that he did not meet the requirements of the revised statute. Najour appealed, hired a lawyer, Willis M.
Everett, and formed an association to assist in his effort to gain American citizenship. His case generated considerable attention in the Atlanta
papers, which began covering the story in November and carried frequent articles through to the December rehearing. "Atlanta Syrians Fight
for Rights," announced an early article in the *Atlanta Journal.* "[They]
have formed a league and employed counsel to resist the efforts now
afoot in many parts of the United States to deny their race the right of

Figure 7. George Shishim, Los Angeles, ca. 1909. Courtesy of the Arab-American Historical Foundation.

becoming American citizens on the alleged ground that they are not Caucasians."[30]

After the first day of arguments at the Fifth Circuit Court, the same paper noted that "Costa Najour ... is still in the dark as to whether or not he is a white man."[31] On December 3, however, after hearing arguments of both sides and listening to the lengthy questioning of the petitioner until, as Najour phrased it, "I became as a drunk," Judge William T. Newman granted him naturalization on the basis of membership in the "white race." The rationale for Judge Newman's decision fell overwhelmingly on the side of what he considered "scientific evidence." He cited, for example, A. H. Keane's *The World's People,* which divided the world's population into four classes: Negro or black, Mongol or yellow, Amerinds, and Caucasians. According to Keane, Caucasians hailed from "North Africa, Europe, Iran, India, Western Asia, and Polynesia." Newman relied on Keane's classificatory scheme to argue that Syrians belonged to "what we recognize, and what the world recognizes, as the white race."[32] He rejected the idea that the naturalization statute referred to skin color and was adamant that "fair or dark complexion should not be allowed to control [the decision]."[33] This construction would be used in other rulings where the judges argued that race was not to be determined by "ocular inspection alone."

Judge Newman's decision in the *Najour* case helped alter the discourse on racial classification by distinguishing between skin color and race.[34] It is important to note, however, that he followed his statement on color with this caveat: "providing the person seeking naturalization comes within the classification of the white or Caucasian race."[35] In other words, color didn't necessarily matter if it could be determined by some other rationale that the applicant was white and possessed the personal qualifications deemed necessary for naturalization. In cases where personal qualifications were in doubt, and the applicant was deemed unworthy of citizenship, color continued to serve as an additional marker of ineligibility. When, for example, Judge Smith denied Syrian applicant Faras Shahid naturalization in a South Carolina district court in 1913, he emphasized that Shahid was "somewhat darker than is the usual mulatto of one-half mixed blood between the white and the negro races."[36]

Even Judge Newman, whose ruling in the *Najour* case seemed to move away from color as the defining marker of race, began his decision with a description of Najour as "not particularly dark." He may have distinguished between skin color and race, but a basic pattern persisted in the racial prerequisite cases: the ascription of darkness increased the

chances of ineligibility, while that of lightness decreased them. The lawyer
for the government in the *Najour* case knew as much. After four hours of
testimony by Costa Najour that seemed only to confirm his eligibility to
naturalize, the exasperated lawyer, desperate to prove that Najour was not
white, asked him to take off his shirt and show his body to the court. Najour began to comply but was stopped in the early stages of undress by
Judge Newman, who wanted no such theatrics in his courtroom.[37] What
was perhaps more important in Judge Newman's ruling—as far as alter-
ing the legal discourse on racial classification goes—was his use of the category "Caucasian." Using the literature on ethnology, he reached the conclusion that Syrians were "part of the Caucasian or white race."[38] The use
of *or* was significant, for it indicated that being Caucasian and being white
were held to be one and the same thing. This equation had been used in
combination with other rationales in previous racial prerequisite cases.[39]
What was different in the *Najour* case was that Judge Newman made it
possible to use membership in something called the "Caucasian race" as
the *sole* criterion for judging whether someone was white for the purposes
of naturalization.

Several judges followed Judge Newman's lead, but an equal number
rejected this formulation and dismissed altogether the relevance of
"scientific evidence." Judge Henry Smith, for example, ruling in the
Shahid case cited above, ridiculed the idea that being Caucasian automatically meant someone was white. The very idea of a Caucasian race
was suspect to him, the result, he would later write, "of a strange intellectual hocus pocus."[40] The ultimate test of whiteness, in his view,
was one of geography, and the deciding factor was whether the applicant was from Europe or a descendant of a European immigrant. There
was, therefore, no need to "examine his [the applicant's] complexion
with a microscope nor measure his skull or his limbs and features."[41]
Since the Syrians were, in his estimation, clearly not European but
"Asiatic," they were not entitled to the privileges of citizenship.[42] To
arrive at this ruling that whiteness was linked to European descent,
Judge Smith relied on two other rationales that would become increasingly popular in the racial prerequisite cases: common knowledge and
congressional intent.

The term *congressional intent* referred to the meaning of the Naturalization Act as it was first formulated by Congress in 1790. In Judge
Smith's words, "The real question is: What does the statute mean, to
whom did the terms 'free white persons' refer in 1790, in the understandings of the makers of the law."[43] He answered the question through

an imaginary journey into the mind of a member of Congress at the end of the eighteenth century. Such a man, he argued, would have known nothing of the ethnological or linguistic theories that undergirded modern racial classification. He would, for example, "certainly have repudiated the idea that a black Ceylonese or dark South Persian was in the language of the enthusiastic supporters of the theory that all speakers of Aryan languages are of one race, an 'Aryan brother.' "[44]

Judge Smith was so sure of his argument that he claimed it was all something to which "an average citizen" in 1790 could agree. Appeals to the racial knowledge of the "average citizen" were made frequently in the racial prerequisite cases. James Farell, for example, assistant U.S. attorney in the *Halladjian* case, argued against the admissibility of Armenians by appealing to the racial knowledge of the "average man." He claimed that "without being able to define a white person, the average man in the street understands what it means, and would find no difficulty in assigning to the yellow race a Turk or a Syrian with as much ease as he would bestow that designation on a Chinaman or Korean."[45]

Despite Farrell's assertion that race could be determined without difficulty, the racial prerequisite cases reveal a lack of consensus about who belonged to what race and why. Judge Smith, for example, shifted from his original position that what mattered was the intention of the framers of the law ("congressional intent") to one that emphasized the understanding of the common man ("common knowledge"). Aware of the ambiguity of his own ruling, Judge Smith concluded with the suggestion that an appeal be taken to the Supreme Court, where a settlement to "this most vexed and difficult question could be reached."[46]

The issue was vexed because the naturalization statute could be interpreted in so many different ways. While some judges relied on scientific evidence, others used congressional intent, common knowledge, or some combination of all three to determine the race of an applicant for naturalization. Complicating matters was the category of personal qualifications, which, like color, was not supposed to figure prominently in the determination of race but was repeatedly used to assist in the decision. Syrian applicant Tom Ellis's religious, professional, and moral profile, for example, clearly influenced the decision on his racial eligibility in an Oregon district court in July 1910. Indeed, so intertwined were the criteria in the judge's ruling that it is difficult to discern where one ended and the other began.

Ellis, described as "a Turkish subject . . . a Syrian, a native of the province of Palestine, and a Maronite,"[47] had to counter the argument that he was ineligible for citizenship because he was not of European descent. Lawyers for the district attorney made no attempt to ague that Ellis was not "of the white race," and they openly admitted that Syrians were considered to be white by immigration authorities. The Immigration Commission, for example, which had conducted extensive studies of the immigrant population in the United States between 1907 and 1910, noted that "physically the modern Syrians are of mixed Syrian, Arabian, and even Jewish blood. They belong to the Semitic branch of the Caucasian race, thus widely differing from their rulers, the Turks, who are in origin Mongolian."[48] The argument against Ellis was that he was not the right *kind* of white: that is, he did not descend from white Europeans. The district attorney emphasized the importance of being of European descent in his interpretation of the statute, arguing that the meaning of the words *free white persons* "comprehended such only of the white races who, from tradition, teaching, and environment, would be predisposed toward our form of government, and thus readily assimilate with the people of the United States."[49]

Whereas Judge Smith had couched his preference for European immigrants in the language of congressional intent, lawyers for the government in the *Ellis* case were much more explicit in their use of race as a marker of a particular cultural and political disposition. In the logic of their argument, whiteness was linked to geography (Europe), which in their opinion produced moral and intellectual traits essential for participation in the American polity. More to the point, they assumed that white Europeans were familiar with, and supportive of, republican forms of government. Non-Europeans were, in contrast, deemed to be dubious products of despotic regimes, politically unsophisticated and likely to taint the cherished pool of American citizenry. The government lawyer's insistence on the connection between whiteness and fitness for self-government was a well-worn strategy that was firmly embedded in the discourse of American citizenship.[50] The district attorney in the *Najour* case had also used this argument, claiming that Najour, as a subject of the Muslim Ottoman sultan, was incapable of understanding American institutions and government. Judge Newman dismissed the argument and claimed that if being a Turkish subject disqualified one from naturalization "the extension of the Turkish Empire over people unquestionably of the white race would deprive them of the privilege of naturalization."[51] Despite a ruling in Najour's favor, whiteness as fitness for self-government continued to figure prominently in the legal debates on racial eligibility for citizenship until the 1950s.

Fortunately for Ellis, Judge Wolverton ruled that if Congress had intended the statute to mean Europeans only, it would have specified such. He granted Ellis citizenship, but his ruling reveals how it was possible to reject the specific formulation of the government argument while accepting its underlying assumptions—that "personal qualifications" were an indication of a person's *racial* eligibility for naturalization. What ultimately tilted the decision in Ellis's favor was Judge Wolverton's conviction that he was "possessed of the highest qualities which go to make an excellent citizen . . . well disposed toward the principles and policies of this government."[52] Having already decided that Ellis was of "Semitic stock, a markedly white type of the race," the judge went on to extol Ellis's personal qualifications, noting that he was a "good and highly respected citizen of the community." Tom Ellis spoke English, was a practicing Christian, and was of "good morals, sober and industrious." In short, he possessed "all the essential qualifications to entitle him to naturalization." He was, in Judge Wolverton's view, exactly the type of person Congress had intended to become a citizen. Remarkably oblivious to the debates—scientific, judicial, and congressional—that suggested otherwise, Judge Wolverton believed that the words *free white persons* were devoid of ambiguity and were of "plain and simple signification."[53] He did not pause to consider how far the "personal qualifications" of the applicant had influenced the legal construction of his whiteness.

TRANSNATIONALISM AND THE SYRIAN DEBATE ON RACE

By 1909, it was clear that the Syrian naturalization cases were generating a significant, if at times contradictory, legal definition of whiteness. Syrians were themselves confused about how best to define their racial status, and they turned to various sources to answer their questions. Elkourie had used English-language dictionaries, while Najour and his supporters found standard works in ethnology convincing. Other Syrians turned to the Arabic-language press in the Middle East. Indeed, partly because of the increase in transatlantic migration, there was within elite Middle Eastern discourse in the late nineteenth and early twentieth centuries a new interest in racial classification. The Cairo-based journal *al-Hilal,* for example, devoted several issues to articles on the scientific categorization of human types, written by the editor, Jurji Zaydan, a Syrian émigré. *Al-Hilal* was a popular monthly magazine that "appealed to readers of different classes and leanings because of its interesting subject matter."[54] The journal had a wide circulation in the Middle East and in the diaspora. "You will not find a country in the five continents of the world in which there are readers of Arabic and they do not read *al-Hilal*," Philip Tarazi asserted in his comprehensive study of the Arabic press published in 1913.[55]

The articles in *al-Hilal* on human classification were drawn from Zaydan's book *Tabaqat al-umam* (Classes of Peoples).[56] The book was based on the "modern sciences" of anthropology and ethnology and drew extensively (often verbatim) from a classic tome of ethnology, A. H. Keane's *The World's Peoples*. Zaydan's title, however, borrowed from the fifth-century *(hijri)* Arab judge Saʿd ibn Ahmad al-Andalusi's book of the same name. Al-Andalusi had divided the world into two types: peoples who had excelled in learning and those who had not. Zaydan set out to modernize and supplant this system by using the new "real" classificatory schemes based on "observation and research."[57] He noted that that the importance of these schemes extended beyond purely scientific realms: "The science of human classification is the basis of the philosophy of history, for it elucidates the morals of peoples and their characteristics . . . and it helps explain their decline and florescence."[58]

Tabaqat al-umam divided the world's population into four main categories arranged from lowest to highest. At the bottom were blacks *(al-zunuj)*, "the lowest and most base," followed by the Mongolian or "the yellow race," the American Indian, or "the red race," and the Caucasian, "or the white race."[59] Within the last category Zaydan placed the Semites, which included the "Arabs, Jews, and Aryans." To support the text, he included numerous pictures representing the different human types and, in intriguing choices to represent the Arabs, featured an Egyptian, Mustafa Kamil (1874–1908), leader of the independence movement against the British, and a "Syrian Lebanese," Yusuf Bey Karam (1823–89), a legendary Maronite leader famous for his nineteenth-century revolt against Ottoman authority in Mount Lebanon.

Zaydan's writings reflect the concerns of educated, cosmopolitan elites who were anxious to forge a modern orientation to the world by familiarizing themselves with European racial theories. Interest in racial classification also stemmed from the experience of immigrants throughout the *mahjar,* whose curiosity on matters of race emerged as they confronted new social realities in new places. Earnest queries about their racial status can be found in the less flowery, more matter-of-fact "Question and Answer" sections of *al-Hilal* and other periodicals.

In 1914, for example, Mahmud Sulayman Bu Karam wrote in from Little Rock, Arkansas, inquiring whether the "Phoenicians were Semites or Hamites." *Al-Hilal* responded that "it is believed they are Semites like the Arabs, Caldeans, Babylonians, Hebrews, Aramaens . . . since the language found on their ruins is very Semitic and resembles Hebrew."[60] From London, England, a young student informed *al-Hilal* that his fellow Egyptians considered themselves among the "colored people" *(min al-shuʿub al-mulawwana)*, a designation he thought wrong. *Al-Hilal* responded, "Yes, this is incorrect. The Egyptians are Caucasian, but there are two types: white and red." For further edification, the editor referred the reader to his *Tabaqat al-umam*. On the same page of the journal, Iskandar al-Khuri wrote in asking about the racial identity of Syrians and referred to their "troubles" in the United States: "I have heard that the United States of America does not consider the Syrians among white people *(min al-shuʿub al-baidaʾ)* or Caucasians, which is a condition for entry into their country. And the Syrians have set out to prove the error of the Americans."[61]

These questions and responses indicate a number of things about racial ideas among Syrians at the beginning of the twentieth century. First, there was confusion over what race the Syrians belonged to as well as disagreement over its importance. Were the Syrians Phoenicians, and, if so, were they Semites, Hamites, or "white" or "red" Caucasians? While Zaydan tried to be precise about racial differences, another leading Syrian journalist of the day dismissed the whole idea of racial hierarchies. Muhammad Kurd ʿAli, editor of the Damascus newspaper *al-Muqtabas,* criticized the idea of white racial superiority, noting that it was the result of narrow-mindedness. "In reality" he argued, "there is only one race, and that is the human race."[62] Second, it is clear that the problem of racial classification in the diaspora engendered debates in the homeland—a reminder that emigration produces a flow across borders not only of bodies and resources but of ideas also. The "troubles" to which al-Khuri referred were the series of naturalization cases in which Syrians attempted to prove their status as "white persons," especially the *Dow* case, which became a cause célèbre for the Syrian American community in 1914.

Like Costa Najour, George Dow was born in the coastal town of Batroun, Syria, in 1862. He immigrated to the United States in 1889, entering at the port of Philadelphia. Seven years later, he filed his declaration to become an American citizen in 1896 in Evansville, Indiana, and eventually made his way to Summerton, South Carolina, where he ran a store with his wife, Saydy.[63] He filed for citizenship in 1913, initiating a legal battle that would generate various opinions on the racial status of Syrians.

Dow's testimony before the court revealed that he was unfamiliar with the U.S. system of government and possessed poor English language skills. To questions posed to him about U.S. politics, for example, he responded that there were about thirty houses of Congress and that the difference between the government in Turkey and the United States was that he would like to be a citizen of the United States. It was on the basis of this lack of knowledge (and not his race) that the lawyer for the government asserted that Dow was not a worthy candidate for citizenship. However, Judge Smith ruled, not on this basis, but on the grounds that Dow did not meet the racial requirement of the naturalization statute.

His petition refused, Dow gained the assistance of the Syrian American Association (SAA), which had been founded by Naoum Mokarzel, owner and editor of *al-Hoda* (The Guidance) in 1909. Determined to settle the question of eligibility for citizenship once and for all, the SAA and Dow's lawyers formulated an elaborate defense of Syrian whiteness. Their argument for why Dow should be included in the category of *white persons* had five points:

1. That the term "white persons" in the statute means persons of the "Caucasian race," and persons white in color.
2. That he is a Semite or a member of one of the Semitic nations.
3. That the Semitic nations are all members of the "Caucasian" or white race.
4. That the matter has been settled in their favor as the European Jews have been admitted without question since the passage of the statute and that the Jews are one of the Semitic peoples.
5. That the history and position of the Syrians, their connection through all time with the peoples to whom the Jewish and Christian peoples owe their religion, make it inconceivable that the statute could have intended to exclude them.[64]

This complex argument incorporated nearly all the rationales used in previous attempts to prove Syrian whiteness. There was first the three-part equation that Syrians were Semites, hence Caucasian and therefore white. This had worked in cases where the judge had relied heavily on ethnology, but it was unpersuasive in front of judges like Smith who relied on the rationale of congressional intent. The second important component of the Syrian argument was cultural, an insistence that their "history and position" made them eligible for the privilege of citizenship. Interestingly, the argument did not specifically mention the Maronite relationship to modern European interests within Mount Lebanon, referring instead to the "peoples to whom the Jewish and Christian peoples owe their religion." The third part of the argument turned on legal precedent, namely that European Jews (who were also Semites) had been naturalized and that the same should hold for Syrians. This argument, however, played into the hands of Judge Smith, whose definition of "white" turned on the question of European descent. In his opinion, a European Jew was first and foremost a European, "racially, physiologically, and psychologically a part of the peoples he lives among."[65] "A professing Jew from Syria," he continued, "who was not of European nativity or descent would be as equally Asiatic as the present applicant, and as such not within the terms of the statute."[66] Since none of the naturalization cases involved Syrian Jews, Smith's argument was never actually tested in court.

Smith's views on race were of grave concern not only to the Syrian applicants but to members of the Jewish American community also. Many feared that if Syrian inclusion in whiteness were denied, it would be only a matter of time before the same would hold for Jews. Cyrus Adler of the American Jewish Committee expressed these fears in a letter to his colleague Mayer Sulzburger. Once the Syrians and Japanese were declared nonwhite, he noted, "it will not be a very far step to declare the Jews Asiatic."[67] There was already fierce debate within Jewish circles about whether Jews should define themselves as a race and allow government officials to designate them as such. The U.S. Immigration Commission's practice of classifying Jews racially as "Hebrews," for example, worried those who believed that such a designation isolated Jews from white Americans.[68] Two Jewish lawyers, Louis Marshall and Max J. Kohler, who were active in the campaign to reverse this classification and to prevent the Census Bureau from adopting a racial category for Jews on the census were also involved in the Syrian naturalization cases. They viewed the cases as an important test that could have far-reaching repercussions for Jewish citizenship. Marshall and Kohler served as lawyers for the "Syrian interveners" acting as amici curiae (friends of the court) in the *Balsara* case, heard in 1910.[69] Their eighty-four-page brief included a lengthy discussion of prominent American leaders who, since the founding of the republic, had supported broad naturalization principles. In addition, Marshall and Kohler stressed that the Immigrant and Naturalization Act of 1906 emphasized character and the upholding of laws as the primary qualifications for citizenship. Finally, they argued that because other courts had admitted applicants from western Asia to citizenship (Najour, Halladjian) there was ample legal precedent to support Balsara's naturalization.[70]

While these arguments worked in the *Balsara* case, they were unpersuasive in *Dow*. In this rehearing, Judge Smith denied Dow's petition for naturalization, which the SAA had so vigorously supported. Smith actually began his ruling with an acknowledgment of the "deep feeling manifested on the part of Syrian immigrants" but went on to argue that they had misinterpreted the decision of the court. The Syrians claimed that they had suffered "humiliation" and "mortification" in the wake of the decision that they did not belong to the "white race." Judge Smith countered that this had not been the wording of the decision; rather, "a modern Syrian was an Asiatic, and was thus not included in the term 'white persons' as contained in section 2169 of the U.S. Revised Statutes as amended in 1875."[71] He followed this clarification with a telling interpretation of the Syrian position: "The true ground of this supposed humiliation is that the applicant and his associates conceive the refusal of this privilege to mean that they do not belong to a white race but to a colored and what they consider an inferior race."[72]

The judge's musings were not without merit. Syrians did perceive exclusion from naturalization to mean that they were deficient, unwelcome, and uncultured. That is why their early arguments for inclusion in the "white race" revolved around the issue of the contribution of Semitic peoples to the Western world, especially Western Christendom. When George Shishim's eligibility was challenged in the Los Angeles Superior Court, for example, his response was to assert his Christian identity.[73] Costa Najour also based his argument for membership in the white race on the fact that he was a "pure Syrian and a Christian."[74] In both cases, the applicants for citizenship emphasized their Christian heritage to distinguish themselves from the "Asiatic" Muslim Turks who were the sovereigns of the Ottoman Empire.

The claim that the Syrians interpreted the defeat in the courts to mean that they were "colored" and therefore members of an inferior race was different. This was a construction that was familiar to southern whites, but it had to be learned by Syrian immigrants. Elkourie in his defense of Syrian whiteness did not mention color, nor did he resort to the strategy of defining whiteness as the absence of blackness. The "others" from which he attempted to distance Syrians were not blacks and Asians but prostitutes and anarchists, persons whom he deemed morally, not racially, unfit for full participation in the American polity and who were among the classes excluded from entry into the United States. As refusals to naturalize Syrians increased, however, the ways in which Syrian whiteness was defined both within the community and outside it shifted. No longer did Syrians simply claim whiteness by asserting their Christian credentials. Since the majority of Syrians were either Catholic or Eastern Orthodox, doing this was not always effective in the eyes of their Protestant neighbors, who viewed their Christianity as odd and foreign.[75] Instead, Syrians began to claim whiteness in terms that explicitly excluded blacks and Asians.

Evidence of this development can be seen in the letters that poured in to al-Hoda concerning the Najour case. Saleem Shaheen, for example, complained of the "premature rejoicing and claiming of [Najour's] victory while the main stigma has not yet been removed from us and the American people still refer to us with the stigma of Asiatic." He described how a judge in Lincoln, Nebraska, had refused to naturalize a Syrian, Mahmoud Salem, because "he is as the American newspapers referred to him an 'Asiatic' or 'Mongolian.' " Saleem Shaheen also related that he had been told by some Syrian peddlers that they had been refused entry into restaurants and taverns and that some of them had been greeted with the words "Hello, nigger." He then went on to describe another incident that revealed how Syrian racial identity was in dispute, not only in the courts, but in everyday encounters as well. He related in Arabic the story of Syrian cousins, Khaleel and Rasheed Zarzoor, who entered a saloon in Chattanooga, Tennessee. When the bartender served them, one man (described by Shaheen as a "ruffian") objected and asked the bartender: "Why do you serve these Negroes [al-ʿabid] before you serve me?" The bartender responded that there were no Negroes in the bar. The "ruffian" pointed at the two Syrians and said: "Yes, these two are Negroes [zunjian]. . . . You and all your Syrian people are Negroes, so get out of here." At this point one of the Syrians responded, "We are not Negroes. We belong to the white race [sulala al-baidaʾ] more than you do, and we are more honorable." A fight ensued between Rasheed and his detractor in which the latter was "injured plenty" and left the saloon saying, "I'll kill that negro Rasheed some day."[76]

In the Ross area of North Dakota, the small community of Syrian peddlers, homesteaders, and store owners were often referred to as "Black Syrians," "black ones," or "Blackies." Reflecting on their childhood relationships with those who used these terms, Syrians (who now call themselves Lebanese) report that "we're now good friends." One man recalled, however, having had to "fight regularly" as a young man.[77] Whether the perception of Syrians as other than white led to discrimination depended on the context. In many instances, Syrians had supporters. One prominent white citizen of Ross objected to the attempt to declare Syrians racially ineligible for citizenship. "If Syrians are to be barred from citizenship," he declared to the local paper, "the government should not have accepted their first papers and allowed them to file on land."[78] In 1995, an elderly resident of Crookston, North Dakota, was asked by a researcher, "How was the work performance of Syrians on the railroad crews?" He responded that they "worked every bit as good as white people."[79]

For Syrians in North Dakota, the debate on their racial classification was ultimately about property, because many intended to acquire land. To do so, one had to be a citizen or have indicated the intention to become one. In 1909, almost two hundred Syrians had filed their first papers in North Dakota. Many were anxious to acquire citizenship after learning that thirty Japanese who lived close to the Syrian settlement in Ross had lost their homesteads because the government exercised provisions of the Oriental Exclusion Act.[80] Syrian immigrants did not want to suffer the same fate.

These incidents indicate Syrian concern with racial misidentification and, in the case of Rasheed, a willingness to challenge comparisons to black Americans. Over time, and particularly as Syrians faced problems in the courts, these attempts to distance Syrians from blacks in the discourse on race became more frequent. Nowhere was this more evident than in the letter-writing campaign initiated by the Syrian Society for National Defense (SSND) in the wake of George Dow's first defeat. The society was organized in March 1914 in Charleston, South Carolina, to "defend our [Syrian] historic, civil and social rights."[81] The immediate goal of the SSND was to reverse Judge Smith's decision in the *Dow* case and support an appeal at the circuit court level.[82] SSND secretary Najib al-Sarghani kept readers of the popular Arabic-language paper *al-Hoda* up to date on the case and made repeated appeals for money to support the legal defense. The society received fifty contributions, the majority of them from Syrians in North and South Carolina in the amounts of one to five dollars. The largest contribution, however, came from Mansur Helu and Sons in New York City in the amount of fifteen dollars. *Al-Hoda* listed the names of the contributors, along with the size of their contributions, in the pages of the paper.[83]

Al-Sarghani's appeals for support were first and foremost appeals to defend the Syrian sense of honor *(al-difaʿ an al-sharaf)*. "We have found ourselves at the center of an attack on the Syrian honor," he wrote, and a concerted effort was needed to reverse the shame of the decision excluding Syrians from citizenship.[84] Al-Sarghani and other members of the SSND were especially worried about the ramifications of a yet another ruling (possibly at the Supreme Court level) that Syrians were not white. In their view, this would affect Syrians' commercial undertakings, restrict their ability to travel, encourage slander, and bring embarrassment to Syrian children.[85] While he too emphasized the religious credentials of the Syrians, noting that "their [the "Americans"] savior is our savior, and from us came their prophets and messengers," he also began to make arguments rooted in racial hierarchies. He argued, for example, that worse than the insult that a ruling against Dow would bring to Syrians was the possibility that they would be "no better than blacks [al-zunuj] and Mongolians [al-mughuli]. Rather, blacks will have rights [to vote, for example] that the Syrian does not have."[86]

Al-Sarghani's statements reveal the development in Syrian thinking on race, whereby the claim to whiteness was framed explicitly against other racialized groups, namely blacks and Asians. He argued that there could be no worse dishonor than for these groups to have rights that Syrians did not yet fully possess, an argument that boosted the Syrian claim to citizenship while it simultaneously called into question the appropriateness of black and Asian citizenship. Securing status as "white persons" was no longer just about securing the right to naturalize; it was about distancing Syrians from blacks and Asians in the discourse on race. Hence the argument in favor of Syrian whiteness in the Arabic-language press became more and more about defending the Syrian's status as "a pure Caucasian," racially distinct from two other groups of people understood (both in the understanding of the common man and according to scientific rationales) to be emphatically not white.[87] To be sure, there were attempts to modify this position. The Syrian New York paper *Meraat ul-gharb,* for example, translated Judge's Smith ruling in full and reaffirmed that being Asian did not necessarily mean one was not white, but these parsings lost their relevance for Syrians as they fought to claim whiteness.[88]

This shift to a more racial, rather than a purely religious or civilizational, understanding of Syrian whiteness was further evidenced in a book that appeared in the midst of the *Dow* controversy. Published in both English and Arabic, it aimed to clarify (before Dow's case went to the circuit court of appeals) the racial classification of the Syrians. The book was written by Kalil A. Bishara at the urging of Naoum Mokarzel, editor and owner of *al-Hoda* and president of the SAA. The goal of the book in the English introduction was to "set forth with a fairly high degree of precision, the evidence conducive to the determination of the racial identity of the modern Syria."[89] The Arabic introduction dispensed with the niceties and stated the purpose more forcefully. The book was a "reply to those who have denied that the Syrian emigrant is Caucasian and have made him out to be of Mongolian origin, whereby they have made him ineligible for American citizenship."[90]

This was not the only place where the English version differed from the Arabic. In an impressive list of figures described as evincing the Semitic "pliability combined with iron fixity of purpose," Bishara cited Moses, Elijah, Hannibal, Amos, Paul, Peter, and John. The Arabic version was identical except that it also included the name of the Muslim prophet Muhammad. The omission was an interesting and strategic move. Having already made gains by promoting the Christian credentials of Syrian immigrants, Bishara probably did not want to jeopardize their standing by aligning them with Muslims, especially not at a time when the Anglo-American judiciary and the American public's perception of Islam was steeped in ignorance and superstition.[91] Like others before him, Bishara stressed the Syrian connections to the Holy Land, Christianity, and "Western" civilization. But the larger argument in his book (especially the Arabic-language version) conveyed a new development in the debate on Syrian racial identity. The early Syrian arguments for inclusion in the white race had emphasized industry, religiosity, and sobriety—qualities that proponents put forward as measures of a group's ability to contribute effectively to the American nation rather than of membership in the "white race" specifically. Increasingly, though, Syrians saw the denial of their whiteness to mean that they were Asian or black, and not, as Elkourie had seen it, heathens, derelicts, and drunks. Syrians thus generated a different definition of their whiteness, one that hinged on the question of who was "not white." It was this argument that carried the day in George Dow's final appeal in 1915, where it was affirmed at the federal court level that he was indeed a "white person."

The presiding judge in the *Dow* case argued that the original act of 1790 had been repealed through successive amendments and new acts. He moved away from congressional intent and argued that the decision of the court must be controlled by the "generally accepted meaning of the words used at the time of the passage of the new statute."[92] "With its amendment of 1875," he continued, "it seems to be true beyond question that the generally received opinion was that the inhabitants of a portion of Asia, including Syria, were to be classed as white persons."[93] Judge Wood conceded that the present inhabitants of Syria had "racial descent from many different sources. Yet as the consensus at the time of the enactment of the statute now in force was that they were so closely related to their neighbors on the European side of the Mediterranean that they should be classed as white, they must fall within the term white persons used in the statute."[94] This decision established a weighty legal precedent for Syrian whiteness based on affinity with Europe.

THE PROBLEM WITH BEING WHITE

Taken as a whole, the Syrian racial prerequisite cases heard in federal courts between 1909 and 1915 demonstrate that buried beneath the reasoned rationales of the legal rulings lay contradictions, ambiguities, and discrepancies. Quite simply, the courts were having difficulty deciding who was a "white person." There was, however, a basic pattern amid the confusion. Judges were turning more and more to the rationales of congressional intent and common knowledge (and away from science) to determine racial eligibility for naturalization. While, for example, ethnological classification had assisted Costa Najour in his request for citizenship, it was completely discarded in *Ex parte Shahid.* This move away from scientific explanations of race was evident in other cases as well and would culminate in the 1923 U.S. Supreme Court decision in the case of South Asian applicant Bhagat Singh Thind. Since the *Thind* case would significantly redefine racial eligibility for citizenship, a brief outline of the case and its relevance for Syrians is in order.

Thind was born in India, immigrated to the United States in 1913, and petitioned for naturalization in 1920. He was successful at the district court level, but lawyers for the federal government appealed, and in January 1923 the case eventually reached the U.S. Supreme Court, where the decision of the lower court was reversed. The Court claimed that although science considered Indians to be "Caucasian," Thind was not a "free white person" in the "understanding of the common man."[95] He was therefore ineligible to acquire citizenship. Paradoxically, only a few months earlier, in the *Takao Ozawa* case, the Supreme Court had affirmed the power of what it called "scientific authorities" when it argued that Japanese persons were not Caucasian but Mongolian and therefore not white.[96] In the *Ozawa* case, *white* and *Caucasian* were synonymous, but in the *Thind* case clearly they were not.[97] These two Supreme Court rulings suggest that when science failed to reinforce popular beliefs about racial difference it was discarded but that when it confirmed them it was conveniently embraced. This was not a mere subtlety in an arcane legal tradition but a decision that had real and often disastrous consequences in the lives of immigrants.[98] At least sixty-five Indian immigrants—a class of people previously admitted under the provisions of the 1790 Naturalization Act, amended in 1870—were stripped of their citizenship between 1923 and 1927, prompting one, Vaisho Das Bagai, to commit suicide.[99]

Mention must also be made of a secondary ruling given in the *United States v. Thind* case. When the circuit court of appeals submitted its certificate to the Supreme Court, it requested instruction on two questions. The first was whether a "high-caste Hindu, of full Indian blood" was a white person within the meaning of section 2169 of the Revised Statutes. The second concerned the applicability of the Act of 1917, which had designated certain geographic areas, the inhabitants of which would be barred from entering the United States as immigrants.[100] Specifically, the lower court wanted to know whether the Immigration Act disqualified from naturalization "Hindus" who had entered the country legally: that is, prior to the passage of the said act. It was, in fact, the Supreme Court's response to the first question that generated the lengthier and weightier response, but the second question was not ignored. In the final paragraph of the ruling, the Court made an explicit connection between eligibility for immigration into the United States and suitability for naturalization. "It is not without significance," Justice Sutherland wrote, "that Congress, by the Act of February 5, 1917, . . . has now excluded from admission into this country all natives of Asia within designated limits of latitude and longitude, including the whole of India. This not only constitutes conclusive evidence of the congressional attitude of opposition to Asiatic immigration generally, but is persuasive of a similar attitude toward Asiatic naturalization as well, since it is not likely that Congress would be willing to accept as citizens a class of persons whom it rejects as immigrants."[101]

The inclusion of India in the Asiatic "barred zone" had thus informed Justice Sutherland's thinking on racial eligibility for naturalization. Significantly, Syria had fallen outside the zone, a decision that furnished additional proof for the Syrian claim of whiteness. In 1923, for example, when a poorly informed Judge Smith tried once again to prevent the naturalization of a Syrian applicant, he was confronted with the same argument made by Justice Sutherland, only in reverse: Syrians were eligible to immigrate to the United States, so they were therefore eligible to naturalize. Smith was forced to naturalize the applicant, F. W. Basha, and the Syrian eligibility question never again reached the courts.[102]

The examples cited above are among the many that reveal the intricate connections between immigration and naturalization law and, specifically, their shared racial logic. Both the Act of 1917 and the Supreme Court rulings of 1922 and 1923 on eligibility for naturalization deployed a racial construction of Asians that was narrow and rigid, while simultaneously allowing for flexibility in determining the racial status of European immigrant groups. This led to a reconstruction of racial categories whereby race and nationality were conflated for Asians (and Mexicans) but disaggregated for "white" Europeans.[103] The legal construction of Asians as nonwhite would continually mark them as "outsiders," thus rendering them targets of discriminatory legislation.[104]

The demise of scientific explanations of race in favor of those rooted in congressional intent and common knowledge did not bode well for South Asian and Japanese immigrants. The same cannot be said for Syrians, whose encounter with naturalization law during roughly the same period led to a legal consensus that they were white. It is especially curious that the Syrians did not meet the same fate as the South Asians, since, in cases where their whiteness was affirmed (*Najour,* for example), judges had relied overwhelmingly on the conclusions of the contemporary "science" of race to argue that Syrians were Caucasian and therefore white. The Supreme Court ultimately rejected this logic in the *Thind* case, but it continued to apply to the Syrians. Parallels between the Syrian and the South Asian cases had been apparent not only at the level of legal argumentation. As mentioned above, influential Syrians in New York had actually assisted the naturalization of a South Asian applicant in 1910 by hiring counsel and serving as "friends of the court." They hoped that this case would influence future rulings in Syrian cases, and they were right.[105] The case of Bhicaji Franyi Balsara, described as a "Parsee" from India, was cited as a precedent in at least two federal cases affirming the whiteness of Syrians and hence their eligibility for naturalization.[106] The Supreme Court, however, overlooked the case of Balsara as a legal precedent in the most important case involving a South Asian, that of Bhagat Singh Thind. The twisted labyrinth of legal reasoning on the question of whiteness had led to a position that was patently absurd: some South Asians, notably non-Hindus, remained white, and their whiteness, in the form of a legal precedent, could help prove the whiteness of *other* immigrant groups like the Syrians but not—as the *Thind* case clearly demonstrated—the whiteness of fellow South Asians.

What explains this apparent discrepancy? Why did the courts begin to place Syrians in the category of those "commonly understood" to be white and not South Asians (labeled, often erroneously, as "high-caste Hindus")? An important piece of the explanation for this Syrian "victory" lies in the record of their involvement in the racial prerequisite cases. Armed with expert lawyers, "friends of the court," and a belief in their special status as the mediators of the Christian tradition, Syrians had actively participated in arguments for their inclusion in the "white race." The exclusion of Syria from the Asiatic barred zone helped consolidate it. Thus the legal construction of Syrian whiteness became part of a larger story of their disassociation from Asia and of the creation of a new category, the "Middle East" (which is, in fact, West Asia).

Why, though, had Syria fallen outside the Asiatic barred zone? When Syrians first began to arrive in the United States, immigration officials classified them not as Syrians but as persons coming from "Turkey in Asia." Yet the 1917 Act constructed a different Asian space, one that lay beyond West Asia and that delineated not just a geographic location but the peoples that had triggered American anxieties about the "yellow peril." As Sridevi Menon argues, fears of the imminent "Mongolianization" of the United States focused initially on Chinese immigrants, but these fears soon expanded to include the rest of East and Southeast Asia's population. In the early twentieth century, South Asia was incorporated into this topography largely because of concerns over Sikh settlement in California. The erection of the Asiatic barred zone marks an important moment of differentiation between Europe's Asia—which included India and West Asia—and America's Asia, in which India occupied a liminal space and West Asia (the "Middle East") was absent.[107]

With the ruling in *Dow v. United States* supporting Syrian whiteness, the race crisis for Syrians subsided—but only temporarily. The periodic violence inflicted upon Syrians and the popular and political characterizations of them as a suspect immigrant group suggested that their whiteness was inconclusive, particularly in a South still steeped in the politics of Jim Crow.[108] Indeed, the seemingly provisional quality of Syrian whiteness, despite *Dow v. United States,* prompted Syrian immigrants (especially the elite among them) to reaffirm their coveted racial status as whites. They did not challenge the premise that whiteness was a legitimate prerequisite for citizenship and the privileges it afforded, only "that their rightful share in whiteness was being denied them."[109]

Advancing arguments in favor of Syrian suitability to "share in whiteness" was certainly on Naoum Mokarzel's mind when, in 1920, he wrote a letter to the French consul in New York City, beseeching his intervention on the part of Syrians in Panama. The Panamanian government had passed a restrictive law on immigration that barred Syrians and "other

Asians" from entering the country. Mokarzel asked for Consul Liébert's intervention: "Will you take charge of the matter yourself and see that the Lebanese and Syrians are treated as they ought to be? They are not only from the white race," he continued, "but from the cream of that race, and I am sending you a book written on the subject."[110] The book was no doubt Kahlil Bishara's—the same one Naoum Mokarzel had commissioned to serve as evidence in the United States' racial prerequisite cases. By this time, Syrian arguments for inclusion in the "white race" based on their Christian credentials were being augmented by arguments rooted in the language of racial hierarchies.

"To enter the white race," Noel Ignatiev reminds us, "was a strategy to secure an advantage in a competitive society," and whiteness was, ultimately, the "result of choices made."[111] Syrians had written letters, published articles, hired lawyers, formed associations, and raised money, all to support the claim of whiteness. The legal decision in *Dow v. United States* corresponded to, and was even made possible by, a decision on the part of individual Syrians to think of themselves as white in the "popular" sense of the term, or, as the legal phrasing of the day put it, "in the understanding of the common man." Ultimately, this demanded that Syrians construct and make sense of their whiteness in relation to others who were nonwhite, for historically whiteness had little meaning unless it stood in opposition to a racialized Other. Perhaps that is why, forty years after he was granted naturalization and deemed to be a "free white person," Costa Najour described the verdict as one that refuted the idea that he was "yellow."[112] Slayman Nimmee did the same when he recalled the naturalization controversy to historian Alixa Naff. In his words, "President Wilson said that the Syrians are of Chinese race and can't get citizenship papers. I was one of those that got hurt—I was refused. When this happened, the community in New York united, collected money, and sent a lawyer to Washington, D.C. He argued that if Syrians were Chinese then Jesus who was born in Syria was Chinese. They won the case, and so I went here and got my citizens [sic]."[113]

For Costa Najour, Slayman Nimmee, and many other Syrians, being classified as white encouraged them to participate in the racialization of those who remained nonwhite. While this may have helped Syrians assimilate more quickly, it helped perpetuate a discourse of exclusion in which other immigrant groups were marked as "Others," ineligible for citizenship and full membership in the American nation. Thus one of the unfortunate, if unintended, consequences of the Syrian struggle for whiteness was that it helped refine the legal arguments that repeatedly called into question the suitability of non-Europeans to "become American." Not until 1952 did Congress pass a new Immigration and Naturalization Act (also known as the McCarran-Walter Act) eliminating the racial prerequisite for citizenship. Passed in the midst of anti-Communist agitation, however, the act continued to apply the restrictive national-origins formula of 1924, so as to prevent the nation from being "overrun, perverted, contaminated, or destroyed," according to the law's backer, Senator Pat McCarran.[114]

The National Origins Act of 1924 recognized that there was now a national entity called "Syria" and set the annual quota at one hundred persons. What the act did not recognize was that the idea of a Syrian nation was contested, particularly in the wake of the demise of the Ottoman Empire and the establishment of French colonial rule in the Levant. Mokarzel's appeal to the French consul (requesting that he intervene to save the Syrians in Panama from exclusion based on their race) was a request to a colonial power that was now the overseer of Syrian domestic and foreign affairs. According to the Treaty of Lausanne, signed between the Allies and Turkey in July 1922, residents of Syria and Lebanon became ipso facto nationals of these countries that were "detached from Turkey." The treaty stipulated that persons living abroad "may opt for the nationality of the territory of which they are natives, if they belong by race to the majority of the population of that territory, and subject to the consent of the Government exercising authority therein. This right of option must be exercised within two years from the coming into force of the present Treaty."

Syrian immigrants in the United States were slow to respond to the provisions of the treaty or failed to follow them altogether. The French consul in Chicago noted with some frustration the low number of applications for Syrian or Lebanese nationality, adding that most immigrants had naturalized as Americans "with the aim of more readily finding work." He blamed unfavorable American press coverage during the 1925 Druze revolt against the French in Syria for this situation, claiming rather condescendingly that "the Syrian and Lebanese population in this country, which is generally poorly educated, has accepted without hesitation the most fantastical assertions in the American papers and has since turned against us [détournée nettement de nous]."[115] Two years earlier, the French consul in Chicago had been more hopeful. He was under the impression that the Syrians could not naturalize as Americans because "geographically they are considered Asiatic, in the same category as the Japanese and the Hindous, to whom the Supreme Court has denied the ability to naturalize." The French diplomatic corps should more than ever, he argued, "reinforce the bonds that connect the Syrians to their country of origin and to us."[116]

The bond of colonial citizenship was clearly something Syrians in the United States were willing to give up. According to the U.S. Census, by 1930 slightly over 50 percent of the Syrian foreign-born population had naturalized as U.S. citizens—the same percentage as the southern Italians.[117] In the state of New York, for example, the percentage of naturalized Syrian men rose from 27.2 to 58.2 between 1920 and 1930. The naturalization rate for Syrian women rose from 22.7 to 37.1 percent in the same period.[118] In 1920 the average rate of naturalization in the main areas of settlement had been 25 percent. The French consul was indeed correct that many Syrians did not share Mokarzel's enthusiasm for French support and were "turning against" the Mandate power. In the Syrian diaspora, because of the saliency of racial categories, the debate around the question "To what nation do we belong?" was also a racialized one. This question would have far-reaching impact on the course of Arab nationalism.

CHAPTER 3

Nation and Migration

Emergent Arabism and Diasporic Nationalism

But we are more than Syrians. Like Janus, the old Roman
god, we are double-faced—and that in no slanderous sense.
We have one face looking backward and another forward.

Philip Hitti (1928)

The renaissance of the Syrian nation was brought about by
the World War. The Syrian immigration was particularly active in transmitting to the native country the idea of democracy and national self-determination which started the Syrians on the way to racial self-consciousness and solidarity.

J. Ray Johnson (1928)

The racial prerequisite cases had underscored for Syrians the salience of
race in the United States. They emerged from the legal controversy believing in the importance of whiteness for securing their future as citizens in America. As Syrians contemplated naturalization and permanent
settlement in the United States, however, they were drawn into new debates about the future of their homeland. The first two decades of the
twentieth century witnessed the emergence of Arab nationalism, based
not so much on yearnings for full-fledged independence from the Ottoman Empire as on a desire for greater parity within its institutions.
Syrian emigrants in the United States voiced concerns that echoed those
of their compatriots in Cairo, Beirut, Damascus, Paris, and elsewhere
who had begun to advocate political reform and greater national autonomy for their homeland at a time when the empire itself was en-
forcing greater centralization. On both sides of the Atlantic, Syrians
were redefining the nature of the bonds that held the Arab peoples

together and the type of political arrangements that would honor and protect these solidarities.

The history of the Arab national movement has been studied, analyzed, and mythologized for over fifty years, and it is not the goal here to discuss the historiographical debates that have focused on questions of origins and scope of the movement in the pre–World War I period.[1] The purpose of this chapter is to bring the Syrian diaspora into the discussion of the early phase of Arab nationalism, sometimes called the "protonationalist" phase because its proponents were not yet committed to the creation of an Arab nation-state but instead sought national autonomy within the Ottoman Empire.[2] This chapter elucidates the connections between emergent national and diasporic identities. The focus is on how nationalism and migration interacted with each other and how emigrants became part of the debate on the "Arab nation" while, at the same time, national sentiment shaped *mahjar* politics and identity. For even as Syrian emigrants chose to become American citizens they also participated in the struggle for national independence of their homeland. They joined secret national societies, attended congresses, and raised money to support a movement that was broadly unified around the goal of opposing the centralizing policies of the Ottoman government. Their participation points to the wide geographic base of Arab nationalist politics in the prewar period. More relevant still was the way that the diaspora became part of a new Arab national imaginary among Syrians in the United States.[3]

CITIZENSHIP AND NATIONAL BELONGING

In 1924, Philip Hitti argued in his pioneering study of his fellow Syrians living in the United States that they lacked a developed sense of national identity because they understood themselves first and foremost in religious terms. "A Syrian is born to his religion, just as an American is born to his nationality," he wrote, coining a phrase that has been appropriated many times over.[4] Hitti was clearly ambivalent about this attachment to religion. On the one hand, he deemed it the wellspring of morality, sobriety, and "social purity" among Syrian immigrants; on the other hand, he considered religion a source of division and a barrier to more unified national solidarity. In particular, social organization around religious sect promoted "clannishness" and "factionalism," and "in political matters its results are a disintegrated and inharmonious national life."[5] According to Hitti, Syrian patriotism was defined by love of religious sect, and as admirable as this was in the eyes of "tourists and Orientalists," it was patriotism devoid of national feeling, "to say nothing about international feeling."[6] Hitti's friend Syrian émigré Reverend Abraham Rihbany also bemoaned the lack of national solidarity among Syrians in the United States, although his criticism focused more on their material concerns. "The trouble with our people," he wrote to Hitti from Boston, "is that they are more ready to spend time and money on their wedding feasts than on their national ideals."[7]

Hitti was certainly right that religious factionalism existed within Syrian communities in the United States. As early as the 1890s, Syrian writers complained about sectarianism in the *mahjar* and lamented that emigrants let religious differences stand in the way of unity.[8] One emigrant wrote in to the popular Cairo journal *al-Hilal,* complaining of the "division and factionalism, which springs from ugly narrow-mindedness." The call for cooperation between the different sects became a recurring theme in the writing of some of the most famous Syrian poets in the United States, including Kahlil Gibran and Amin al-Rihani, although behind this often lay a thinly veiled anticlericalism.[9] Religious factionalism was part of *mahjar* politics, and even non-Syrians knew about the quarrels that pitted Orthodox against Maronite and sometimes the latter against the Greek Catholics and Protestants. The English-language press often sensationalized fighting within the Syrian community in New York City, in one case describing a controversy over the appointment of the first Syrian Orthodox bishop in the United States as provoking "wild-eyed Syrians, . . . the glint of steel in two hundred swarthy hands."[10] J. Ray Johnson's 1928 study of the Syrian community also emphasized religious divisions. He noted that "religion has drawn the deepest lines of cleavage in the Syrian national community, but at the same time each of the different churches has been the cohesive power for its own membership and has inspired the believers with loyalty, devotion and solidarity reminiscent of state patriotism."[11]

Was Hitti really correct in his claim that religious identity obstructed the development of national identity? Or, in Johnson's formulation, was religious solidarity "reminiscent" of attachment to the state? A closer examination of the sources suggests that Syrians in the United States *did* possess a national consciousness (although not a unified one) in the prewar period that was not simply a reflection of their sectarian identities. Indeed, the question of naturalization in the *mahjar* had encouraged Syrians to think about citizenship and their attachment to the Arab nation and the Ottoman state in new ways.[12]

To be sure, by 1915, in the wake of the *Dow* decision, many Syrians became interested in pursuing American citizenship, an action that would
seem to indicate their willingness to abandon ties to the Ottoman state.
The weight of legal precedent was in their favor, and a network of community organizations stood ready to defend and support Syrian applicants
should they encounter difficulties in the naturalization process. There were
compelling practical and political reasons for becoming an American citizen, including ease of travel, the purchase of property, and access to the
voting booth. Moreover, as the Ottoman Empire, under the leadership of
the Committee of Union and Progress (CUP), plunged into World War I
on the side of the Central Powers in November 1914, incentives for Syrian emigrants to keep their citizenship in the empire diminished.

The CUP's crackdown on the leadership of the Arabist movement during the first two years of the war was devastating.[13] Members of this movement had disagreed with the direction of the war and had worked to rally
support for the independence of the Arab provinces of the empire. Many
of them paid with their lives for doing so. Syrians at home and abroad
would not easily forget the public hanging of eleven Arab notables in
Beirut in August 1915 and twenty-one more in May 1916 (fourteen in
Beirut and seven in Damascus) on trumped-up charges of treason.[14]

The Syrian press in the United States conveyed a growing disillusionment
with, and in many cases outright hostility toward, the Turkish regime. *As-
Sayeh,* for example, compared the CUP rule in the Arab provinces to that
of the infamous eighteenth-century tyrant Ahmad Pasha, better known by
his nickname, al-Jazzar ("the Butcher").[15] In fact, it was worse: "Syria did
not see during the reign of al-Jazzar the kind of injustices and losses that it
now sees."[16] After the executions of May 1916, *as-Sayeh* described the
regime as "a demonic government" *(hukuma shaitaniyya).*[17] Thousands of
Syrians in the United States chose to display their rejection of the Ottoman
state by joining the U.S. Armed Forces, a choice that a contemporary American sociologist cited as evidence of the community's "straight Americanism."[18] The New York branch of the Lebanon League of Progress urged the
French ambassador in Washington to support stationing an invasion force
in Lebanon to which the league would send, with proper arms and ammunition, thousands of volunteers.[19] The French preferred to recruit a much
smaller number in the Légion d'Orient, which was based in Cyprus under
French command and accepted Syrian and Armenian volunteers from Europe, the Americas, and Egypt.[20]

An overemphasis on Syrian wartime support of the Allied cause
tends, however, to underestimate the dilemma that acquiring American

citizenship could present to Syrians in the prewar years. Many decided to forsake their Ottoman citizenship toward the end of the war, when the demise of the Ottoman Empire was at hand and when the malevolence of the Turkish regime was more clearly evident to Syrians everywhere. In the prewar period, however, alienation from the Ottoman state was by no means universal, and there were compelling reasons for Syrian emigrants *not* to become American citizens. On a purely formal level, taking this step meant losing their Ottoman citizenship, since neither U.S. nor Ottoman law allowed for dual citizenship. Naturalization as Americans also signaled a departure from the ideals of Ottomanism, the sense of belonging to a multiethnic Ottoman citizenry.[21] Thus, even before Syrians in the United States became racially suspect in the federal courts, the issue of citizenship had provoked intense debate within Syrian emigrant communities. Typical of *mahjar* politics, the debate was waged in the pages of rival Arabic newspapers. The editor of the New York paper *al-Ayyam* (The Times), for example, criticized the owner of *al-ʿAlam* (The World) for printing editorials that discouraged naturalization. *Al-Ayyam* cited the following editorial as proof of *al-ʿAlam*'s allegedly "un-American" position: "Oh Ottomans, we are in a strange country, and must some day return to our native land, if only for a visit. Keep ever in mind the land of your birth and of your ancestors, and give no heed to the counsels of foreigners. Loyalty to your country and your Sultan are commanded of the Faith."[22]

Al-Ayyam went further and accused *al-ʿAlam* of being the "mouthpiece of the Turkish Legation in Washington" and, in an effort to embarrass George Jabour, *al-ʿAlam*'s owner, submitted translations of the paper's allegedly offensive sections to the *New York Times,* which ran the story under the title "Lively War between Syrians." Jabour responded by sending a letter to the *New York Times* claiming that neither he nor *al-ʿAlam* espoused un-American views. "He declares," the article read, "that he is in no way interested in preventing Syrians, or other foreigners, from becoming American citizens."[23] Indeed, Jabour was himself a naturalized American and a founding member of the Syrian-American Club, which, he argued, worked for "the promotion of the naturalization of Syrians."[24]

Jabour's earlier exhortations in the pages of *al-ʿAlam* may have been a classic case of journalistic rivalry in which a new newspaper deliberately incited the editors of other already-existing popular Arabic papers in order to gain more readers. Quite possibly he was encouraged to make appeals to Ottomanism with the help of a subsidy from the Turkish

Legation—at least that is what *al-Ayyam* claimed. But Jabour was not a lone voice of support of the Ottoman ideal. For every denunciation of the Ottoman regime and exhortation to enjoy the privileges of American citizenship in the Arabic papers, there were sincere appeals to remain loyal to the Ottoman state. The debate on citizenship began in New York Arabic papers, but it soon spread beyond the borders of the United States. In 1904, for example, two popular *mahjar* newspapers, *al-Munazir* (The Interlocutor) published out of São Paulo, Brazil, and *al-Muhajir* (The Emigrant) of New York, took opposing positions on whether Syrians should become citizens of nations in which they lived in the Americas. The editor of *al-Muhajir*, Amin al-Gharayyib, argued that Syrians should naturalize and "mix completely with Americans." Na'um Labaki, founder and editor of *al-Munazir*, opposed the move to naturalize and called for Syrians to "remain loyal to Ottomanism and committed to Syrian patriotism *[wataniyya]* so that they can return to Syria."[25]

Labaki's argument, refreshingly concise amid the verbose editorial style of the day, reveals an interesting connection between Syrian and Ottoman identity in the *mahjar*. In his view, remaining an Ottoman citizen was an act of Syrian patriotism—a position shared by other writers of the *mahjar* who still conceived of Syria as inseparable from the larger Ottoman polity. To be Syrian meant that one was also an Ottoman, and, as the writings of Labaki suggest, this confluence of identities would be undermined if Syrians began naturalizing in the Americas.

Labaki's prideful prewar Ottomanism and the jostling over the meaning of Americanization in the pages of *al-Ayyam* and *al-'Alam* point to the complex political allegiances that animated debates on citizenship in the *mahjar*. The Syrian diaspora's engagement with Ottomanism also helps dispel the notion that emigrants were politically unsophisticated or, at best, disengaged from politics because they were caught up solely in the pursuit of economic gain.[26] And while there is a tendency to assume that emigrants were all too happy to see the demise of the Ottoman Empire, disengagement from the Ottoman ideal (particularly in favor of an Arabist one) was gradual and not without inconsistencies.

In this regard, it is important to distinguish between opposition to the policies of the Ottoman government and repudiation of the Ottoman polity, for the latter did not always follow the former. Syrian emigrants frequently denounced the actions of the Ottoman central government even before the imposition of the infamous Turkification policies of the CUP. However, they held in high regard the imperial realm of which their homeland was a part. It was a minority faction that wanted to see an independent Syrian nation emerge out of a dismembered Ottoman Empire. The secret society Suriyya al-Fatat (Young Syria) did, among other Syrian groups, support separatist aims before World War I and call for "creating a revolutionary movement for the independence of Syria as a republic."[27] Such explicit appeals to an independent Syria, however, were few and far between. Even as Syrian emigrants began to embrace the goals of Arabism, which in the prewar period focused on issues of maintaining the primacy of Arabic in education and administration in Syria, they were committed to the idea of reform within an Ottoman framework. This position was expressed in the *mahjar* press and, more significantly, at the First Arab Congress held in Paris in 1913.

ARABISM IN THE DIASPORA

The congress was the brainchild of a small group of Syrian émigrés in Paris, including ʿAbd al-Ghani al-ʿUraysi, Jamil Mardam, and ʿAwni ʿAbd al-Hadi, all of whom were members of the secret Arabist society al-Fatat. The primary goal of the congress was to attract international attention to the reforms being advocated by a growing number of Ottoman Arabs who were disillusioned by the policies of the CUP government. Chief among their complaints was the imposition of Turkish as the language of administration and instruction in the state schools of the Arab provinces, a policy that they referred to as *tatrik*, or Turkification.[28] The Paris members of al-Fatat, along with two other prominent members of the Syrian Paris community, Shukri Ghanim and Nadra Moutran, formed a planning committee for the congress, which then sought and attained the support of the Ottoman Administrative Decentralization Party, head-quartered in Cairo.[29]

News of the congress spread throughout the Arab provinces of the empire and the *mahjar*, thanks to a manifesto circulated by the planning committee. Addressed to the "Sons of the Arab Nation," the document informed its readers of the principles behind the congress. Organized by Syrians, it would "be attended by delegations of notables from the Arab lands and by intellectuals from among the Syrian emigrants of Egypt, North and South America, and Europe so that the entire Arab nation, spread across the world, will be represented."[30] The participation of Syrian émigré leaders at the Arab Congress points to the fluidity between Ottomanism and Arabism and to the weakness of an argument that depicts Syrian emigrants as predisposed toward abandoning the Ottoman ideal, either because they were sold on the virtues of Americanization or because they were indifferent to the fate of the Ottoman polity. Indeed, for a diaspora that is characterized as politically apathetic in the pre–World War I period, Syrian emigrants showed great interest in the congress. Telegrams of support arrived from various corners of the United States: from the Society of Zahalni Youth in Cleveland, Ohio, the Society for Syrian Reform in Lowell, Massachusetts, and the Committee of Syrian Reform in Oklahoma, to name a few.

The organizers of the congress welcomed the support and penned a resolution "thanking the emigrants for their patriotism."[31] Among the delegates from the United States were Naoum Mokarzel and Najib Diab, editors of the two most popular Arabic papers in New York. 'Afifa Karam, also from New York, was among the handful of Arab women who attended the conference. Karam was born in the village of 'Amshit, just north of the Lebanese coastal town of Jubayl, in 1883 and was the daughter of a doctor in the Ottoman army. She immigrated to Louisiana as a bride of thirteen and later moved to New York, where she worked as an editor at *al-Hoda*. In 1912, she bought the license of one of Salloum Mokarzel's journals, *al-'Alam al-jadid* (The New World), and changed the name to *al-'Alam al-jadid al-nisa'iyya* (The New World: A Ladies' Monthly Arabic Magazine), which catered to female readers throughout the *mahjar*.[32]

The congress convened in the auditorium of the French Geographical Society, on the Boulevard St. Germain, between June 18 and June 23, 1913, and was attended by over three hundred participants. This was a significant achievement for the leaders of the Arabist wing of the reform movement. Held in the heart of a European capital, it attracted the attention of foreign observers and initiated a flurry of diplomatic correspondence by French and British officials, who had no clear idea how to respond to the congress. The French Ministry of Foreign Affairs received several delegates, and the British—anticipating a call from the congress organizers at the London Foreign Office—initially decided to pattern their reception on that of the French. A meeting in London never did occur, however, because the leadership of the congress was caught up in negotiations with a representative of the CUP, for the developments in Paris had also attracted the attention of Istanbul.[33]

An agreement between the CUP and the reformers was eventually reached that met the most important demands of the congress. The CUP promised, for example, that education in Syria would be in Arabic in primary and middle schools, that the provincial administrative councils would be strengthened, and that Arabs would make up a significant proportion of the top provincial posts. Addressing what were more popular grievances, the agreement stated that military service in Yemen, ʿAsir, and Hijaz would be shared by Ottoman soldiers of various nationalities in proportion to their numbers in the empire's population.[34] Syrians of military age had a special reason to celebrate this provision, for they believed that the central government deliberately sent a disproportionate number of Arabs into what was popularly called "the cemetery of the Turks."

The CUP government failed to ratify the agreement reached in Paris, and the one that was eventually accepted was a watered-down version of the first. It was full of conditions and qualifications. The CUP's about-face dismayed supporters of the Arab national movement, and many became convinced that the possibility of achieving greater autonomy within an Ottoman framework was remote if not impossible. Others, including the president of the Arab Congress, ʿAbd al-Hamid al-Zahrawi, believed that accommodation was still possible, and in this spirit he accepted a senate position in the CUP government in 1914. Less than two years later, he was rounded up, along with other members of the Arab reform movement, and sent to the gallows.

The CUP's wartime policies in the Arab provinces, especially Cemal Pasha's "reign of terror" in Syria, alienated Arabists from the Ottoman ideal.[35] Prior to and during the 1913 Congress, however, supporters of Arabism believed that the most promising way to implement reform in the Ottoman Empire was through administrative decentralization. The list of topics for discussion at the congress combined this interest in administrative reform with more ardent appeals to Arab national rights. Three of the proposed issues for debate were principal concerns of the Decentralization Party and the Beirut Committee of Reform, the two most openly Arabist organizations of the prewar period. As listed in the invitation to the congress, they were "National Life and Opposition to Occupation" (munahada al-ihtilal), "The Rights of Arabs in the Ottoman Empire," and "The Necessity of Reform on the Basis of Decentralization." A fourth and little studied issue on the agenda for the congress was "Migration from Syria and to Syria." Shaykh Ahmad Hasan al-Tabbara, a delegate from the Beirut Reform Party, addressed this topic in one of the major speeches given during the five-day-long proceedings.[36] Two other speeches also addressed the issue of emigration and were given by delegates to the conference from the United States, Najib Diab and Naoum Mokarzel.

Al-Tabbara's speech conveyed the vast scale of the emigration wave from Syria, consisting, in his estimation, of 550,000 persons, or roughly one-fifth the total population.[37] The principal cause of this migration was "the difficulty of life under poor administration." He then cited the success of Syrian emigrants abroad as proof of their promise and potential when they were allowed to prosper free of the constraints of bad government. His musings on the effects of misrule were followed by a plea for Ottoman reforms "so that we may live as those among the advanced nations do."[38] In essence, al-Tabbara was calling for a rejuvenated Ottomanism in which all subjects of the empire could find meaning in their shared citizenship. "We are a people who were born Ottomans, grew up as Ottomans, and want to remain Ottomans," he exclaimed, and "we will not be pleased should our Ottoman state be replaced."[39]

The call for reform within the framework of the Ottoman state had also been a theme in the speech given the previous day by Najib Diab, entitled "The Aspirations *[al-amaniy]* of the Syrian Emigrants." Diab was the owner and editor of the popular New York newspaper *Meraat ul-gharb* (Mirror of the West), which had been established in 1899 and which published the works of *mahjar* poets Kahlil Gibran and Ilya Abu Madi.[40] He was a leading figure in the New York émigré community, and his paper was known for its sharp criticism of Hamidian rule. His editorials and political activism resulted in a death sentence being passed against him by the Ottoman sultan, although he was granted clemency under provisions of the 1908 Constitution. Diab was also a member of one of the largest Syrian associations in the United States, the Association of Syrian Unity, and attended the congress as its representative.[41]

In his speech to the delegates of the congress, Diab repeated what had become standard in *mahjar* oratory—the emphasis on the indissoluble bond between emigrants and their homeland. But underneath the embellished eloquence was a straightforward political message: Syrian emigrants wanted to remain in the fold of Ottomanism *(fi hidn al-ʿuthmaniyya),*[42] provided that the rights of all Ottoman subjects could be safeguarded. Moreover, Diab believed the specific reforms advocated by the Arab national movement could be implemented within the framework of the Ottoman constitution.[43]

It is curious that a man who had once been condemned to death by the Ottoman sultan (and who was still considered a "political criminal") should have desired to remain within the "Ottoman fold." Diab's allegiance to the Ottoman political system makes more sense, however, if we take into consideration the alternatives with which informed Syrians believed they were faced in 1913. Diab, for example, despised the Turkification policies of the CUP, but he was more worried about the designs

of the European powers on the Ottoman Empire and on Syria in particular.[44] The defeat of the Ottoman armies in the Balkan Wars and the surrender in North Africa had troubled many Arabists, for it pointed to the
shaky sovereignty of the empire.[45] Rather than contemplate its dissolution, Diab and other reformers at the congress wanted to strengthen the
empire's constituent parts. In the case of Syria, this meant fighting for
semiautonomous status, for only then could Syrians begin to challenge
European domination of the economy. To help them achieve this goal,
Diab promised that Syrian emigrants would return to their homeland because they too wanted a land that was self-sufficient and that "did not
buy the necessities of life from Europe, even the needle and thread."[46]

Interestingly, Diab did not touch on the issue of immigration into
Syria, which was supposed to be on the agenda. A few months earlier,
however, his paper, *Meraat al-gharb*, had published an article, entitled
"Reformist Awakening in Syria," that addressed the issue directly. Again,
attention focused on the peoples of the Balkans. The author accused the
Ottoman government of transferring huge numbers of people of the
"Turkish race" from Macedonia into Syria in the wake of the Balkan
Wars. In language that revealed a growing animosity toward "outsiders,"
he asked, "How will the Syrians manage if millions of that barbaric race
occupy their land?"[47] This rather xenophobic statement reveals one of the
uncomfortable elements of Arabist discourse, indeed of many protonationalist discourses, namely the simultaneous construction of *emigrants* as
members of the nation and of certain *immigrants* as outsiders who compromised the integrity of the nation. Anxieties over immigration emerged
in the context of Arab disaffection from the CUP regime (the result of po-
lices perceived as "Turkification") and, in the case of Palestine, increased
settlement by European Jews. However, it is worth noting that opinions
varied on how best to resolve the immigration question. Al-Tabbara, for
example, criticized those "who reject the immigration of non-Arabs into
Syria because they fear they will mix with the local population and corrupt
their morals." He wanted a nation that would welcome newcomers, and
he did not object to immigration "provided it is regulated."[48] Still, immigration served an ideological function in Arabist circles. As van der Veer
notes, "Nationalism needs the story of migration, the diaspora of others,
to establish the rootedness of the nation."[49]

The views expressed in Diab's speech were consistent with the platform of the Decentralization Party, and like the majority of the delegates
at the conference he was a committed Arabist in the sense that he believed that the language and shared history of the Arab peoples were the

basis of their national identity. He was also an Ottomanist because he believed that Arab national aspirations could be achieved within the framework of the Ottoman state. ʿAbd al-Hamid al-Zahrawi, president of the congress, also emphasized that Arabs were interested in strengthening their position within the empire, not outside it. In an interview for the French newspaper *Le Temps,* al-Zahrawi dismissed the claim that the Ottoman government would be angered by the demands of the congress. "The government would have the right to be angry," he argued, "had we demanded secession from the empire, for example. But we want the opposite. Our demands would improve the condition of the [Ottoman] state *[daula]* and the Arab race *[unsur]* at the same time."[50]

The records of the congress demonstrate that delegates from the *mahjar* advocated greater autonomy for Arabs within the Ottoman system. There were, however, important nuances in this position, the significance of which would become clearer during and after the war. Naoum Mokarzel, for example, attended the conference as the representative of the U.S. branch of Jamʿiyya al-Nahda al-Lubnaniyya (Lebanon League of Progress), the only association at the conference to carry the name of Lebanon in its title. The main goal of the society in the prewar period was to safeguard the special status of Mount Lebanon guaranteed to it by the Règlement organique. Its members were overwhelmingly Maronite, residing both inside and outside Mount Lebanon.[51] One of the most active members outside Lebanon was Ibrahim Salim al-Najjar, who established a branch of the society in New York in 1911, to which Naoum Mokarzel was elected president. According to Basil Kherbawi, priest of St. Nicolas Syrian-Greek Orthodox Cathedral in Brooklyn, New York, the Nahda had eight thousand members by 1913, five thousand of whom were members of the fifteen branches in the Americas.[52] Mokarzel was the publisher of *al-Hoda,* chief rival to Diab's *Meraat ulgharb,* and he was active in the defense of Syrians in the racial prerequisite cases.[53]

Mokarzel's speech, entitled "The Progress of the Emigrants, and Their Support of the Arab Reformist Awakening," described a diaspora mobilized by "national feeling" and willing to devote its intellectual and material resources to the cause of reform.[54] He too pledged allegiance to the moderate platform of the Decentralization Party, but he was more provocative on issues of strategy. He made several references to the "revolutionary" character of the movement, and he recognized that the struggle for freedom might require martyrs and not just "printer's ink."[55] Unlike Diab, Mokarzel made no appeals to the "Ottoman fold," although he did acknowledge that the Lebanese were already enjoying administrative independence within the Ottoman system and encouraged Lebanon's "neighbors" to pursue the same.[56] Mokarzel would eventually become an active supporter of a French mandate over Lebanon, and at the war's end he hurried to Paris to lobby on behalf of the Nahda's separatist goals.[57] As a delegate at the Arab Congress, however, he had still been a supporter of decentralization, not Lebanonization.

Syrian emigrants did develop a new understanding of the Syrian nation in the *mahjar*, but it was a part of a larger whole. Moreover, at the Arab Congress, as well as in the *mahjar* press, emigrants were beginning to articulate a specific relationship between the diaspora and the nation. This was a relationship rooted in the practical matters of remittances, but it was also based on a new imaginary in which the *mahjar*, and the emigrant's place within it, came to represent Arab modernity.

EMIGRANTS AND A "NEW SYRIA"

Linking the development of Arab nationalism to a modernizing impulse is not a new idea. This analysis began with George Antonius's classic account *The Arab Awakening*, which posited a dividing line between the modern westward-looking members of the nineteenth century Lebanese *nahda*, or literary renaissance, and a stagnant Ottoman past.[58] According to Antonius, the Arabs were awakened from their "torpid passivity" by the guiding hand of French and American missionaries, the "foster-parents of the Arab resurrection."[59] Albert Hourani also emphasized the atmosphere of "westernization" among early Arab nationalists, describing their desire for reform in the empire as a yearning to "participate in modern civilization."[60] Hourani was careful not to denigrate the Ottoman past as so many others did, but he continued to conceive of late nineteenth- and early twentieth-century Arab intellectual activity as primarily a project to assimilate European thought—a "coming to terms" with the power and thought of the West.[61] Despite revisions in both the Antonius and Hourani theses, many scholars continued to view Arab demands for national rights as motivated by a desire to emulate a modern Europe.[62] As Hourani succinctly put it, "To be modern was to be in communion with her."[63]

The argument that Arab nationalists were driven by a need to catch up to Europe is easily supported by the published sources of the movement's leading theoreticians. Even a casual reading of the writings of Arabists reveals that the language of rights, autonomy, and reform existed beside broader appeals to the "modern" and the "civilized." Rashid Rida, for example, in his introduction to the published proceedings of the First Arab Congress in Paris, proclaimed that "this is the age of groups [jama'at]. Everything in this age that is civilized and advanced in terms of science, production, and political administration is the result of group activity. Those who do not form groups—in the name of associations, parties, congresses, companies, and unions—have no chance to partake in the civilization of the age."[64] The characterization of the nation as a new, intrinsically modern, and civilized political form recurred frequently at the congress. Al-Tabbara argued that the implementation of the reforms in the Arab provinces would show the world that the "East is civilized." Like other Arabists, he believed that the fulfillment of Arab national aspirations would mean the implementation of European-styled parliamentary structures and the birth of a new political culture. That the Arabs were capable of participating in such a culture was never at issue, for, as al-Tabbara asked rhetorically, "Are we of one species, and they [the West] of another?"[65]

In addition, and in contrast to the Phoenicianists who detached themselves from Arab history, Arabists invoked a glorious Arab past to argue that they had once been the leaders of a sophisticated, scientific, and inventive civilization and that they could therefore reclaim this position in the world of nations. Echoing what had become a popular argument in Arabic thought in the mid–nineteenth century, al-Tabbara reminded his audience that Arabs had excelled in technological and scientific fields when Europe was stagnant: "When the West had descended into the shadows of ignorance, the East was flourishing in its knowledge and civilization."[66] It was only when corruption and ignorance were allowed to go untrammeled that the East lost its position of supremacy (a stage that a more radical group of Arabists associated with the advent of Ottoman rule) and "the professor became the student and the student the professor."[67] To prove that Arabs were being held back by the Ottoman regime, al-Tabbara cited their success abroad in Paris, Egypt, and elsewhere, "where they have succeeded as well as Europeans." "Is not this proof," he argued, "of their capabilities, and of the potential to build their own country if they were granted a stable political life?"[68]

Here al-Tabbara suggests how the *mahjar* and the Syrian emigrants who inhabited it were cast as the mediators of a modernity deemed essential to the construction of the "Arab nation." Najib Diab's speech to the Arab Congress also positioned emigrants within a discourse of the modern. He described emigration as a transforming experience. Emigrants to the Americas, he argued, were given work opportunities by governments that welcomed them and treated them fairly. They learned new techniques of farming, became familiar with modern machinery and, most importantly, "learned the meaning of civilization in Europe and America and witnessed with their own eyes how to protect their individual rights."[69] The emigrants' hope was to take this knowledge and expertise that "they learned in the land of emigration" and apply it to the growth and modernization of Syria.

The motif of transformation was a recurring one in the writings of Syrian emigrants. It was captured visually in a full-page advertisement placed in *al-Hoda* by the Moshy Brothers in New York. Pictured in front of their five-story supply store at the heart of the Syrian enclave on Washington Street are two men, both with peddler's packs on their backs. One is disheveled and downtrodden. The caption above his head reads, "I am in this poor, miserable condition because I did not do business with the Moshy Bros." On the other side is an upright, crisp-suited man with a bowler hat and cane. His caption reads, "I am in this happy condition with lots of money because I did business with the Moshy Bros."[70] The visual is powerful: the Syrian peasant, through smart business practices, has evolved into a "new" Syrian, adorned in the clothes of the middle-class male. One author likened emigration to a transformation in the Syrian personality, adding, "It was hard to believe they [the emigrants and those who stayed behind] were from the same blood."[71] He argued further that emigrants were responsible for the reformist awakening *(al-nahda al-islahiyya)* in Syria and cited their efforts at the Arab Congress in Paris as proof of their commitment to the struggle for change.

Yusuf Jirjis Zakham, a frequent contributor to the *mahjar* press, also pointed to the benefits of emigration to the Syrian "character." The majority of emigrants, he argued, left as illiterate, unpolished peasants and became educated members of a polite bourgeoisie in America. They left ignorant of national and foreign politics and became politically aware beings. Finally, and related to concern with the virility of the Syrian nation, America could make men of Syrians. Whereas Eastern parents suffocated their sons and tried to keep them close to home, Americans encouraged their sons to learn and struggle on their own. If Syrians took only one thing from America, Zakham argued, it should be this method of rearing children—"With this basic principle they could build an exalted nation *[ummatun ʿaliyatun]*."[72] The Rev. Abraham Rihbany echoed these sentiments a few years later in his autobiography published in English and entitled *A Far Journey*. In the closing lines of his preface he

Figure 8. The Moshy Store, advertised in *al-Hoda,* 1899.

wrote: "So to Syria, my loving, untutored mother, as to America, my virile, resourceful teacher, I offer my profound and lasting gratitude."[73]

This emphasis on the *mahjar* "making men" out of Syrians, coupled with the claim that they would sometime in the future return to build an independent nation, helped to counter the argument that emigration had emasculated Syria by draining it of its able-bodied men. Muhammad Kurd ʿAli, better known for his Arab nationalist stance and political activism in Damascus,[74] raised these concerns in a set of articles published in his journal *al-Muqtabas*. Troubled by the rising tide of emigration to the Americas, he criticized men for holding on to naive fantasies about America's wealth and offered sobering statistics that for every thousand persons who left Syria only one or two would succeed in a life that was significantly better than what was possible at home.[75] Why not migrate to other areas within the Ottoman Empire badly in need of human resources, he suggested? With an exodus of healthy men, who would be left to till the soil, plant the mulberry trees, and cultivate the vines?[76] While he was aware of the potential benefits of remittances, he lamented the rush to emigrate on the part of workers, especially those of the key industries of agriculture, silk, and weaving.

Muhammad Kurd ʿAli's dire analysis was exaggerated and at odds with his earlier favorable view of the United States. His inaugural edition of *al-Muqtabas* had in fact extolled the economic opportunities of the United States in a series entitled *al-Nahda al-amrikiyya* (The American Florescence). One article celebrated "American greatness" and attributed this to "the mixture of people . . . innovation, lack of attachment to tradition . . . and appreciation for peace."[77] A few years later, however, Muhammad Kurd ʿAli viewed immigration to the Americas as a drain on the national potential of Syria. It was not just the negative economic impact of emigration that troubled him. The massive loss of manpower, he argued, was devastating the Syrian economy, but it was also wreaking havoc in another way by dotting the landscape with villages of unmarried women. Later historiography resolved this problem by arguing that men returned to marry or sent for wives, but Kurd ʿAli believed that this would not be the case. He feared that men had departed for good and that no amount of cajoling would bring them back.[78] He even accused them of falling prey to the seductive power of Western materialism and ridiculed their desire to be "civilized" at the feet of American women.[79]

In Kurd ʿAli's early *al-Muqtabas* articles we see how his idea of a modern, strong Syria was compromised by the torrent of emigration. The country was being depleted of men, but worse than the loss of their labor was the loss of the authority they commanded as husbands, brothers, and fathers. In short, emigration had produced a crisis in patriarchy and had upset the social, economic, moral and political order.[80] Men were (at least in theory) the heads of families and of the polity, and as the Jesuit journal *al-Mashriq* captured the problem in 1902, "Woe, to the body that is separated from its head."[81] To counter this image of an emasculated Syria, émigré writers like Yusuf Zakham proposed the figure of the virile male emigrant, charting a new course for the nation. It was this image that Arabists incorporated into nationalist discourse, revealing how, as Anne McClintock argues for most nationalisms, "men . . . represent the progressive agent of national modernity (forward-thrusting, potent, and historic), embodying nationalism's progressive, or revolutionary, principle of discontinuity."[82]

The recurring themes of progress, transformation, and virility in the evolving discourse of Arab nationalism demonstrate how the *mahjar* was being linked to "the modern." In other words, the Syrian diaspora helped Arabists establish a claim to modernity.[83] This was an argument that could easily lead to chauvinism, and it did in its Lebanese variant, where the emigrant was cast as a conduit of all things Western, a civilizing influence on a backward, parochial homeland society. Nadra Moutron, writing in 1916 in *La Syrie de demain* (a book dedicated to Paul Deschanel, president of the French Chamber of Deputies), argued that emigrants "hastened the march of progress, they serve as intermediaries between civilized areas by putting them in communication with less advanced races."[84] This tendency to conceive of difference in civilizational and westernizing terms would eventually become a component of Lebanese nationalism. Maronite Archbishop Khouri, writing on behalf of Lebanese committees in America, epitomized this position when he came out emphatically against union with Syria after World War I. Lebanon should remain separate, he argued, because "the Lebanese person believes, and is in fact, superior to the Syrian with respect to science, morality, and civilization." To render Lebanon part of Syria, he continued, "would be to submit light to shadows, intelligence to ignorance."[85] The earlier idea that the *mahjar* represented the Syrian modern was one that, in its best form, was full of vision and promise for a new Syria that hoped to see its diaspora return to build a new nation. The notion was romantic and idealistic, but it served to define Arab nationalism in the pre—World War I period in terms that made sense to a people who had been migrants before they were nationalists.

These observations support the argument that modern nationalisms involve a temporal paradox—a simultaneous assertion of newness and antiquity.[86] People commit to the idea of the nation in the belief that they are participating in the modern march of progress, and they affirm their membership in the nation by invoking old (invented) traditions of wholeness and unity, culled "from the depths of a presumed communal past."[87] This temporal paradox was clearly evident in the rhetoric of Arab nationalism. Al-Tabbara's speech at the Arab Congress, for example, was a perfect combination of this simultaneous claim to modernity and antiquity. Moreover, because national claims emerged in a context of intense emigration, the story was far more complicated and perhaps even more paradoxical. As argued above, the Syrian diaspora served an ideological function in the discourse of Arab nationalism in that it both symbolized and justified the assertion of Arab modernity. That this happened at a point in time when Syrian emigrants were beginning to reap the fruits of their labor and transitioning out of the peddling phase into store ownership and manufacturing is interesting. How eager would Arabists have been to see in the features of the *mahjar* the modern face of the nation had the diaspora still been predominantly working class? If the Arab Congress is any indication, the answer is, not very likely. More to the point, the *mahjar's* position in the discourse of Arab nationalism complicated notions of national space. Emigrants, who were only metaphorically rooted in the soil through their absence, were nonetheless thought of as members of the national community. As the manifesto of the First Arab Congress claimed, the entire Arab nation was "spread across the world." The boundaries of the Arab nation in the prewar period were thus configured along a space-time axis that was powerfully rooted in the experience of migration. In spatial terms, the *mahjar* was positioned within the imagined community of Syria, not outside it. In temporal terms, the *mahjar* became a symbol of the future and the Arab modern.

The war changed all of this. Hopes of remaining within the Ottoman fold were dashed by the draconian measures of an embattled central government. Talk of compromise turned to talk of confrontation, separation, and full-fledged independence. Naoum Labaki, former editor of the newspaper *al-Munazir* (The Interlocutor) and once a proud Ottoman, became an open and active opponent of the Ottoman regime upon his return to Lebanon from Brazil. After the empire's demise, he served in the administrative council of one of the territories shoehorned together from a fragmented Syria: le Grand Liban (Greater Lebanon).[88] Even Syrian emigrants who had advocated complete assimilation as Americans changed their minds. The editor of *al-Muhajir*, Amin al-Gharayyib, returned to Syria to publish a journal called *al-Haris* but was exiled by the Turks. He returned to Syria after the Ottoman defeat and worked in the short-lived government of Prince Faysal.[89]

The dissolution of the empire had a profound effect on how Syrian emigrants thought about national identity. Philip Hitti's observation, quoted at the beginning of this chapter, provides an important clue as to the nature of the postwar shift in Syrian conceptions of home, nation, and citizenship: "Like Janus, the old Roman god, we are double-faced. . . . We have one face looking backward and another forward." In one sense, his analogy conjured the familiar divisions between ancient and modern. In another, this division was infused with new meaning as the Syrian diaspora contemplated its future in America in the age of immigration restriction, as well as its commitment to the homeland in the age of colonial rule. Syrians in the United States began to construct new boundaries between the *mahjar* and the nation and between old and new in the immediate postwar period. For the war, and the settlement that followed, would cause Syrians to rethink their relationship to the homeland and to the United States. The political and economic situation in what was now *colonial* Syria deeply concerned Syrians who had hoped for a greater degree of independence in the postwar order. The passage of restrictive laws on immigration in the United States, and in other parts of the Americas, was also confounding to Syrians.[90] Once again, they found themselves assessing the doubleness of their identity, as emigrants increasingly alienated from their communities of origin and as immigrants trying to define their Americanness—an Americanness that hinged on their ability to claim white citizenship. The dilemma of identity in the postwar years was captured in the question posed in *al-Hoda:* "Who are we in our homeland and who are we abroad?"

A NATION DIVIDED

Competing visions of post-Ottoman Syria were part of the heated debates at the Paris Peace Conference held in the wake of the war. The settlement reached there would fulfill few of the Arab nationalist demands, for while the Great Powers had deemed the Arabs capable of fighting the Ottoman army, they were thought to be insufficiently prepared for full independence. Arab leaders were humiliated by French and British demands and by blatant backtracking on earlier agreements. Perhaps the worst affront was against Prince Faysal, who attended the conference to pursue the cause of Arab independence. He had been encouraged to do so by British officials, especially the "blond Bedouin," T. E. Lawrence, whose convoluted involvement in the Arab Revolt has become the stuff of legend.[91]

Faysal, son of the Hashimite amir of Mecca (Sharif Husayn), had led the forces of the Arab army into Damascus and set about organizing what he and his father believed was their reward for assisting the Allied war effort: an independent Arab state. In March 1920, Faysal was proclaimed king of Syria, an event that harked back to the days of the Ummayads, when Damascus was the capital of a great Arab-Islamic kingdom. Faysal's rule over Syria would last a mere five months, however, for an independent Arab kingdom was not what the Allied victors had in mind as they negotiated the fate of the former Ottoman territories. France asserted its claim to Syria along the lines of the secret agreement made with Britain in 1916.[92] Britain, knowing full well that the agreement with France compromised and even contradicted promises made to Sharif Husayn, chose to preserve a delicate relationship with an imperial rival. As Colonel Meinertzhagen of the Peace Conference staff put it, "It was now preferable to quarrel with the Arab rather than the French, if there was to be a quarrel at all."[93]

The San Remo Conference in April 1920 thus affirmed France's claim to the northern half of geographical Syria and Britain's to the south (Palestine) and to Iraq.[94] Syria became a class "A" Mandate, which in theory was purely administrative, an apparatus to guide the native inhabitants toward self-rule or, as French high commissioner Robert de Caix described it, "a provisional system designed to enable populations which, politically speaking, are still minors to educate themselves so as to arrive one day at full self-government."[95] In practice, it was an occupation pure and simple, and like all occupations it began with a chilling show of force. In July 1920, French troops, reinforced with Senegalese soldiers, moved toward Damascus to wrestle control from Faysal, which they did after defeating his forces at Maysalun. They then marched on to the capital and paraded through the streets in celebration of their victory.[96]

"Syria," so long the prized possession of empires, from the Roman to the Ottoman, had been seized by a new imperial power: Mother France and her civilizing mission.[97] Barely two years after President Wilson had proclaimed his famous Fourteen Points, the Arab provinces of the Ottoman Empire had been carved and divvied up along the lines of the secret agreement of 1916. The Mandate system was formally recognized in Article 22 of the Covenant of the League of Nations. In language that masked the political and economic interests of the Mandatory powers, the covenant declared the Mandate to be a beneficial and civilizing form of governance for "peoples not yet able to stand by themselves under the strenuous conditions of the modern world."[98]

The reaction in the *mahjar* to the imposition of the Mandate was mixed. In the United States, among the Maronites, there was support and celebration of France's reconfiguration of the *mutasarrifiyya* as "Greater Lebanon"—a territory considerably larger than the old Ottoman governorate.[99] Naoum Mokarzel, who had been more cautious at the Arab Congress, became an outspoken advocate of French intervention in Syria and was pleased by the developments at the Peace Conference. In a dispatch to *al-Hoda* on September 28, 1919, he was ecstatic about the prospects of French control of the Levant: "This is the most important telegram I have sent to you and the most beautiful to fall on your hearts. The conference has decided to send French forces to take the place of the British army in Syria, and all of Syria will be under the guardianship *[wisaya]* of France, and Greater Lebanon will be autonomous within the lines of its original borders."[100] He was obviously pleased by what he called "Faysal's total failure" to negotiate a deal at the conference,[101] and he was impressed by the Lebanese delegation, headed by the Maronite Patriarch Elias Pierre Hoyek, who argued that "the Lebanese have always constituted a national entity, distinct from their neighbors on account of their language, their customs, affinities, and their Western culture."[102]

There was, in fact, little enthusiasm among the Syrian Christians in the United States for Faysal's Arab government. When Damascus fell to the Allied forces in 1918, celebrations erupted in New York. Joseph Khoury, editor of *ash-Shaab*, announced in the "Victory Edition" of his paper that "the Crescent vanishes and its light will not shine again in the Orient, which is the Cradle of the Educator of Humanity. . . . Hail to Syria, who has been longing for the army of salvation and liberty."[103] Mokarzel's Francophilia, however, represented an extreme position. More typical was the guarded support of the French Mandate expressed by the Orthodox editor of *as-Sayeh*, ʿAbd al-Masih Haddad, who argued that the Mandate was a practical necessity. France's role was to train and supervise Syrians in the methods of good governance, he wrote, "and this is the only way to achieve our real independence."[104]

Meraat ul-gharb's special correspondent to the Peace Conference also urged his readers to support French "guardianship" over Syria as a way to avoid the country's "domination by Muslims."[105] He carefully distinguished between "guardianship" *(wisaya)* and "protectorate" *(himaya)*, claiming that "the age of protectorates is over!" He appeared optimistic that if France's supervision of Syria could resemble that of the United States over Cuba, independence would be forthcoming. Like Haddad, he adamantly opposed the division of geographical Syria into separate states.[106] This was a position consistent with the Alliance Libanaise and the Syria–Mount Lebanon League of Liberation, with which Haddad had become associated during the war.[107] The league had been founded in New York in 1917 under the leadership of the dynamic émigré Ayyub Thabit, former member of the Beirut Reform Society and future president of the Lebanese Republic.

Thabit had headed to New York after the 1913 Arab Congress to campaign for liberation– of Syria from Ottoman rule, a position that resulted in a death sentence in absentia being issued against him by the CUP.[108] By the end of the war, he had come out forcefully in favor of a French protectorate over a *united* Syria. The insistence on the administrative integrity of Syria (including Mount Lebanon) would place him at loggerheads with Naoum Mokarzel and the Lebanon League of Progress. The rift between the two groups became blatantly obvious in October 1918 when they hosted separate parties in New York to celebrate the Allied victory in Syria and Palestine.[109] Mokarzel's vision of a postwar Syria would ultimately prevail, and he went to great lengths to ensure that the U.S. government recognized the independent status of Lebanon. In this regard, minor details mattered. When, for example, the U.S. Postal Service decided to accept letters to Mount Lebanon only if the address read "Mount-Lebanon, Syria," Mokarzel went to the French ambassador in Washington and asked him to persuade the American postal authorities that "Mount Lebanon" was all that was needed.[110] He soon embarked on a new campaign to change the name of the immigrant community from "Syrian" to "Lebanese," a program that, at this stage, was only partially successful. A few clubs did introduce a hyphen to their name and thus became "Syrian-Lebanese," but the separatist zeal of Mokarzel was not widely shared.[111]

Disagreements over the status of Lebanon and the French Mandate steadily increased in the *mahjar,* a development with which French diplomats were none too pleased. As early as December 1920, high commissioner Robert de Caix complained to the French Ministry of Foreign Affairs about "the anti-French propaganda coming out of [the Syrian colonies] in America." "The Syrian American press counts at least fifteen to twenty newspapers, which are almost all anti-French," he continued. "They come into Syria in great numbers, where they are widely read and commented upon." He cited evidence of a number of proclamations intercepted in Beirut from New York and Buenos Aires calling for Syrians to unite and fight for the liberation of Syria.[112] The French could, however, always find supporters among the Maronites. D. Hederi, for example, president of the United Maronites Society in New York, denounced "the nefarious propaganda in this country directed against the French Authority in Lebanon and Syria." "It is our duty," he continued, "to refute these lies [prétention mensongère] so that it is not said that the sons of Lebanese emigrants are detached from their brothers in the homeland and have renounced the historic love and protection of France."[113] For members of the Syrian American Society, however, France was exercising imperialist designs that were inconsistent with the age. They wrote a twenty-eight-page memorandum to U.S. president Calvin Coolidge urging his support for an independent Syria based on Wilsonian principles and on the recommendations of the King-Crane Commission.[114] The memorandum appeared to fall on deaf ears.

Other important issues besides the status of Lebanon drew immigrants into debates about the homeland. The question of Palestine, for example, was very much on the minds of many Syrians in New York. Indeed, concern over Jewish settlement prompted what was perhaps the first major demonstration by a coalition of Arab American groups. Immediately after the issuance of the Balfour Declaration in 1917, a number of Syrians in New York established the Palestine Anti-Zionism Society. The society's first foray into activism came on November 8, 1917, when, along with the Ramallah Young Men's Society, it held a demonstration at the Hotel Bossert that attracted five hundred Syrians.[115] After a debate on the situation in Palestine, a resolution was passed: "Resolved that we protest against the formation of any Government or body politic based on religious principles, by a minority, contrary to the principles of the majority. We further protest against the usurpation of the homes and property of a people weakened and impoverished by centuries of misery, by a race rendered more powerful and wealthy through contact with the western civilization thus applying might against right. We further protest against any scheme of artificial importation of Zionists flooding the country against its natural capacities and thus forcing an emigration of the rightful inhabitants."[116]

One of the most active members of the Palestine Anti-Zionism Society was Fouad Shatara from Jaffa, Palestine, a surgeon and instructor at the School of Medicine of Long Island College Hospital. He became a forceful critic of the British Mandate in Palestine. Before it was imposed, Shatara had written twice to Robert Lansing, secretary of state under President Woodrow Wilson, with the sincere hope "that our cause may not be left unchampioned at the forthcoming peace conference."[117] In 1922, Shatara appeared before the House Committee on Foreign Affairs to reiterate the concerns over the Balfour Declaration and Zionist settlement in Palestine. He called for an investigation of the situation by a "neutral commission" but found little support among members of Congress. Senators and House representatives held overwhelmingly favorable views of the Zionist movement. Representative W. Bourke Cockran of New York, for example, likened Jewish immigration into Palestine to the white man's arrival in the New World, underscoring how the debate on Palestine was viewed through the lens of racial hierarchies.[118] The Arabs were seen as inferior, unfit for self-determination, and in this case not white.

Analyzing the reaction to the Mandatory regimes is indeed one way to assess the diaspora's connection to postwar Syria, and the active involvement of emigrant elites in nationalist politics is a subject that warrants more thorough study. There is, for example, much to be learned about opposition to French intervention in Syria among Syrians in Latin America and the United States.[119] However, the question of immigrants' connection to and support of postwar Syria was addressed in less overtly political ways. The issue of return migration, for example, acquired new resonance after the war. Although short-lived, the intensity of the debate, as well as the terms in which positions were cast, conveyed a new development in Syrian ethnicity.

MYTHS OF RETURN

What was markedly different about the postwar identity debates was the focus on the second generation, the children born of first-wave immigrants. Forums that had typically chronicled homeland events or the achievement of Syrians in the *mahjar* began to tackle questions that had more to do with Syrians' relationships to each other, specifically along the lines of generation. The clearest example of this shift in terms of the debate on Syrian identity could be found in a new publication called the *Syrian World*. "Conceived in the spirit of service to the Syrian-American generation," the journal was published monthly in English with the explicit aim of serving "as a forum for the discussion of existing problems among Syrians in America in an effort to arrive at their best solution."[120] These problems were addressed in lengthy essays written by the editor, Salloum Mokarzel (brother of Naoum), and other prominent members of the Syrian immigrant intelligentsia. The journal also contained a lively "Readers' Forum" where readers across the United States voiced their concerns and asked for advice. In addition, the *Syrian World* was the first publication to provide translations from the Arabic-language press as a service to its non-Arabic-speaking readers, Syrian and non-Syrian alike. This helped make the journal a great success among educated Syrians (particularly those concerned with the situation of the second generation), as well as government agencies, charitable associations, and other organizations interested in the nation's foreign-born population. One of the journal's enthusiastic supporters, for example, was Rose Davidson, national director of the Department of Racial Groups of the Woman's Christian Temperance Union.[121]

Salloum Mokarzel argued that the most pressing problem facing Syrians in the United States was the steadily widening cultural divide between immigrant parents and their children. The *Syrian World,* he hoped, would foster a new dialogue between them.[122] The broad question at hand was how the second generation could embrace their American identity yet still retain a connection to Syria, its culture, language, and history. The question provoked a divisive set of responses, for there was disagreement over what it meant to be Syrian at a time when the very contours of the homeland were being redefined in a classic example of "divide and rule," while the second generation had become more self-consciously Syrian *American.* These tensions were exposed in the pages of the *Syrian World* as community members debated the merits of return migration.

The debate was sparked by a letter submitted in February 1927 by Michael Shadid, a medical doctor living in Elk City, Oklahoma. Entitled "Syria for the Syrians," it encouraged Syrians to migrate back to Syria to assist in the country's postwar development. To many readers of the journal this seemed an odd suggestion, since Shadid was established professionally in Elk City and appeared to be an unlikely candidate for return migration. In 1898, at the age of sixteen, he had left his mountain village of Judayda for New York, where, after learning how to peddle from his cousin's wife, he promptly began his own rounds as a peddler of jewelry.[123] He saved enough money to bring over his brother and sister in 1900 and, after a dizzying tour peddling through "all of the United States east of the Rocky Mountains, with the exception of New England," turned to his studies.[124] With five thousand dollars in hand, he enrolled at Tarleton State College in Stephenville, Texas, graduated in 1902, and went on to Washington University's medical school. He practiced medicine (interspersed with peddling) in Missouri and Oklahoma between 1906 and 1923, when he took the post of chief surgeon at a hospital in Elk City, Oklahoma. Concerned by the high rate of illness among the poor in the area, he turned the hospital into the first cooperative facility in the United States—a hospital owned by the people it served. In

Elk City a family of four could get its medical care for $25 a year, with low extra charges for hospitalization and medicine.[125] Despite his service to the Elk City community, Shadid believed he would remain an outsider, and worse, that his children, who were born in America, would face discrimination and ridicule at the hands of "peoples belonging to the Nordic branch of the White race."[126] The only real solution, in his opinion, was for Syrians to leave the United States and transfer their skills and know-how to a new Syria in-the-making.

The article provoked an incendiary response. Shadid's optimistic view of Syria was described as misguided and naive. Salloum Mokarzel, in one of the more conciliatory responses, claimed that the economic conditions in Syria had not improved but only worsened and that since those conditions had precipitated the emigration in the first place returning would be folly. He argued that Syrians had begun to reap the rewards of the early years of hard work and should not "forsake positive results to risk a doubtful experiment."[127] Numerous other letters contained the same skeptical view of Syria's economic potential, and Shadid's agricultural proposals were repeatedly deemed impractical.

However, Shadid had justified his "back to Syria" crusade in other than economic terms. He argued that Syrians should return to their homeland because they would never be fully welcome in the United States. He described his own unease, living in a town where so many members of the professional class, including his doctor neighbors, were Klansmen, who, he wrote, "recognize me professionally but ostracise [sic] me socially." He reminded his readers that Syrians in other parts of Oklahoma had fared worse, and he gave the example of the burning of a Syrian dry goods store by the Ku Klux Klan as a case in point. "It may be said," he argued, "that among native born Americans there is more prejudice against foreigners in general, and Syrians in particular, than in any other country of the wide world."[128] For this reason, Shadid argued, Syrians should make Syria, not America, their home.

Shadid's argument touched a sensitive chord among immigrant elites because he challenged their convictions, made so strikingly clear during the racial prerequisite cases, that Syrians were eminently suited for integration into the American mainstream. His troubling claim that there was a deep-seated animosity toward Syrians in the United States was handled in two ways. One group of writers argued that the attitudes described by Shadid were an aberration from the norm of tolerance in America and that those persons who held them were not "true Americans." A. N. Adwon, for example, wrote in from Wilson, Oklahoma (a

town of 2,500 inhabitants with only three Syrian families), to praise the
way that Syrians and other immigrants had been made to feel welcome
in the Southwest. "I want to say," he declared, "that there is no better
locality for a man who attends to his own business and obeys the laws
of the country to live in."[129]

A second group agreed with Shadid that Syrians would continue to
face bigotry and prejudice in the United States but that this in itself was
not a good enough reason to return to Syria. Joseph David, for example,
from Jacksonville, Florida, chastised Shahid for "his spirit of pitiful defeat." Syrians, he argued, had for millennia endured persecution at the
hands of tyrants and were able to preserve their "noble traditions."
"Shall we, then, surrender to an isolated, insignificant, bigoted band of
individuals, planted here and there in this great land of liberty and within
this great right-loving nation?"[130] What Syrians must do, according to
David, was not return to Syria but challenge those who demeaned and
defamed them.

The controversy surrounding Shadid's letter prompted the American
Syrian Federation of New York to call a special meeting to discuss the
subject of "whether the Syrians in the United States are being discriminated against." The minutes of the meeting, which were excerpted in the
Syrian World, reveal that it was primarily an occasion for speechmaking
and not a discussion of practical solutions to the problems raised by Shadid. Several prominent members of the New York community, for example, spoke of the virtues of the Syrians in the United States and encouraged the audience to take pride in the Syrian "race." Fouad Shatara
did acknowledge that Syrians faced discrimination in rare circumstances
but suggested that they were often to blame for their misfortune. "What
are those characteristics of ours that are the underlying cause of the trouble?" he asked.

The overwhelming tone of the meeting was positive. The minutes conveyed a broad optimism on the part of the participants that Syrians' contributions to America, as well as their appreciation of American values,
would be fully recognized and honored. In short, there was no real problem of discrimination. Indeed, what was remarkable about the forum
was the way it made the concerns that were obviously paramount to men
like Shadid a nonissue. The more pressing problem for Syrians in the
United States, according to the closing remarks at the forum, was assimilation, not discrimination. The children and grandchildren of Syrian
immigrants were becoming "indistinguishable from other Americans,"
Shatara argued. "If your children are going to forget entirely that they

have any Syrian blood in them, that will be a great pity."[131] And so, in the face of evidence that Syrians were being ostracized and excluded from American communities for being, in effect, "too Syrian," the federation chose to focus on the problem of those who had become "too American." Just how they would remember that they had "Syrian blood" would be the topic of future debate.

As for the question of returning to Syria, it quickly receded in the *Syrian World*, and there was no great return migration in the decade after the war's end. This did not mean that Syrian immigrants severed ties to the homeland. On the contrary, Syrian immigrants took great pride when they could host a homeland leader or support a "national" cause. What constituted a worthy cause was, of course, hotly contested, as attested to by the uproar in the Syrian American papers regarding the visit of Amir Shakib Arslan to Detroit in January 1927. Arslan was the representative of Sultan Atrash, leader of the insurgency movement against the French in Syria, and his visit to Detroit, under the auspices of the New Syria Party, was condemned by the heavily Christian-identified papers like *al-Hoda* and *as-Sayeh*, while it was happily received by the Druze, anti-imperialist paper *al-Bayan*.[132] The New Syria Party had chapters throughout the United States. In the summer of 1927, members bombarded the Ministry of Foreign Affairs in Paris with telegrams demanding independence from France. From Grand Rapids, Michigan, Hamad Atrash wrote, "It is about time for the French Government to see the faults of the militaristic policy in Syria. France should listen to the just demands of the Syrian nationalists and long ago put an end to bloodshed in Syria, the martyred." Sayah Hamood in Arkansas noted that the French government was working on a new constitution for Syria, and he hoped that it would not be "saturated with the spirit of colonization and that [France] would give Syria its freedom and independence."[133]

In terms of financial support of the homeland, remittances to communities of origin soared. According to a report commissioned by the Mandatory government, "Lebanese" emigrants remitted over $8.5 million to two banks alone between 1926 and 1927.[134] In fact, Syria's dependence on remittances provoked sharp criticism from emigrant leaders. Najib Diab, who at the Arab Congress had dreamed of a Syria freed from dependency on Europe, printed an article that criticized Syrians for depending on earnings from the *mahjar*.[135] Salloum Mokarzel, writing as A. Hakim, took aim at those who came to the *mahjar* (particularly clergy) to collect money, only to enrich themselves rather than the churches, schools, and hospitals they had promised to support.[136] The Beirut paper

Lisan al-hal was somewhat more diplomatic, commenting that such a high rate of remittances "does not show a healthy condition in a country striving for economic independence." The paper reminded its readers that money from abroad should go toward investment and not "reckless spending on necessities and luxuries which should be amply covered by native production."[137]

The Syrian American press continued to feature news reports on developments in Syria, and letters from immigrants who did return were eagerly anticipated and read. Often these letters conveyed the distance between aspiration and reality, or the difference between imagining what the homeland was like and actually returning to it. Philip Hitti, for example, returned to take a post at the American University of Beirut and wrote frequently to his friend Reverend Abraham Rihbany. In one letter, he complained about the excessive materialism of postwar Beirut. Rihbany replied, "It must have been rather amusing to you to see so many dressed in *franji* [European dress]. You know that the thing which I regret is the fact that that poor mother country has to array itself in the borrowed garments of an imported civilization, instead of rooting itself in a civilization evolving out of its own soul. But this is a big subject, and a task which Syria probably never can face."[138] Joseph Ferris, president of the American Syrian Federation in New York, replied to another of Hitti's letters in this way: "The idea that prevailed heretofore to the effect that Syria was the promised land for a lot of our young men is becoming somewhat stale and more particularly insofar as it pertains to the opportunities it offers. Quite a few of our friends who were insistent in their support of the idea have somewhat modified their point of view and attempt to state numerous exceptions."[139]

Michael Shadid also returned to Syria with his daughter and was so disappointed by what he saw that he wrote an "Explanation and Retraction" to the *Syrian World* and reversed many of the arguments he had initially made in his article "Syria for Syrians." Significantly, he would not make Syria his permanent home, citing the country's "economic ruin" as a deciding factor.[140] While Shadid admitted a change of heart on the question of return, he held fast to his belief that Syrians would never be considered fully American. Just how right he was, and how premature the optimism of the federation meeting in New York had been, was made clear in 1929 during a Senate debate in which Senator David Reed of Pennsylvania referred to the Syrians as the "trash of the Mediterranean" and singled out Arabs as unfit for immigration to the United States.[141] "How can anyone expect an Arab, who has lived under some patriarchal government where he did not even dare whisper his views, to come here and participate intelligently in the American processes of democracy?" Reed asked of his Senate colleagues.

Michael Shadid felt vindicated and said as much in a letter to the *Syrian World*: "The outburst of Senator Reed only substantiates what I have repeatedly asserted in what I have contributed to a previous issue of The Syrian world *[sic]*, that the Syrian people are discriminated against in this country on account of racial prejudice."[142]

Senator Reed's comments incensed Syrian community leaders, and they were quick to mount a defense. Reed's claim that the Syrians were a mongrelized race, part of "all the Levantine stock that churns around through there and does not know what its own ancestry is," had especially goaded them. For immigrant elites, the charge that Syrians were somehow "impure" was nauseating, especially since the question of racial identity had already been settled in the naturalization cases, or so they believed. Salloum Mokarzel sounded another wake-up call: "This is a direct and open challenge to Syrians to develop a little more knowledge of their ancestral background that they may be able, when the necessity arises, to defend and prove their racial extraction."[143] The response of Syrian community leaders to Reed was to defend their heritage, assert the purity of their "race," and establish their credentials as a productive, loyal, and Americanizing population.

Not since the racial prerequisite cases had Syrians felt so maligned by a government official, and they employed many of the strategies that had helped them make their case a decade and a half earlier. They debated the issue in the Arabic-language press, submitted letters to the English-language papers, and conferred with legal counsel. In Massachusetts and Ohio a new tactic was employed: Syrians lobbied their senators. The campaign was quite successful, since Senators Walsh and Burton took Syrian concerns to the floor of the Senate. This action prompted Senator Reed to backtrack on earlier comments and to carefully parse what exactly he had meant by "trash."[144]

The *Syrian World* covered the controversy over Senator Reed's comments at length. Readers were outraged by the slanderous way that the senator had dismissed them, and they marshaled evidence to prove him both bigoted and wrong. Juxtaposed against the "Readers' Forum" was another story that put Senator Reed's comments and the Syrian reaction to them in jarring perspective. Under the title "Has the Syrian Become a Negro," the *Syrian World* printed a translation from the New York paper *ash-Shaab*. The article described the killing of a Syrian immigrant and his wife in Lake City, Florida, and while it was sparse on details, it was clear from just one word that this was an unusual murder, for the man had been lynched. More than the comments of Senator Reed, this brutal killing substantiated Michael Shadid's claim that Syrian immigrants had reason to worry about their status in America. Both these events were terrible reminders that the path to "becoming American" was strewn with obstacles. The lynching in particular confirmed that the "race crisis" was far from over for Syrians and that their status as American citizens was suspect. In this post–World War I period in which they were being asked to choose between being French colonial subjects or American ones, the question of whiteness resurfaced. Chapter 4 examines the reiteration of the crisis in racial identity.

The Lynching of Nola Romey

Syrian Racial Inbetweenness in the Jim Crow South

The white brutality that I had not seen was a more effective control of my behavior than that which I knew.

Richard Wright (1945)

[Lynching] is a specie of mob violence which results in the death of a man whose guilt has not been judicially ascertained; but in addition to that, there are the judicial lynchings—the rapid, unfair trial and railroading of men to prison or to the gallows.

W. E. B. Du Bois (1948)

All of my life I still live in fear. I look over my shoulders thinking are they looking for the survivors of my family?

Surviving daughter of Nola and Fannie Romey, 1968

The lynching occurred in Lake City, Florida, where it was covered extensively in the local paper. Newspapers across the nation also carried the story in various degrees of detail. "Man Lynched after Wife is Slain by Cop" announced the bold-type headline of the *Tampa Tribune* on May 18, 1929.[1] The *Chicago Defender* ran the story on the front page under the title "Florida Mob Lynches White Storekeeper," while the *New York Times* and *Los Angeles Times* printed Associated Press reports under the heading "Grocer Is Lynched at Lake City, Fla."[2] *Meraat ul-gharb*, published in Arabic in New York City, printed an article with the title "Syrian Killed at the Hands of a Mob after His Wife Is Killed by Chief of Police."[3] The reports in the English- and Arabic-language press revealed that the lynched man was Nola Romey, who, with his wife Fannie and their four children, was a member of one of two Syrian families living in Lake City.[4] Early in the morning of May 17, 1929, a group of men took him from the local jail where he was being held and shot him. "Pierced by 13 bullets," his body was found in a ditch two miles south of the town by a local farm boy.[5] Some of the wounds were dry, indicating that they had been inflicted after his death.

The obvious question is: Why was Nola Romey in police custody in the first place, and what could have been so egregious about his alleged offense that it prompted a mob to take him from jail, circumvent state authority, and lynch him? What was the connection, as the papers suggested, between his death and the killing of Fannie Romey at the hands of the police? Like so many instances of extralegal violence in the South, the circumstances surrounding the lynching are not entirely clear. Once the event receded from the headlines, the lynching began to fade into the silence of the past. It was never systematically researched, and it received no attention in the substantial literature on the subject of lynching. Scholarship on Arab Americans rarely mentions it, despite the claim by community leader Salloum Mokarzel in 1929 that the lynching was "one of the saddest tragedies in the history of the Syrians in America."[6]

This chapter lifts the cover of silence off this tragedy that left Nola and Fannie Romey dead and their children orphaned. It pieces together the events leading up to the lynching and analyzes the response by the Syrian and non-Syrian community in Lake City and nationwide. What was the impact of this lynching on Syrian Americans' perceptions of race and of their place in the U.S. racial order? What did the editor of *al-Shaab* mean by his question "Has the Syrian become a Negro?" in the context of the newspaper coverage that described Romey as a "white man"?

RACE AND LYNCHING IN THE JIM CROW SOUTH

In 1929, when the Romeys were killed, lynching had had a long history in the United States. Early dictionary definitions claimed that the term derived from Charles Lynch, an eighteenth-century neighborhood leader in Virginia who advocated punishment of local Tories without proper trial. Lynching came to encompass a range of practices used to punish and intimidate persons of different political and religious persuasions as well as persons accused of violating community standards. Although not always described as such, lynching included beating, whipping, tar-and-feathering, and, occasionally, killing. *Webster's Dictionary* of 1848 defined "lynch law" as "the practice of punishing men for crimes or offenses by private, unauthorized persons, without a legal trial."[7] In the mid-nineteenth century, as antislavery activity rose, mobs lynched abolitionists as well as Mormons and Catholics. In the West, lynching was part of vigilante frontier "justice" inflicted disproportionately, and often indiscriminately, on the American Indian, Latino, Chinese, and African American populations.[8]

Lynching changed dramatically during and after the Civil War when it became a practice used primarily in the South to punish and terrorize newly enfranchised African Americans. When blacks attempted, for example, to assert their rights through the Populist Party, whites united across class lines to crush them.[9] With the failure of Reconstruction, lynching accompanied the passage of Jim Crow laws that erected a rigid structure of racial segregation, disenfranchised blacks, and encouraged the exercise of frequent and horrific violence against those who allegedly went against community norms. Indeed, community approval, either explicit, in the form of participation by local citizenry, or implicit, in the form of acquittal of the lynchers with or without trial, is what distinguished lynching from murder.[10] And while historians and sociologists have noted the varying types of lynchings (depending, for example, on the size of the mob and the method of execution), the underlying intent of the vast majority of lynchings in the post–Civil War era was the same: to enforce a system of white supremacy. Lynchings occurred in the North, Midwest, and Far West, but the highest numbers were in the South, where lynch mobs killed an estimated 3,943 persons between 1880 and 1930.[11] In the 1920s, 95 percent of all lynchings occurred in the South in a culture that was "saturated with the ethic of mob violence."[12] Florida had the highest per capita lynching rate in the country. Between 1921 and 1946, Florida witnessed sixty-one recorded lynchings—more than twice the number in Alabama and Louisiana and only slightly less than the number in Georgia.[13]

Blacks accounted for nearly 85 percent of the victims lynched between 1880 and 1930.[14] They were killed for "offenses" such as arguing over crop settlements and wages and not showing sufficient deference to whites.[15] The most heinous lynchings—those that involved prolonged torture, mutilation, hanging, and burning of the victims—were unleashed upon black men accused of alleged rape and murder. These lynchings were "feasts of blood" that acquired a sacrificial nature.[16] They were fueled by a late nineteenth-century ideology of white supremacy that held blacks to be inferior in all ways. Unlike antebellum white perceptions of blacks as docile and childlike, this more virulent white supremacism held them to be aggressive and dangerous.[17] Supporters of lynching viewed the practice as a lethal punishment and as a deterrent to the perceived threat posed to them by blacks.

Lynched blacks thus became the "strange fruit" that Billie Holiday sang about in her haunting 1939 recording: hanging from the poplar trees, their bodies tortured and defiled, left for public display and, increasingly, public consumption in the form of commodified spectacle and dismemberment.[18] Thousands came to be spectators at Sam Hose's lynching in Newman, Georgia, in 1899—many in specially chartered trains. A crowd of men, "souvenir seekers," rushed to cut off pieces of his body, parts of which were sold at "inflated prices" in the market that developed for such macabre memorabilia. Sam Hose's knuckles were later displayed in a grocery store window, an event that became seared on the mind of the scholar W. E. B. Du Bois and undoubtedly thousands of other African Americans.[19] Twenty-four years after the Hose lynching, the gruesome tradition of dismemberment was still being practiced. After the lynching of two black men in Georgia, a drugstore in Milledgeville proudly displayed a severed finger and ear along with a sign reading, "What's left of the niggers that shot a white man."[20] Spectacle lynchings were made possible by the rise of consumer culture in the South. They were advertised in the press, announced by telephone, arrived at by train and by automobile. Photographs of lynchings were circulated, commemorated, and sold. While the actual number of lynchings declined in the early twentieth century, the cultural impact of the killing increased as more and more people participated in watching the drawn-out and grisly deaths of the accused.[21]

THE LOCAL CONTEXT: LAKE CITY

Lake City and the surrounding area did not escape the epidemic of lynching that spread throughout the South in the late nineteenth and early twentieth centuries. The town lay in an area that was predominantly rural and agricultural, focusing on the cultivation of fruits and tobacco. Although relatively small, Lake City had an ice factory, a bottling works, cotton ginneries, tobacco-packing warehouses, a sawmill, a public market, baseball fields, and an opera house. It was situated at the junction of the Seaboard Air Line Railroad and the Plant System, with several trains arriving and departing daily.[22] According to a souvenir pamphlet prepared by the Florida Tobacco Fair Association in 1897, Lake City was "growing steadily, substantially and permanently."[23] The pamphlet boasted that Lake City was "the healthiest town in Florida" and occupied the highest point on the peninsula. "The population is thrifty and prosperous, including the colored portion, between which and the white there is perfect peace, harmony and good will."[24]

In the early 1920s, Lake City benefited from the Federal Highway Act, which provided funds for the building of a concrete highway from Jacksonville to Pensacola. Passing through Lake City, Highway 90 was the first concrete highway in the state and rapidly became a popular route for thousands of automobile visitors or "tin can tourists" traveling throughout the state. A *Saturday Evening Post* article featuring Lake City in 1925 described the town as a "flourishing North Florida community . . . surrounded by pecan groves, towering live oaks and rolling hill slopes whose contours suggest southern Maine or Vermont rather than tropical Florida."[25] Because so many of the automobile tourists entering the state passed through Lake City during the height of the tourist season—1,700 cars a day according to a tally by the Boy Scouts of Lake City—the *Post* referred to Lake City as "the Gateway to Florida."[26] It was perhaps the bustling character of Lake City that prompted Nola Romey to move his family there sometime after 1923 and to open a fruit and fish market in the heart of downtown on North Marion Street. Moreover, his Syrian cousin, Ellis Moses, operated a grocery store in Lake City and assisted in the Romey family's transition to a new environment.[27]

Nola had immigrated with his wife Fannie from Zahle, Lebanon, to the United States in 1906. They settled in Valdosta, Georgia, and became naturalized citizens in 1916.[28] Nola's experience in Valdosta had not been pleasant. While listed in the 1920 census as a retail merchant with a fruit stand, he engaged in other business activities on the side.[29] He was arrested and charged twice for gambling-related offenses. In 1916 he was charged with operating a slot machine and in 1923 was charged for running a "punch board" (a game of chance). In both cases, he was sentenced to labor on a chain gang, although in the first case there is a record of his payment of a $25 fine instead.[30] Nola was also targeted by members of the Ku Klux Klan (KKK) in Valdosta, who flogged him, an experience that no doubt encouraged him to think of alternative places to live.[31]

Nola Romey arrived in Lake City with a history of run-ins with the law and with firsthand knowledge of the tactics of white supremacists. Not only had he been harassed by the KKK, but Georgia had been the site of a particularly gruesome rampage of lynching in May 1918. In the area between Barney and Morven in Brooks County, twelve African Americans were lynched on suspicion that they were involved in the planning and execution of a plot to murder their abusive employer. One of the victims,

Mary Turner, wife of a man allegedly involved in the plot, was eight months pregnant at the time. A mob killed her one day after lynching her husband, apparently to silence her protestation over his death. The lynchers set her on fire and cut her unborn baby from her stomach. They then fired hundreds of bullets into her body. The barbarism continued on into Valdosta, where Sidney Johnson, the alleged ringleader of the plot, was hunted down and shot to death in a shootout with the police. Walter White, who investigated the lynching for the National Association for the Advancement of Colored People (NAACP), reported that the crowd that had gathered "took the body, unsexed it with a sharp knife, [and] threw the amputated parts into the street in front of the house."[32] The body was then dragged behind an automobile down Patterson Street, where the Romeys had their store. It is impossible that Nola Romey did not know about this frenzy of violence. Perhaps it influenced his decision to leave the town and settle in Lake City. But here too he could not escape a tradition of extralegal violence. Indeed, it is difficult to square the rosy picture of harmony painted of Lake City by the Florida Tobacco Fair Association with the history of lynching in and near the town.

Lake City was situated in the middle of lynch-prone Columbia County, the county that registered more multiple lynchings (involving the killing of more than one person) than any other county in the state.[33] These lynchings typically followed challenges to white authority, which were interpreted as a threat to the system of privilege and white domination over a more populous black segment of the community. Lynching was a way to preserve this domination and perpetuate "the ascendancy of an entrenched group."[34] In Lake City, where in 1929 there were only twenty people of foreign birth and the census showed that 57 percent of the total population of 1,682 was black, native whites were concerned primarily with maintaining their ascendancy over blacks.[35] They had already demonstrated a willingness to use intimidation and violence in order to do so. In 1893, three blacks were lynched near the town on suspicion of homicide.[36] Two years later, a mob of men dragged a young black preacher, Robert Bennet, from the pulpit and lynched him five miles southwest of Lake City. He was accused of "acting improperly" toward the daughter of his employer.[37] In 1900, Spencer Williams, described in the press as a "negro gambler," was literally shot to pieces when a posse tracked him down and killed him. He had allegedly wounded a city marshal who had tried to arrest him. His body, filled with approximately two hundred bullet holes, was brought into town and displayed in front of the courthouse, where it was surrounded by a crowd.[38]

Lynching continued into the new decade when, in 1911, six black men were killed after a mob gained entry to the Lake City jail where they were being held, removed them to the outskirts of town, and shot them.[39] According to a press report, the shooting lasted an hour, and at daybreak citizens from Lake City found the men "mutilated beyond recognition."[40] Extralegal violence erupted again in 1920 when B. J. Jones, a black dry goods store owner and chairman of the Columbia County Republican Club of Lake City, barely escaped with his life when he challenged the political status quo. Jones had angered white citizens of Lake City and Jacksonville with his efforts to encourage blacks, particularly newly enfranchised black women, to vote. He was reported to have visited churches, lodges, and night schools and to have threatened to have black women expelled if they failed to exercise the franchise.[41] In an effort to silence him, a mob snatched him from his home at night and carried him several miles from Jacksonville. They put a noose around his neck, but "after being allowed to think he would be lynched, [he] was allowed to escape."[42] It is not clear why in this instance the mob decided against lynching, although by the early 1920s some Florida government officials openly discouraged lynching and insisted on the use of the criminal justice system to try persons accused of alleged offenses—a position that, as we shall see, many Columbia County citizens supported.

Still, several months before the killing of Nola and Fannie Romey, Lake City was by no means committed to eradicating lynching and the white supremacy that supported it. As the November 1928 election approached, the local paper cited southern newspapers that decried the possibility of a victory by the Republican Party and "its anti-lynching plank." The *Atlanta Constitution* combined gendered and racist rhetoric to sound the alarm: "In the pending national campaign, the question of white supremacy is paramount and supersedes every controversial issue—it strikes at the very hearthstone of every white man's home in the South."[43] The Republican Party did win the election, an event that angered many white Floridians. Two weeks later, perhaps to soften the blow and reassert racist imagery, the Elks Club of Lake City hosted a blackface minstrel show and urged attendees to "lay aside your worries, and enjoy the occasion."[44]

Given this background, in which lynching became a ritualized form of violence inflicted primarily on black male bodies, how are we to understand the lynching in Lake City, Florida, in 1929, of a Syrian immigrant whom the newspapers described as a "white man"? Was this, to use Christopher Waldrep's term, a "non-racial lynching," an aberration from the norm of lynching blacks? Was Romey one of those whites who historian Fitzhugh Brundage would argue was perceived to have "merited lynching" because he violated community standards? If so, what were those standards? I argue below that the lynching of Nola Romey should not be placed simply on the list of nonblack victims of lynching or, conversely, understood as a moment when Romey was mistaken for a black man or racialized as black. Rather, I explore how Romey could be described as a white man in the press while at the same time his death underscored his inbetweenness, or the inconclusiveness of that white identity. Put another way, the lynching of Nola Romey and the murder of his wife *were* about race and the work that race did in a town where they were foreigners and outsiders.

THE CIRCUMSTANCES OF THE LYNCHING

The Romeys, like so many of their compatriots in the South, operated a grocery store, outside which they displayed produce for sale.[45] On Wednesday, May 15, 1929, John F. Baker, Lake City's chief of police, appeared at their store and ordered Fannie Romey to remove some of her vegetables from the sidewalk. At this point, the reports of the incident begin to vary widely. The local paper, the *Lake City Reporter*, indicated that the chief of police had had "trouble with Mrs. Romey" over her use of the sidewalk.[46] According to the *Miami Herald*, Fannie Romey "resented the order" to remove her produce and warned Baker: "We're going to kill you before Sunday."[47] The *Syrian World*, which based its report on the investigation conducted by Syrian lawyers Joseph W. Ferris of New York City and F. S. Risk of Jacksonville, provided a substantially different account. According to its version of events, Fannie Romey had protested the order to remove her vegetables from the sidewalk, but her defiance was met with swift action on the part of Baker and several other police officers, who began to drag her across the street toward the patrol car. However, the arrest was stopped by the intervention of some of the town's "leading citizens."[48]

The *Syrian World's* report contained additional information on events leading up to the vegetable dispute, and this report shed light on why Baker had gone to the Romey store in the first place. One week earlier, the eldest Romey child, Icer, had taken his three siblings out for a drive in the family car around the local lake.[49] They were struck by a speeding car, which later turned out to have been stolen. The police arrested the occupants of the stolen vehicle, absolved Icer Romey of all blame, and promised him that the reckless driver would be responsible for covering the cost of repairs to the damaged car. This last piece of information is crucial, for it led to the dispute between Baker and Fannie that ultimately ended in tragedy.

His car fixed, Icer called on Baker to honor his promise, but the police chief denied having made it and refused to discuss the matter further. Fannie then challenged what must have appeared to her as blatant unfairness and abuse of power: she confronted Baker and called him a liar. The chief of police did not take lightly this charge from a Syrian woman and quickly decided on a course of action to assert his authority and, it would seem, his masculinity. He headed for the Romey store and asked to see either Nola or Icer. Finding neither there, he began arguing with Fannie Romey and demanded that her vegetables be taken inside, a strange request, since other grocers also had outdoor displays of fresh produce, and therefore a special punishment for Fannie's outspoken behavior. Her initial refusal to do so resulted in Baker's attempt to arrest her. However, on the basis of the reports of what followed, she eventually placed the vegetables inside, although the dispute with Baker was far from over.

Several sources related that the chief of police's altercation with Fannie Romey infuriated Nola. Most likely feeling that his own male honor was at stake, he phoned Baker to convey his anger and informed him that he had again put his vegetables out on the sidewalk. This conversation resulted in a second and more deadly visit from the chief of police. Again the newspaper reports differ, particularly over the question of who fired the first shot. The *Syrian World* claimed that Baker and his men returned to the Romey store and began firing "without the least provocation, but presumably for purposes of intimidation only."[50] When Nola Romey attempted to hide behind the counter, one of the policemen struck him in the head with a gun, causing him to fall to the floor. The *Valdosta Times* carried a similar version of events, noting that when the police arrived at the store an argument ensued with Nola, "the result being that the officers placed him under arrest, and began clubbing him into submission." When Romey fought back, one of the police officers fired into the floor of the store to intimidate him.[51] At this point, Fannie Romey rushed to the front of the store. Seeing her husband lying in a pool of blood and believing the police had killed him, she shot at Baker with a gun they kept in the store. He returned fire, mortally wounding her. While she lay on the floor admonishing her son, Icer, not to intervene, one of the policeman shot at her several more times "with a curse and the exclamation 'Aren't you dead yet?' "[52]

The Florida newspaper reports and the testimony given by the police officers and a witness claimed that Fannie Romey had fired at Baker first when he attempted to remove her husband from the store. In response, as the *Florida Times Union* put it, "Baker was said to have fired five times, several of the shots taking effect in the woman's body."[53] Nola Romey was taken to the local jail, where he was "reported to have made threats to get even for the shooting of his wife."[54] Later that night, a mob removed him from his cell and lynched him. The fact that Fannie Romey had already been gunned down was apparently not retribution enough for the killers, and they directed their rage at Nola in retaliation for her defiant behavior. Indeed, the headline in the *Lake City Reporter* called attention to the close connection between their deaths: "Woman Killed in Pistol Battle with Police Chief; Husband Taken from Jail, Lynched."[55]

According to the *Miami Herald*, "An examination of Romeo's [sic] cell in the city jail failed to show any marks of an instrument having been used to pry off the lock," although the *Lake City Reporter* noted that the sheriff had found a "heavy iron pipe" and a "twisted and bent lock" in front of the jail cell.[56] As was typical of so many lynchings at this time, both Sheriff Douglass—who lived in the jail—and the chief of police claimed to have no clues as to the identity of the lynchers.[57] Members of the coroner's jury impaneled to hear the investigation of the lynching determined that "Romey came to his death at the hands of persons unknown to us."[58] This phrase was a tired formula in the South and represented the unwillingness of white jurors to view lynching as a punishable offense. Moreover, the fact that a police officer had been wounded in the altercation with the Romeys made the likelihood of a fair trial nearly impossible. Whites developed a sense of debt and obligation to the police, who were seen as "caretakers of the color line and defenders of the caste system."[59] In addition, even those whites who objected to the lynching may have felt intimidated by the police and unable to voice their opposition openly. Challenges to police authority were costly, particularly for those who could not count on the law's protection.

The Romeys' decision to confront Baker and to challenge his authority suggests that they did not view themselves as among the powerless, unable to talk back to the police. This was their fatal mistake. Indeed, as the report in the *Syrian World* indicates, Fannie Romey originally expected fairness from Baker after her son's car was damaged. She did not receive it. Without the information provided by the *Syrian World*, the Romeys appear in the newspaper reports as unruly immigrants who disobeyed the law. With it, they are hardworking people who had a legitimate grievance and took it to the authorities, who responded with harassment and fatal violence.

THE SYRIAN AMERICAN RESPONSE

News of the lynching traveled quickly to Valdosta, Georgia, the Romeys' former place of residence. The *Valdosta Daily Times* ran a boldfaced headline on the front page that read, "Lynch Romey at Lake City." Below it, in smaller type, was the other important news of the day: "Scarface Al Capone Gets Year for Carrying Gun."[60] Valdosta had several well-established Syrian families who mobilized to protect the Romey children. George J. Lahood, representing a number of Syrian citizens, sent an anguished telegram to Florida governor Doyle E. Carlton urging him to intervene and ensure the safety of the eldest Romey child, Icer, who had been taken from the scene to the jail.[61] "We ask that you have Esau Romey [sic] removed from jail Lake City to jail Tallahassee for protection," the telegram requested. "We do not uphold wrong but simply ask this young boy, who is innocent, be removed as to be protected from probable mob violence."[62]

The Syrians in Valdosta had good reason to be afraid for the life of Icer. Not only had the police taken him to the county jail, but three men "whom he knew" came to tell him that they were going to lynch his father.[63] Moreover, as described above in the lynching of Mary Turner, it was not uncommon for lynchers to target the family members of their intended victim. In Wagoner County, Oklahoma, for example, a mob of white men came to lynch Marie Scott's brother, who had allegedly killed one of two white men who had assaulted her. Finding that the brother had already escaped, they lynched the seventeen-year-old African American woman instead.[64]

Governor Carlton responded to the telegram of George Lahood by ordering Sheriff Douglass to conduct an investigation into the killings.[65] One day later, Douglass responded to the governor with a telegram informing him that Icer Romey had been released from his jail. "If I think or see that there will be any more trouble about the boy," he wrote, "I will see that he is protected as far as I can."[66] Less than six months into his term, Governor Carlton was tackling the economic problems of the state of Florida, including those brought about by the invasion of citrus groves by the Mediterranean fruit fly.[67] He believed that lynching sullied the reputation of the state and would later speak out forcefully against it. At the time of the Romey lynching, however, his priorities lay elsewhere.

George Lahood's appeal to Governor Carlton was only one of several responses by Syrians to the lynching nationwide. While his cautious wording that "we do not uphold the wrong" was issued while the fate of Icer was still of paramount concern, more forceful letters condemning the lynching soon arrived at the governor's office. The president of the Moral Progress Society of Minneapolis, Joe M. Joseph, sent a letter that expressed outrage and demanded an investigation into the lynching. "Syrian Americans throughout the country . . . have been shocked at the malicious and atrocious treatment which the Romeos [sic] received at the hands of the hair trigger or drunken and blood-thirsty policemen of Lake City," the letter read. "If the preponderance of testimony shows as we believe, that the policemen involved were to blame, we hope you will immediately suspend them pending the outcome of their trial."[68] This letter appears to have served as a form letter, for other Syrian organizations, including the Southwestern Syrian Merchants Association of Forth Worth, Texas, and the Syrian-Lebanon-American Association in Hazelton, Pennsylvania, sent identical texts to the governor. Members of the Syrian community in Jacksonville attempted to organize a committee to bring the case to trial, but it soon folded due to lack of "public support."[69]

Syrian leaders in New York City, home of the largest Syrian community in the nation, also mobilized to investigate the lynching after receiving news of the deaths of Nola and Fannie Romey. Najib Diab, editor of the Arabic-language paper *Meraat ul-gharb,* ran the story of the lynching and closed with an appeal to George Lahood to send more information on the killings. This request revealed how the Arabic-language press operated as a message board as well as a purveyor of news.[70] Naoum Mokarzel, veteran defender of Syrian rights and owner and editor of the popular Arabic-language paper *al-Hoda,* hired lawyers Joseph Ferris and F. S. Risk to investigate. Thanks to this investigation, the complicated back-story of the lynching was made public, although in publications with limited circulation. It was the information gathered by F. S. Risk that revealed that the Romeys had had a prior history with Baker and that the dispute with him was not really about the vegetables at all.

While Naoum Mokarzel was obviously concerned about the deaths of Nola and Fannie Romey, he cautioned his readers against a rush to judgment, especially in a case that involved police officers. His brother, Salloum (editor of the *Syrian World*), was also reserved and wrote in an editorial that "a certain feeling of prejudice undeniably exists against the Syrians in some parts of the South and any rash action on their part might tend to aggravate matters unnecessarily."[71] The careful, at times tentative, response by the Syrians in the South to the lynching suggests that they hoped that the incident would fade from memory. They did not want the Romey lynching, and specifically Nola's and Fannie's altercation with the chief of police, to reflect badly on the Syrian community. Moreover, with brutal lynchings continuing to occur all around them, they no doubt feared that agitating for justice could bring a violent response. They were therefore cautious to confront the powerful men who had reminded them that their assimilation in America could be obstructed by mob violence.

Syrians were not, however, the only persons to claim that members of the police force had been involved in Nola Romey's killing. Several citizens of Lake City wrote to Governor Carlton implicating Chief Baker in the lynching, but none chose to sign their name out of fear of reprisal. One letter, written by "an American and citizen of Lake City," described how Baker, Deputy Sheriff Leo Cox, and Arthur Hall had "beat Romey down the street with their pistols." When they began to drag him away from the store, Fannie Romey fired at Chief Baker. According to this letter, it was not Baker who returned fire but Leo Cox. "If you investigate this matter you will find out," the letter continued, "[that] Deputy Cox killed this woman and the balance of the Police force killed Romey next morning . . . and if you will investigate you will find out that it was a click [sic] between Sheriff Douglass and his deputy and Police Force to kill the bunch because they was afraid of them." In a postscript the author of the letter added, "I will like also to advise that the man they lynched never resiste [sic] arrest."[72]

Another letter from "the People of Lake City" asked the governor "to look in the way things are going on here, it is a shame for the officers of this town to take people out and Shoot [sic] them. We are suposed [sic] to live up to the Law and they are to pertect [sic] us and it is a plain case they killed Romie for nothing."[73] And a third letter began in this way: "Please allow us citizens of this little town a few lines as to the man that was uncalled for linched [sic]. We are people that wants and trys to do the right thing [and] we regret such occurred." The author[s] of the letter argued that Carlton's request to Sheriff Douglas to investigate the lynching was "asking the guilty parties to investigate." They urged Carlton to get the testimony of "those negroes that was in jail" [beside Romey], adding that it would be necessary to "get them away" to safety first. The letter also disputed the reports published in the papers, noting that "this women was draged [sic] through the streets and in no shape for such so Dr. says they new [sic] so. . . . After they killed her they began

beating on him [Romey] on the head then taken [sic] him off later."[74]
The letter's reference to Fannie Romey being in "no shape for such" was
a euphemism. A conversation in 2006 with an eyewitness to the shooting at the store revealed that she was pregnant.[75] Like the previous letter, this one insisted that Baker was not the police officer who killed Fannie Romey. The "American citizens of Lake City," closed their letter by
asking for protection: "Please give all the help possible, the ones that
done this should be protecting instead of being guilty. Hoping this comes
to light and other thing that are smuggled in this town."[76]

The involvement of police officers in a lynching was nothing unusual in
the South. Arthur Raper's case studies of lynchings in 1930 showed that
sheriffs and their deputies routinely failed to resist lynch mobs effectively
and later reported under oath to the grand jury that they did not recognize
a single member of any of the mobs.[77] However, the letters to the governor from the citizens of Lake City revealed not only dismay at the killing
of Nola and Fannie Romey but a conviction that the police were not performing their duties properly. These complaints were in fact the first of
many sent to the governor over several months (an entire stack of them are
organized under the heading "Columbia County, Complaint, Sheriff" in
the Florida State Archives). The recurring complaint was that the sheriff
and his police force were involved in bootlegging and in the "doling out of
confiscated liquor for gifts." One letter, written by someone who claimed
to be one of the sheriff's best friends, noted that "murder, bootlegging,
white slavery and numerous other crimes are going unpunished." "Mrs.
Romey brought her trouble on even if she was in delicate condition," the
letter continued, "but Mr. Romey was murdered and why I ask you was
he put in a separate jail than his son if it wasn't on purpose?"[78]

These letters demonstrate that the community approval that typified
lynchings in the South was muted in the Romey case. Not only did citizens of the town write to the governor complaining about the killings,
but an entire delegation went to Valdosta to attend the funeral of Nola
and Fannie. The delegation consisted of members of the Lake City Kiwanis and Rotary clubs and a "minister of the gospel."[79] "These visitors
did not have much to say about the tragedy, except that it was deplor-
able," noted the Valdosta Daily Times. In addition, they did not think
that Romey intended to be impudent to Chief Baker when he called him
to ask him to come to the store and show him how to arrange his fruits
and vegetables. Rather, because he and his black driver had just returned
from out of town with a load of truck, he did not want to unload it until
he had received proper instructions from the police.[80]

Three Lake City clubs, the Woman's, Rotary, and Kiwanis, published editorials in the local paper condemning the lynching. The Rotary Club regretted that "the peace and dignity of our community have been shamefully and grievously violated." Be it resolved, the club continued, "that the legal authorities of our community be urged to use every resource at their command to bring to justice the perpetrators of this heinous crime." The Lake City Woman's Club, which held its final meeting of the year on May 19—two days after the lynching—announced that "such disregard for law is repulsive to all right thinking people and brings great reproach upon our community."[81] Members of the club passed a resolution that condemned "such lawlessness" and pledged cooperation "in every effort to bring about respect for law in our community." The Kiwanis also met and condemned the manner in which "unknown parties took the law into their own hands and removed a citizen from the city jail and killed him before he had been brought before any court for hearing." None of the denunciations mentioned Nola Romey by name; instead, they referred to him as "the prisoner" and "a citizen . . . killed before he had been brought before any court for hearing."[82] Each of the clubs focused on the lawlessness of the lynching and not on the fact that the lives of two immigrant members of the community had been extinguished. While the Woman's Club did express "sympathy for the family of children left orphaned by the violent deaths of their parents," no concerted effort was made to provide for them. Ellis Moses became the guardian of the four Romey children, Icer, Emeline, Leila, and Lucile, and was therefore given the right to administer the $8,500 Metropolitan Life Insurance policy held by his cousin Nola. Ellis was already guardian to three other children in addition to his own.[83] When he moved the family to Birmingham after the lynching, there were fifteen members in his household.[84]

The opposition to the lynching voiced by these three prominent Lake City clubs echoed themes of a growing antilynching movement in the South. The movement had many strands, some more moderate than others. It began with the pioneering work of Ida B. Wells, who, at great threat to her personal safety, investigated and published reports on lynching in which she debunked the theory that the majority of lynching victims had sexually assaulted white women. Building on the research of Wells, the NAACP adopted lynching as one of its key issues and worked to mobilize support for the (never-passed) Dyer Anti-Lynching Bill. In 1919, the organization published a pathbreaking book based on thirty years of research on lynching that it hoped would "bring home to the

American people their responsibility for the persistence of this monstrous blot upon America's honor."[85] Three years later, the Anti-Lynching Crusaders was formed under the aegis of the NAACP. Headed by Mary Talbert, this was an organization of black women who continued the tradition of campaigning against lynching begun by Ida B. Wells.

Not until after World War I did white southerners begin to organize around an antilynching platform. At the center of this movement was the Commission on Interracial Cooperation (CIC). Founded in 1921 in Atlanta to improve racial tensions in the South, the commission incorporated antilynching work into its broad program aimed at reducing black migration from the South to the North, improving the profile of the southern states internationally, and promoting respect for the law. As historian Jacquelyn Dowd Hall argues, the CIC's paternalistic nature—the "interracial" committee did not at first admit blacks into the organization—shaped its early cautious approach, which focused on improving "interracial attitudes out of which unfavorable conditions arise."[86] The CIC embarked on a program of research and education to investigate these "unfavorable conditions," including lynching. In 1930, Will W. Alexander, a former Methodist minister and director of the CIC, received a grant from the Rosenwald Fund to establish a "Southern Commission on the Study of Lynching." The grant allowed the CIC to assemble a team of researchers who went on to publish what became standard works in the study of extralegal violence.[87]

While the southern commission busied itself with research on the subject of lynching and with spreading the message of interracial cooperation, a more dynamic strategy to combat mob violence took root in one of the CIC auxiliary committees. Jessie Daniel Ames, director of Woman's Work of the CIC, launched a separate organization in 1930 called the Association of Southern Women for the Prevention of Lynching (ASWPL). Ames had moved up the ranks of the CIC, serving as an energetic and effective organizer in Texas. She moved to Atlanta in 1929 to take up her new post as director of Woman's Work for the CIC. Ames then decided to devote her energy to a single-focus organization consisting of white women who would use their moral authority as respectable ladies to work against lynching. The resolutions of the group's first meeting held in Atlanta read: "We are profoundly convinced that lynching is not a defense of womanhood or of anything else, but rather a menace to private and public safety and a deadly blow at our most sacred institutions."[88] The group focused on educating white southerners through letter-writing campaigns, petitions, and speeches that exploded the myth of black male criminality. The main purpose of the group was to "hammer home the argument that black men did not provoke lynching by raping white women."[89]

The lynching statistics compiled by Ames for 1922–31 (totaling 225 cases) showed that of the nineteen alleged offenses the top five were "murder (including attempted), rape and attempted rape, improper conduct and insulting language," and "resisting or wounding officers of the law."[90] One person was lynched for "trying to act like [a] white man and not knowing his place."[91] The group also worked with other antilynching organizations to refine the definition of lynching. In 1937, they agreed that lynching consisted of "death . . . at the hands of a group acting under the pretext of service to justice, race, or tradition."[92] By 1942, the ASWPL had over forty-three thousand signatures to its antilynching pledge. While the original Plan of Action of the organization in 1930 did not have any endorsements from Florida, by this time there was an active Florida Council of the ASWPL chaired by Dorothy Havens of Jacksonville.[93]

The reaction of the Woman's Club of Lake City to the Romey lynching should be understood within the context of this emerging antilynching movement. The club's position on the Romey lynching echoed the dominant antilynching discourse of the day, which condemned the practice as an act of lawlessness. Ames claimed, for example, that the ASWPL was "not an interracial movement, but a movement of Southern women interested in law observance and law enforcement."[94] Governor Carlton exchanged letters with Jessie Daniel Ames and affirmed his opposition to lynching precisely in these terms. In 1931, after the lynching of Richard and Charlie Smoaks, he declared that the killers "lynched not only Negroes but the State of Florida."[95] It is unfortunate that the ASWPL formed one year after the Romey lynching. The case could have benefited from the group's rigorous approach, as laid out in its "Plan of Action," to "study the character, reputation and life of every man lynched."[96]

THE SIGNIFICANCE OF RACE AND ETHNICITY IN THE ROMEY LYNCHING

Brundage argues in his important work on lynching that "the typical response by whites to most lynchings by private mobs was a brief spasm of condemnation followed by silence."[97] The Romey lynching falls into this pattern. The condemnations did not lead to prosecution of the killers, compensation for the victims' surviving children, or even analysis. Syrians who knew about the lynching remained reluctant to speak about it openly. A member of the other Syrian family in Lake City at the time of the lynching revealed in a 2006 conversation that he had not told his children or grandchildren about the tragedy. Although willing to talk about the events that he witnessed as a young boy, he was not sure the story needed to be made public.[98] The surviving daughter of Nola and Fannie is haunted by the memory of the brutal killing of her parents, yet she worries—eighty years after the event—that sharing her story will jeopardize her safety.[99]

The silence surrounding the lynching of Nola Romey and the shooting of his wife suggests a reluctance to probe deeply into the racial meanings of their deaths. But race and ethnicity were at work in this story in significant ways. First, at a time of native white anxiety over their hold on political and economic power, Romey's killers drew on a familiar white supremacist script that advocated the punishment of blacks who challenged the southern caste system by "talking back"—the same offense that Romey committed. The killing of Romey not only connected him to black disempowerment but also sent a message to the black inhabitants of Lake City, and the few foreigners there, that attempts to combat injustice, or any challenge to white authority, could be, and in this case were, met with terror. The lynching of Nola Romey sat squarely within a tradition of extralegal violence aimed at preserving white power in a town in which blacks formed the majority.

Second, it is significant that the two incarcerated black men who might have served as witnesses to Romey's abduction from jail claimed that they had seen and heard nothing. The point is that for blacks—those who had the most to fear in the Jim Crow South, and for whom lynching had acquired its terrifying significance—the lynching of Romey was a reminder of their own vulnerability in Lake City, where they were excluded from white-controlled spaces and institutions and where they endured the psychological burden of being under threat of violence. In contrast, Romey was vulnerable because of his foreignness, because he was an outsider and lacked roots in the community and belonged to a "suspect" immigrant group. While Syrians had won the legal battle for their whiteness in the naturalization cases, it nonetheless remained provisional, subject to scrutiny. They continued to be targeted by a reinvigorated nativism and reminded of their precarious status in the American racial hierarchy. In 1920, a candidate for a political campaign in Birmingham, Alabama, circulated a handbill that read: "They have disqualified the negro, an American citizen, from voting in the white primary. The Greek and Syrian should also be disqualified. I DON'T WANT THEIR VOTE. If I can't be elected by white men, I don't want the office."[100] A few years later, terrorists from the KKK dynamited the home of a Syrian family in Marietta, Georgia,[101] and only a few weeks before the Romey lynching, Syrians were outraged by Senator Reed's infamous comment that they were "the trash of the Mediterranean, all that Levantine stock that churns around through there and does not know what its own ancestry is."[102]

The bombing and the derogatory comments were representative of a wider anti-immigrant feeling in the nation. It is possible that in a town like Lake City, with a white minority unaccustomed to seeing immigrants, let alone non-European ones, Romey's Syrian-ness, his cultural distance from the town's inhabitants, made him a "not quite white" outsider, vulnerable to extralegal violence.[103] Although he was not particularly dark, his olive skin, his wife's dark hair and eyes, and their Arabic language marked them as different.[104] The southern papers that covered the lynching repeatedly referred to Romey as Syrian, reminding the readers that he was not an "ordinary" white man but a foreigner. In contrast, northern papers emphasized in their headlines that Romey was white. Neither the *Chicago Defender* nor the *New York Evening World,* for example, mentioned that he was Syrian.[105] In addition, Nola Romey's death echoed themes of earlier lynchings where the victims' foreignness rendered them inconclusively white. When eleven Italian men were lynched in New Orleans in 1891, for example, the *St. Louis Republic* argued that they were slain "on proof of being 'dagoes' and on the merest suspicion of being guilty of any other crime."[106] The *New Orleans Times-Democrat* countered that "desperate diseases require desperate remedies. . . . Our justification was—necessity; our defense is—self preservation, nature's primal law."[107]

The targeting of a white person considered to be an outsider to the community was again at work in the lynching of Leo Frank in Atlanta, Georgia, in July 1913, sixteen years before the Romey killings. Frank, a northern Jew and manager of a pencil factory, was accused on weak circumstantial evidence of raping and murdering a young female employee, Mary Phagan. A jury convicted him of the crime and he was sentenced to death. After two years of legal appeals, Georgia's Governor John Slaton commuted Frank's sentence to life imprisonment. Two months into this new sentence, a group of men broke into the prison where Frank was being held, drove him to Mary Phagan's hometown of Marietta, and lynched him. Ten years later, when members of the KKK targeted the home of a Syrian family in the same town, they were reconnecting to the practice of extralegal violence made so visible in the lynching of Leo Frank.

The Frank case precipitated the formation of the Anti-Defamation League of B'nai B'rith to fight against American anti-Semitism. Frank's lawyers believed that his Jewishness was at the heart of the public attack of his character and the assumption made by so many that he was guilty. Their response was to portray Frank as an upright, decent white man—the type of man who was to be distinguished from the other suspect (and later witness against Frank), Jim Conley. Frank's lawyer, Luther Rosser, characterized Conley as a murderous brute, a "dirty, filthy, black, drunken, lying nigger."[108] This defense strategy relied on racist language to shore up Frank's innocence and to portray him as the opposite of Conley, whom Rosser assumed jurors would automatically convict because of his black underclass status. Frank's lawyers underestimated, however, the extent to which their client's northern capitalist origin and his position as manager of a factory that employed young women were at work in the community's populist rejection of him.[109]

Just as the lawyers for Frank viewed his case through the lens of race, so did members of the Syrian community when they reacted to the Romey lynching. As they had done during the naturalization controversy of 1909–15, they responded by affirming their whiteness. The reasons for this development should be obvious enough—whiteness meant access to citizenship and the privileges it afforded, while nonwhiteness could render persons vulnerable to disenfranchisement and degradation. Anxious to avoid the latter, Syrian elites reacted defensively to any act that called into question their racial status. It is in this light that the question posed by the editor of al-Shaab—"Has the Syrian become a Negro?"—should be understood. Answering the question, he continued: "The Syrian is not a negro [sic] whom Southerners feel they are justified in lynching when he is suspected of an attack on a white woman. The Syrian is a civilized white man who has excellent traditions and a glorious historical background and should be treated as among the best elements of the American nation."[110] The commentator in al-Shaab was arguing that Romey had been the victim of racial misidentification and that his lynchers had not understood what he believed to be true: that Syrians were *fully* white. His use of the adjective *civilized* was significant and harked back to the arguments made by candidates for naturalization in the racial prerequisite cases that asserted Syria's place as the birthplace of Western civilization. But the main purpose of the article was to argue that the Syrian was "not a negro [sic]." In doing so the writer appeared unconcerned that black persons were regularly the victims of extralegal violence.

The lynching of Nola Romey demonstrates how the racialization of Syrians made sense or acquired meaning in relation to a racialized Other, in this case African Americans. Romey's "whiteness" mattered to Syrians because his lynching summoned fears among them that they had become, in that instant, surrogate blacks. Understanding the link between the racialization of Syrians and blacks helps explain why a common pattern among Syrians was to reaffirm and invest in whiteness. They did so in letters, court cases, newspapers, interviews, and, although it is much harder to document, social relations. Like other immigrant groups (the Irish, Italians, and Jews), Syrians "grasped for the whiteness at the margins of their experiences"[111] rather than challenge the *premise* that whiteness was a legitimate prerequisite for social, economic, and political privilege. When confronted with violence and discrimination in the period of Jim Crow, the response of community leaders often reinforced racist and even eugenicist discourse instead of challenging it. All this confirms what is unfortunately obfuscated in everyday discussion of race in the United States: that whiteness is not a biological fact but a result of long-standing social structures *and* of choices made within a particular historical context.[112] The aftermath of the Romey lynching suggests that Syrians in the South increasingly supported and reinscribed their position on the white side of the color line. There is evidence, for example, that they participated in one of the major processes of white confirmation: movement into neighborhoods that excluded nonwhites in the post–World War II period.[113]

A great deal of work still needs to be done on the kinds of choices made by Syrians and the implications of these choices for their relationships with other racialized groups. Why, for example, did influential Syrians get involved in assisting the naturalization of a South Asian immigrant but not lend help to the NAACP antilynching campaigns?[114] The simple answer is that Syrians were a small immigrant community, lacking in power and trying to make a difficult life better by defending their right to naturalize as citizens and a earn a decent living. As a minority group in the segregated South, they had to "know their place" and not risk losing the security of their whiteness by voicing opinions that were contrary to the prevailing views of the majority of whites. Other groups made similar decisions. Eric Goldstein argues, for example, that when the racial position of southern Jews came under scrutiny and they were denied entry to social clubs and resorts, many reacted by rejecting any comparison between themselves and African Americans. Herbert T. Ezekiel, editor of Richmond's *Jewish South*, argued in 1898 that "our people, though persecuted and driven from pillar to post do not possess the criminal instincts of the colored race. . . . The comparison of Jews and negroes is, we had had always thought, a pastime of our Christian neighbors, and one which we, of all people should not countenance."[115]

What would rejecting whiteness have implied for Syrians and for other groups at this time and at other historical moments? These are the types of questions that investigations of other cases of Arab engagements with race would help to answer. In sum, the Romey lynching reveals the racially ambiguous status of first-wave Arab immigrants in the United States, but it also demonstrates how immigrants strove to resolve that ambiguity by affirming their whiteness. It is yet another instance that proves that whiteness is not an ahistorical, self-evident category but one that was historically construed and contested and has had different implications for different groups—including those that were not allowed to claim it. The Romey lynching was a crisis in whiteness for the Syrians. It suggested that in the eyes of many they were "in between" or "not quite white." Syrians responded by using their ethnic institutions to assert their whiteness and, at the same time, their Americanness. This was ultimately about constructing the boundaries of Syrian American identity, which, since the naturalization cases, had had a racial component connected to it. Distancing Syrians from blacks and Asians in the discourse on race was one way to protect the boundaries of identity. Yet another was the promotion of endogamous marriage.

CHAPTER 5

Marriage and Respectability in the Era of Immigration Restriction

Marriage, which is the foundation of happy family life, which in turn is the basis of the prosperity and progress of the nation, should be our principal concern in our present stage of transition.

A. Hakim (1928)

Every one of us married somebody who was European, and many of them were blond. I don't think that was an accident. It was really clear to us that to be white was better. I don't think we ever questioned it.

"Catherine," interviewed in Bint Arab (1997)

Concern over the institution of marriage in the context of migration and settlement in the United States was not new. Syrian religious officials had been quick to express alarm in the early period of transatlantic migration. The problem in their view was twofold: emigrant men were shirking their patriarchal duties in the homeland and were engaging in extraofficial relationships in the diaspora.

Publications in Syria expressed this anxiety as thousands of young men departed for the Americas. Commentators were troubled not only by the scale of the exodus but also by the potential for wayward conduct. This conduct, they argued, would compromise spiritual and familial duties and carry dire consequences. In letters, published sermons, and announcements, men of religion warned that irresponsible behavior began when men were seduced by stories of instant wealth in distant lands. In 1902, the journal of the Jesuit University in Lebanon, *al-Mashriq* (The

East), described in sordid detail the demise of one such man. It told the story of ʿAbdallah Qazma, a Lebanese villager who left his wife and children behind to pursue the dream of wealth and freedom in America. Related in the style of a sermon, the story, titled "The Surprise Encounter," casts the emigrant as a figure of moral laxity and reveals the clergy's stance against emigration.

The story begins innocently enough in a Lebanese village on a spring day in 1884. A group of men gather after church and listen as a young man "dressed in the style of a European" dazzles them with stories of streets paved with gold. Inspired by his example, the men decide to leave for *Amirka*, and, in a matter of months the village is depleted of every male above the age of ten.[1] ʿAbdallah, ignoring the advice of his priest, who tells him it is un-Christian behavior to leave his wife and children behind, is among these men. Only the women, the old, and infirm remain in the village.[2]

A tragic set of events ensues. ʿAbdallah goes to New York City promising to stay only a year or two but does not return. He stops sending money, and soon his wife does not know whether he is alive or dead. She encourages the son to leave, then the daughter, and eventually sells the house to finance her own trip. Hers is not, however, a story of happy family reunification. When she arrives, a friend takes her to the Syrian enclave along Washington Street. As they pass the local courthouse they see a group gathered, most of which is Syrian. They stop and watch as the judge exits and reads a sentence. It is her son who is condemned to death for killing his employer, while her daughter is sentenced to ten years in prison for stealing the jewelry of her employer. The mother collapses, as does the father, who, unbeknownst to her, is also in the crowd. Mother and father recognize each other in the hospital, but they are stricken with grief and die. The son is hanged, and his sister dies shortly after in prison.

And so the imaginary tale ends by showing how the dreams of wealth and happiness can lead to a nightmare of alienation, poverty, and death. It is fundamentally a moral tale, a warning by the Catholic journal of the evils that lurk in America. The descent into turpitude—which culminates in the son's murderous act—begins with the father's desire to make his fortune outside the homeland. In other words, the son becomes corrupted because the father leaves and abandons his responsibilities as moral exemplar. The author of the story implies that leaving sons in the hands of their mothers undercuts patriarchal authority.

The motif of irresponsibility also appeared in Orthodox publications as senior religious officials chastised emigrant men for violating norms of responsible Christian behavior. The Antiochian Patriarch residing in Damascus, for example, drew attention to the problem in an announcement published in the official journal of the patriarchate, *al-Ni'ma* (The Blessing). Directed to "our young emigrant men," the notice denounced those "who leave their wives and children behind . . . and marry and live as if they have no wife and children."[3] The Patriarch threatened to announce the names of men who had abandoned their duties as husbands and fathers in Syria by taking new wives in the *mahjar*. The instances of "extraofficial polygamy" were so numerous that religious authorities, both Christian and Muslim, began demanding official documents from men returning to Syria stating that they had not married while abroad, since many tried to marry again in their communities of origin, often with the intention of maintaining a wife or concubine in the Americas.[4] Rev. Iskandar Atallah, writing in the Orthodox publication *al-Kalima* (The Word), published in New York, encouraged the practice in reverse: that is, for immigrants to bring proof of their marital status with them to America.[5]

Anxieties over men's absence from Syria were linked to a broader crisis in patriarchy in the late nineteenth century. The roots of this crisis lay in the profound socioeconomic changes brought about by the incorporation of the region into a capitalist economy and in the consequent changes in the sexual division of labor. Historian Akram Khater describes the intricate renegotiations of the honor code in Mount Lebanon as peasant men allowed their young daughters to become wage earners in the silk filatures.[6] This type of work involved a violation of the peasant code of honor that required men to be the guardians and providers of their womenfolk. As single women ventured from the family home and exposed themselves to the dangers—real and imagined—of the workplace, the honor code came under strain. Khater argues, however, that honor was malleable and that peasant families attempted to resolve this crisis in patriarchy in a number of ways. They tried to ensure that the foremen and managers of the factories were male relatives and that religious authorities played a role in the supervision of their daughters. The most effective way to resolve this upsetting of the gendered order of things was to use the women's wages to preserve, and even augment, *male* honor. Wages were used for the purchase of luxury goods like rice and sugar, payment of debt, and the purchase of land, all of which were makers of higher social status. In this way, men could restore the honor that they had temporarily sacrificed by sending their daughters to work in the silk factories.

Transatlantic migration of men initiated another crisis in patriarchy as husbands, brothers, and sons left their womenfolk behind to journey to the Americas. The alarms sounded by religious authorities represented responses by elites to this problem. They were dramatic, if not hyperbolic, and they circulated throughout the flourishing Arabic-language press. The warnings invoked the tropes of male guardianship and authority and predicted perilous outcomes when both were undermined by men's absence and neglect of their families in the homeland. Finally, they encouraged resolution of the crisis through return migration and the (re)assumption of patriarchal responsibilities.

But the dire warnings of spiritual decay described in *al-Mashriq* proved exaggerated. Far from abandoning their spiritual ties in the homeland, emigrants worked hard to maintain them by sending money to support church activities. On the occasion of an official Russian visit to the Antiochian Orthodox Patriarchate in Damascus, for example, large contributions to pay for the festivities came from communities in São Paulo, Cairo, Santiago—and New York.[7] As early as the 1880s, Maronite emigrants sent requests to the Patriarch in Bkerke, Lebanon, beseeching him to send a priest to minister to communities in St. Paul, Minnesota; Philadelphia, Pennsylvania; and São Paulo, Brazil, to name a few.[8]

Strain on marriage and family relationships undoubtedly did occur. Men routinely spent five to ten years away from wives or fiancées before returning home or sending for them. Some men never returned and instead established new families in the *mahjar*. One Palestinian Muslim immigrant to Chicago remembered in an interview conducted in the 1940s that "sometimes the wives wait one year, five years, ten years, twenty years, even thirty years until their husbands come back. Sometimes they never come back but marry some mulatto [sic] here and forget about the old lady in the old country."[9] He noted that he had not followed this pattern but had returned to Palestine to marry "a nice girl from the *hamule* [clan]."

Women faced the strain on the institution of marriage with creative responses. While the prominent Damascene journalist Muhammad Kurd ʿAli warned of the "villages of spinsters" increasing in the Syrian countryside, many young unmarried women migrated to the *mahjar* (usually with male guardians) because it offered new work opportunities and had became a more viable place to find a mate.[10] Married women also journeyed to join husbands, often after many years of managing the household under great hardship. And of course men did return to their families in Syria, not because they succumbed to the pressure from religious authorities but because they wanted to build a house with a red-tiled roof. These houses were fast becoming a marker of emigrant success in villages and towns throughout Syria. As the French Ministry of War remarked in its comprehensive study of Syria in 1916: "The Lebanese [man] emigrates, sends money home, and returns enriched to build the dream house."[11]

"INTERRACIAL" MARRIAGE

The first wave of Syrian immigrants to the United States came from regions characterized by a high degree of endogamy. In Mount Lebanon, for example, patrilineal cousin marriage was the norm, and when this did not occur preference was for marriage within the clan and village.[12] As in other Mediterranean societies, the rationale for endogamous marriage was connected to issues of land ownership and inheritance. Cousin marriage kept land within a family, thus impeding fragmentation of plots and the disputes that could arise from this.

Endogamous marriage was an ideal for Syrians, but under conditions of intense migration marriage practices became more flexible. In the United States, cousin marriage gave way to marriage with Syrian co-ethnics. Syrians' success in securing marriage partners within the ethnic group is indicated on the 1910 U.S. Census. Out of a total of 13,031 persons born in the United States whose mother tongue was Arabic (the vast majority of whom would have been the children of Syrian immigrants), only 232 came from households where their foreign-born parents did not share the same mother tongue. Among the small number of the "native white of mixed parentage," the census revealed that it was much more likely for the father to be foreign born than the mother—a pattern that continued in the next decade.[13]

Rates of out-marriage appear to have been highest among Muslim immigrants, despite American perceptions to the contrary. The pool of available marriage mates was much smaller for them than it was for Syrian Christians, and Muslim families were less inclined to send their daughters off to an overwhelmingly Christian America.[14] Recognizing this imbalance, the New York Arabic newspaper al-Bayan ran a series of articles entitled "The Emigration of the Druze Woman," in which respondents sent in their opinions from across North America. Some discouraged the migration of women, but others argued that it would promote the stability of the family and solve, in the words of one contributor, the "problem of the man leaving his wife and children in the homeland

and forgetting about them . . . [leading] this woman to commit unfavorable acts."[15] While the author did not specify what these acts were, it is reasonable to infer that he meant extramarital relationships.

In another article on Druze migration—this time published in the Maronite-owned *al-Hoda*—the author criticized men for emigrating without their womenfolk. "Where is the shame of a mother accompanying her son, a daughter her brother, a wife her husband?" he asks.[16] Not only was it "not right that a Druze man should travel to strange lands and stay there for ten years and his wife and children endure difficulties [at home]," but denying her the right to emigrate—presumably out of adherence to Muslim tradition—meant "she will remain in a status *that is inconsistent with the age.*"[17] Elites could, at least initially, argue that women's migration and labor in the *mahjar* served a broader purpose of modernizing the Syrian family.

The articles conveyed anxieties over the emotional costs of migration: the disruption of family life, the loss of communication, the difficulties of travel and work in the *mahjar,* and the fear of losing one's culture in a foreign land. As is so often the case in situations of social and economic strain, these anxieties were expressed in a particular gendered language. How could men be the guardians of women when they were thousands of miles away? What could be done to ensure that marriages remained intact across formidable distances? Would the migration of women and their work for remunerative employment outside the home in the *mahjar* undermine the code of honor?

Debates about the respectability of female immigrants and the authority of their male guardians took place against a backdrop of imagined, and later real, exogamous marriage. While emigrants were able to maintain high rates of in-group marriage in the first two decades of migration, by the second decade of the twentieth century this was no longer the case. The 1920 U.S. Census indicated that the number of Syrians of mixed parentage had grown substantially.[18] This development was not only confined to the United States and the other lands of emigration; it was occurring in the homeland as well. And it was largely the result of new practices among returning emigrants, who returned with capital and different expectations about marriage. They were now able to buy land instead of acquire access to it through marriage, and when seeking a spouse they began to prioritize compatibility, friendship, and social class. By the second decade of the twentieth century, Syrians were transforming the institution of marriage within a transnational framework.[19]

Changes in marriage patterns among Syrians in the United States were linked to the mobility of the second generation, the members of which were attending high school and college and growing up in communities of white ethnics. Many had internalized the message of Americanization, with its emphasis on "becoming American" through literal and symbolic acts of renouncing ethnicity. The children of Syrian immigrants faced pressures to conform to Anglo-American norms in school, in the workplace, and in the domain of popular culture. In 1921, for example, a Broadway play written by Harry Chapman Ford entitled *Anna Ascends* conveyed the "proper" trajectory from Syrian to American. Because of the play's popularity, Paramount decided to release it as a silent film in 1922 around the same time that the studio released its wildly successful production of *The Sheik,* starring Rudolph Valentino.

Harry C. Ford was inspired to write the play after befriending a Syrian family in Washington, D.C. Impressed by "their clean way of living," he decided to write a play set in the heart of the Syrian quarter in New York City during World War I. In Ford's words: "I figured here is a people who could read and write probably six thousand years before the northern blue eyes . . . who had a fine culture along with the great Egyptian dynasties. . . . Hence I figured why not write a Syrian drama?"[20] All that survives of the film are a few reviews. The play's script, however, was later published in the *Syrian World,* and several photographs of the original production are archived. On the basis of a reading of these sources, the play and film appear to break from the prevailing Hollywood pattern of casting the Arab as villain. Jack Shaheen, for example, describes the film as one of a handful that focus on Arab immigrants and present "brave and compassionate Arab women, genuine heroines."[21] While the film certainly deserves praise for promoting a different image of Arabs, the alternative it offered is worth examining in closer detail.

The play and film revolve around the story of Anna Ayyoub, played in both cases by renowned actress Alice Brady. Anna is a young woman, recently arrived from Syria, who finds work in the coffeehouse and general store of Said Coury, played by Gustave Rolland. Anna is a determined, hardworking woman who carries an English dictionary with her at all times so that she may look up new words she hears being used by the store's patrons. Several men have their eye on Anna. One is Howard Fisk, or "Gents," the scion of a wealthy Uptown family who is spending time in the Syrian district ("slumming," as his disapproving sister calls his presence there). The other is Bunch, an Irish American rogue intent on wooing Anna into prostitution. He surprises Anna one night at the store and attempts to rape her. She narrowly escapes, stabs Bunch, and flees to Uptown. In the following act, set several years after this incident, Anna appears to the audience as Anna Adams. She has changed her name, learned perfect English, and found a job as a secretary in the office of . . . Howard Fisk. The two are reunited in work and in life, and Anna's "ascension" is complete. Alice Brady's portrayal of Anna received rave reviews: "The memory of her as Anna," wrote the *Evening Sun's* Broadway critic, "will linger with theatergoers long after this dramatic season has melted away."[22]

Anna Ascends is a classic narrative of Americanization. The two Syrian characters, Said and Anna, are desperate to become American. We are told in the first act that Said is "a thorough American and great patriot. . . . He has bitter contempt for his fellow country-men who have come to America and failed to take out their naturalization papers and refers to them as foreigners."[23] When Anna first appears, her entrance is almost comical in juxtaposing her "old" Syrian ways with her desire to become a "new" American: "She carries a two-gallon olive oil can in each arm. Strings of garlic are around her neck. A small pocket dictionary is under the pit of her left arm and a sheet of paper with an order written on it in Syrian is in her mouth. In her blouse pocket is a small American flag."[24]

It is also quite clear that Anna's ascension is an ascension into whiteness. She appears pale-faced next to Said's browned-up, swarthy complexion, so swarthy that the Irish character Bunch calls him "Wop." "Don't call me das Wop," Said responds, provoking Bunch to add another list of derogatory epithets: "Aw, hell, Ginnie, dago, what your greasy little heart [desires]." Anna's escape to Uptown releases her from this questioning that Said faces as to his racial status, yet her journey has a specific sexualized and racialized logic, for she ends up in the arms (and presumably the bed) of a white, upper-class male.

The film's story of whitening makes more sense if understood within the context of the contentious series of naturalization cases in which Syrians had to prove their whiteness in order to be eligible for American citizenship (see chapter 2). Despite the apparent victory of Syrians in the courts, there was still concern, particularly among Syrian elites, that their whiteness was being scrutinized, and they were thus anxious to reaffirm it. *Anna Ascends* provided them with such an opportunity. A young Syrian American composer, Alexander Maloof, wrote the music for the play, and Salloum Mokarzel, who had formed an association to defend

Figure 9. Photo from the play *Anna Ascends,* printed in the *Syrian World,* 1927.

Syrians' right to naturalize, published the script in his journal, the *Syrian World,* where it has fortunately been preserved.

While *Anna Ascends* does not feature a villain, Shaheen's assertion that it features an Arab heroine needs to be qualified in significant ways. Anna is indeed a strong and likable character, yet her story involves the *effacement* of her Syrian identity, not the retention of it. The film's message was antipluralist and assimilationist: Syrians could become Americans, but they would have to lose their language, history, and culture in order to do so. This was the "price of the ticket" for entry into the American mainstream.[25]

Anna's story, and the way it came to represent an ideal path of assimilation, encapsulated several strands of American normativity. Not only does Anna relinquish her Syrian culture, but she is also tamed in the process. She loses her accent as well as her independence. This same spirit of independence, this position outside bourgeois norms of female domesticity, had startled American commentators on the Syrian immigrant community. Female peddlers, for example, raised eyebrows because they ventured beyond the confines of the home, were often unmarried, and returned from work to unorthodox living arrangements. This kind of labor did not conform to the needs of the new industrial order. Syrian women were not refining traditional homemaking skills by spending long hours away on the road selling the contents of their *kashshi*. As they did for other immigrant groups, and most especially for African Americans, American sociologists construed these arrangements as aberrations from the normal family economy.[26]

Americanization programs thus targeted female immigrants in an effort to win them over to the campaign to create nuclear, male-headed households where the woman was wife and mother and nurturer of a new domestic space. Syrian elites were often eager to argue that their women were perfectly suited to this transition. "In point of social purity they are unexcelled," wrote Philip Hitti. "The women are scrupulously guarded by the male members of the family . . . [and] the proportion of unhappy marriages has always been amazingly small."[27] Syrian immigrants, men and women alike, undoubtedly worked to achieve a level of success that allowed them to be secure in house and home, but the model of assimilation advocated by the proponents of Americanization ignored the creative and painstaking ways they did so. Writing on the tenements in the Syrian quarter of New York, the Industrial Commission on Immigration noted that "it is not extraordinary to find 6 to 8 women making their headquarters in such a garret, their husbands away peddling and their children in institutions."[28] While prone to exaggeration and unduly critical of the Syrian community, the Industrial Commission's comments on the reorganization of Syrian families in the context of migration were supported by other sources. Moreover, for many Syrian families, entering the middle class remained elusive. Tahafa Laham al-Tin recalled working as a seamstress in a factory while her husband, unable to find work, "sat around." She worked for seven years, eleven hours a day, and until 2:00 p.m. on Sundays for twenty-four cents an hour. She did not learn to hang white curtains, but she could make a dollar's worth of meat last all week.[29]

Emerging as popular entertainment during a period of heightened immigration restriction when "normal" Americans were considered to be white, middle-class men and women, *Anna Ascends* was a text of both fact and fiction. Elite Syrians supported the play's emphasis on Syrians' ethic of hard work and their ability to learn English and become loyal, flag-waving, white Americans. But the issue of marriage outside the ethnic group remained controversial. Aware that the ideal of in-group marriage was under serious strain, Syrian commentators on both sides of the Atlantic began to address the issue of what was often called "interracial" marriage. In the United States, the *Syrian World* became a forum where differences of opinion on the "marriage question" were eloquently voiced. Sparking the debate was the especially thorny issue of Christian-Muslim marriages, which, according to the journal, were "peculiarly Syrian American in character." One incident in particular provoked an outcry from members of the Syrian immigrant elite and demonstrated how ideas about respectability and proper marriage were important pillars of community identity.

THE MUSLIM "OTHER"

In a lengthy article printed in April 1928, the *Syrian World* related the true story of a prominent Brazilian doctor who had traveled to Syria and learned of the plight of a number of his countrywomen. According to his report, the women had accompanied their husbands back to Syria and were being held against their will in conditions "tantamount to slavery." In Baʿalbek, for example, seven Brazilian women were allegedly confined to the "harems" of their Syrian husbands, who had reverted to the practice of polygamy. The outraged doctor sent a letter to a newspaper in Rio de Janeiro, and within a matter of days the story was circulating in the Brazilian press, accompanied by denunciations of these peculiar Syrian "habits." The Syrian community in Brazil responded with letters defending the Syrian name. Then, in an effort to show their disapproval of the alleged offenses committed against the Brazilian women, several Syrian industrialists in São Paulo (including millionaire Basil Jafet), offered to provide the necessary funds to repatriate the women.[30]

It is difficult to judge the veracity of the doctor's report, although it seems reasonable to assume that both he and the Brazilian women disapproved of polygamous arrangements. What is more interesting, for the purposes of this discussion, is the reaction to the case among Syrians in the *mahjar*. The Syrian elite in Brazil deemed the matter serious enough to jeopardize the community's image and worth the expense of a transatlantic rescue. In the United States, the *Syrian World* described this intervention as a victory and a defense of the Syrian sense of honor: "The adoption of energetic measures succeed[ed] in restoring the shaken confidence of the Brazilians in the Syrians as a race."[31] The resolution of the crisis rested on the claim of respectability. Syrians in Brazil redeemed themselves by rescuing Brazilian womanhood from the clutches of the polygamous Muslim "other."

The mistreatment of women, according to the *Syrian World,* was a peculiar Muslim problem, its damage magnified when it involved American women. Indeed, a few months after running the Brazilian story, the *Syrian World* printed another tale, this time involving Argentinean women married to Syrian men who had returned to the al-Qalamun region north of Damascus. Citing the report of a Syrian correspondent for an Egyptian paper, the journal announced that "these women are really unfortunate and complain of their plight to every stranger they happen to meet in the hope of securing relief from their bondage."[32] They had been made to perform "menial work on the farms as is the custom of the native women," and many had contracted the infectious eye disease trachoma. According to the Egyptian report, the women wanted mainly to return to Argentina, but the *Syrian World* extrapolated from this that "the comment of the Syrian newspapers discloses a courageous attitude towards the unpleasant disclosures, especially when it becomes known that all the complaints are wives of men of the Moslem faith."[33]

These stories must have encouraged Salloum Mokarzel, editor of the *Syrian World,* to think more seriously about marriage among Syrians in the United States, for he soon began to publish a series of articles under the pseudonym of A. Hakim on "The Marriage Problems among Syrians."[34] Written in the form of an imaginary interview with the "Sage of Washington Street," the articles tackled the issue of "interracial" marriage and provided words of wisdom from the mythical "Sage" of the Syrians.[35] The Sage opined that in-group unions were preferable to "interracial" ones, citing the advantage of "the psychological affinity between members of the same race brought up in similar surroundings."[36] In this regard he was echoing the concerns of an earlier contributor to the *Syrian World* who claimed that "matrimonial unity . . . is the only race preservative conceivable."[37]

What was meant by *race* here? Written in English, these elite formulations appear to appropriate a common American usage in which *race* equaled national group. The U.S. Industrial Commission on Immigration, for example, noted that it used *race* in a "broad sense . . . the distinction being one of language and geography, rather than one of color or physical characteristics."[38] But the fact that Syrians used racial idioms to describe Christian-Muslim marriages revealed how—as in the naturalization cases—*race* carried religious significance as well. In Syrian circles, "interracial" marriage referred to marriage outside one's religious community and/or ethno-national group. If the latter occurred but the spouses were of the same religion, censure by the community was not as great. As Naff argues, "Crossing the ethnic line was far more pardonable in Syrian society than breaching the denominational barrier."[39] When Syrian Christians married non-Syrians, they tended to marry white ethnics from the same religious background. This was particularly true of the Eastern Catholics, whose integration into dominant Roman rite churches (the process of latinization) increased their exposure to other ethnics and facilitated marriage across national boundaries but *within* Catholicism.[40]

In an effort to promote "matrimonial unity," Syrians urged the reform of certain practices. The Sage, for example, criticized "the pilgrimage to Syria in quest of brides" and argued that men who did this were "only a relic of our old order of things."[41] He also condemned "the whole system of marriage by bargaining" and urged Syrians to focus on issues of compatibility, not finance.[42] On this issue, he found enthusiastic supporters among the readership of the *Syrian World*. Albert Aboud from Detroit, Michigan, argued that the problem was not so much "interracial" marriages as the elaborate codes of courtship that Syrians were expected to follow. The assumption that courtship of a Syrian woman must necessarily lead to marriage, combined with financial obligations, discouraged second-generation men from pursuing Syrian mates.[43] Matilda Absi agreed, calling prenuptial demands "quite ridiculous."[44] Mary Soloman, of Mishawaka, Indiana, boldly argued that "girls must be given more freedom." She complained bitterly that women had little say in the choice of their marriage partners, and she condemned the age difference that was often a characteristic of Syrian marriages.[45]

A spirited debate ensued on the meaning of freedom for young Syrian women in the United States. Some complained that excessive freedom would lead to licentious behavior and the breakdown of the Syrian family.[46] Others, Mary Soloman among them, cautioned readers against equating freedom with impropriety and argued that a woman desires freedom "not because she is immoral, but because she is human."[47] Clara Bishara, from Brooklyn, emphasized that virtuous women would understand the limits of freedom: "Don't raise slaves in your homes, but independent, intelligent ladies with the right perspective upon the problems of life, who appreciate the value of a clean, moral character, and they may be trusted to take care of themselves under all circumstances."[48]

In many respects, Mary's manifesto and the "Sage's" critique of prenuptial arrangements echoed the concerns of an earlier advocate of women's rights in the *mahjar*, ʿAfifa Karam, whose pre–World War I writings are a remarkable testament to the early Arab feminist press.[49] While scholars have focused on Cairo and Beirut as hubs in the production of Arab feminist discourse, New York was also a center of Arab female literary production, and ʿAfifa Karam was among its pioneers.

Karam criticized immigrant men for rushing off "to the home country to fetch a bride as if she were a piece of cloth sold by the yard." She described how, under these conditions, husband and wife-to-be are thrown together in hastily arranged marriages and with only the slimmest knowledge of each other. "What results may be expected of this?" asked Karam. "Endless misery and regret."[50]

Karam's critique of marriage and her more general call for women's rights sat squarely within a discourse of reform that posited a dividing line between the "old" world and the "new." Her division was not, however, a superficial one between an "old" (homeland) and a "new" (America) but a distinction between ignorance and intelligence, oppression and opportunity, debasement and fulfillment. She likened these worlds to two opposing parties: "the party of reform" *(hizb al-islah)* and the "party of retreat" *(hizb al-taqahqur)*.[51] In her opinion, Syrian men and women, immigrant and nonimmigrant alike, should endeavor to join the party of reform. Hence her repeated criticism of men who fell back on practices that evinced nostalgia for the past, for the way they thought things had always been done. Other female critics exposed contradictions within the so-called "party of reform." Sara Abi al-ʿAla, for example, wrote a piece in *as-Sayeh* that criticized men for publicly proclaiming the "reform of woman" (*islah al-maraʾ*) while privately seeking to confine and control her.[52]

Karam's writings and the postwar critique of relations between the sexes in the *Syrian World* were similar in that they both engaged "the woman question" to address larger issues of societal reform. The "woman question," that is, debates about the place of women in a changing society, emerged in the late nineteenth-century Middle East as part of a modernizing discourse. The symbol of the "modern woman" who was educated and well trained in the techniques of household management and child rearing gained currency in urban milieus like Cairo, Damascus, Istanbul, and Tehran. Islamic modernists, including Muhammad ʿAbduh, engaged the "woman question," as did the pioneers of the "women's awakening."[53] Indeed, initial reforms in education and personal status laws were implemented as part of the project of modernizing the national community. In Egypt, where the question of reform was closely tied to the nationalist struggle against the British occupation, women were celebrated as the "mothers of the nation." They, it was presumed, would educate and cultivate the sons of tomorrow.[54]

The "modern woman" was a familiar trope in the writings of men and women who were advocates of change in the political and social order.[55] "She" reappeared in the *mahjar* under different contexts but served essentially the same purpose: to signal a break with the past and embody the possibilities of the future. In this regard, the defense of women's rights and demands for her "liberation" could serve quite different agendas. Naoum Mokarzel, for example, already a critic of the Maronite clergy, found additional ammunition in the plight of women, specifically their lack of education. "Ignorant women are the source of the public's/people's backwardness," he argued, and the clergy was largely responsible.[56] He condemned the codes of "false modesty," advocated female literacy, and encouraged women to read the Arabic newspapers. Like so many men who were turn-of-the-century champions of reforms in female education, Mokarzel envisioned a society where women were knowledgeable mothers, efficient homemakers, and trusted companions. He was not an advocate of equality and believed that "God singled out women for a special role/status which should not be changed."[57] Women's political participation in the life of the nation, for example, was not part of his agenda. Of course, this was hardly a position unique to Middle Eastern men. It was also similar to the views of another champion of "the reform of woman," Lord Cromer. As a top British official of the occupation in Egypt, Cromer (formerly Evelyn Baring) called for the liberation of women from the "shackles" of Islam, while at home in his native Britain he was a founding member of the Men's League for Opposing Women's Suffrage. His paternalism at home and his colonial feminism abroad were intimately related, for both served to perpetuate white male dominance.[58]

There were parallels between the articulation of the woman question in the Middle East and in the United States, but there were also subtle differences. In 'Afifa Karam's critique, men and women were urged to live up to the modernist ideal so as to represent the reform movement that had gripped the Middle East in the late nineteenth and early twentieth centuries. Twenty years later, when Mary Soloman called for reform in marriage practices, it was so Syrians could accommodate the reality of their Americanness. "We are living in America," she argued. "We have adopted America as our country—we must adopt her ideas, and live an American life. We must put away those foolish ideas of the past and the Orient. We must give our girls the freedom which other girls in the world enjoy."[59] One of the "freedoms" she no doubt envisioned was that of marrying outside the Syrian community. Although rarely presented as such, marriage to an Anglo white man was one way to avoid scrutiny and to end the probationary racial status assigned to Syrians. These desires may have increased after episodes of violence against the community, such as the lynching of Nola Romey and the murder of his wife in 1929. Was it merely coincidence that their daughter married a native Anglo and took a very common English last name?[60]

The different framing of the problem of reform in Karam's and Soloman's critiques was emblematic of a broader transition in the postwar debate on Syrian identity. Karam had wanted immigrants to be modern *Syrians,* a position that was completely consistent with a woman who was a child of the "women's awakening" and a partner in the Arabist one. She had, after all, gone to Paris to attend the First Arab Congress in 1913.[61] For Mary Soloman, modernity was cast in a completely American frame, and immigrants were encouraged to relinquish practices that marked them as Syrian. But the practices that Mary deemed *especially* Syrian were ones she saw as retrograde, as "the foolish ideas of the past." This was a reversal of the temporality that infused constructions of the *mahjar* in the pre–World War I period: where first- generation immigrants had once been cast as the mediators of the modern, they were now viewed as reminders of the past.

The debate on marriage in the *Syrian World* suggested this shift. Practices such as arranged marriage, payment of brideprice, abnegation of choice, and even the reliance on Arabic were deemed distinctively Syrian and an impediment to the Americanization process. This posed an obvious problem for those who wanted to hold back the march of assimilation to, as Fouad Shatara phrased it, make sure that the children of immigrants would not "forget that they have Syrian blood." Indeed, this was *the* problem of Syrian ethnicity in the postwar period and one that could not be easily solved, for the second generation was reluctant to identify with practices and institutions that were increasingly marked as "old."

There were efforts to adapt Syrian customs, to "Americanize" them. In this spirit, voluntary organizations held yearly *mahrajans,* or "outdoor picnics," that aimed to bring the second and third generations together and to encourage in-group marriage of the young attendees even as it declined.[62] The *mahrajan* also served to mark the "cultural stuff" that would define the group as ethnic, and the cultural expressions that best survived this transition were food, music, and dance.[63]

It is perhaps not surprising that in this period of debate over how to be Syrian American Salloum Mokarzel spearheaded a campaign to organize Syrian clubs and societies into a national federation. "Let our people become conscious of their racial merits and claim their rightful position in the body social and politic of America," he wrote in the November 1928 issue of the *Syrian World*. The following month, Reverend W. A. Mansur lent further support to the idea of a federation. He wrote: "We are Americans first because we made America our home, because it is the home of our posterity and because we owe it to posterity to be for America first. We pledge to give to the United States a pure Americanism, the fullest loyalty, and undivided allegiance. [But] we [also] love our Mother Land, we honor the memory of our illustrious ancestors, and we exalt the contributions our race has made to mankind."[64]

By February 1929, twenty clubs throughout the nation had pledged their support to the formation of a federation. They included, among others, the Syrian Young Men's Society of Los Angeles, the Good Citizenship Club of Birmingham, Alabama, and the Ladies' Syrian Association of Spring Valley, Illinois. Over the July 4 weekend in Port Arthur, Texas, in 1931, Habeeb Amuny, an elder member of the local Young Men's Amusement Club, chaired a "Convention of Young Syrians" out of which the Southern Federation of Syrian Clubs was born. Participants at the convention spent most of their time socializing at a dance that lasted until 2:00 a.m. The three to four hundred conventioneers then went to a sunrise breakfast that was followed by the highlight of the gathering: a baseball game between the YMCA of Port Arthur and the Young Men's Syrian Association team of Houston, Texas. Somewhere during the festivities, delegates found time to charge the YMCA with drawing up articles of federation that would be submitted to Syrian clubs throughout the South for approval.

FORGING A NEW RELATIONSHIP TO THE HOMELAND

What is often missed in the literature on Syrian immigrants in the United States is the conscious attempt to deal with the question of assimilation in the post–World War I period. This chapter has described how Syrians sought to manage the trajectory of their assimilation and not simply capitulate to a process that they deemed inevitable. The debates around marriage revealed how first-generation Syrian immigrants negotiated their commitment to the homeland and to the United States. In each case, concessions were made in favor of Americanization. Immigrants would, for example, give up the idea of returning to Syria but would continue to support the homeland financially and, in the case of a politically active minority, participate in the nationalist struggles of the territories under the French Mandate. They would advocate changes in marriage practices but with an eye to maintaining the ideal of in-group marriage.

In her study on Syrian ethnicity, Helen Hatab argued that the debates in the *Syrian World* took shape within a public/private dichotomy. Concerns with marriage and with instilling in the second generation a sense of pride in their Syrian heritage were "private" matters, while the emphasis on American patriotism and loyalty to an adopted homeland was a manifestation of the group's "public" presentation to the wider society. This division between a private ethnicity that was kept at a level of low articulation and a public Americanism that was celebrated and encouraged impeded the development of organized group solidarity and helps explain the rapid assimilation of Syrians in the United States in the interwar period.[65]

The public/private dichotomy is a useful framework for understanding the transition in Syrian ethnicity in the postwar period, although it does not in itself explain why certain attributes were assigned to the private domain and others to the public. For example, aspects of the culture that were most readily retained as distinctively Syrian, such as food, were reproduced by women in the domestic sphere.

Moreover, this chapter has argued that Syrian ethnicity in the postwar period should be understood as a reworking of ideas about migration's relationship to modernity in the sense that the division between "old" and "new" was central to strategies of ethnicization. Recognizing that the claim to be modern Americans existed alongside reinterpretations of what it meant to be Syrian indicates how the process of assimilation was dialectical. To make the *mahjar* home, and to become American, involved the interaction of homeland and host country identities that were themselves the product of a particular historical context. Immigration restriction, the reconfiguration of homeland national communities, and the aspirations of the second generation powerfully shaped the context in which Syrians (re)interpreted their identity.

By the early 1930s, Syrians in the United States who had emigrated before World War I had begun to forge a new relationship to the homeland. Precisely at a moment when they could have fulfilled the promise of return, for the most part they chose not to. They preferred instead to send remittances home and to support the nationalist struggle (in its multiple meanings) from afar. They preferred, in other words, to imagine their connection to the "real" Syria, while the Syria that they had begun to re-create in the *mahjar*, and the culture that the second generation defined as authentically Syrian, were shorn of their dynamism and rendered more traditional than they had ever been. A new influx of immigrants and a radicalization of politics in the 1960s would be necessary for a new conception of ethnicity to develop—an Arab American one.

Conclusion

Syrian immigrants to the United States were not a unified group but representatives of various regional, local, and religious identities. They could be at once Ottomans, Syrians, Zahalnis (residents of Zahle), Druze, and Maronites; Damascene Sunnis, Greek Orthodox from Beirut, Jews from Aleppo, and many other combinations. They were men, women, and children who could claim they had little in common yet—because they were immigrants—everything. Recognition of solidarity in the face of difference most often began on the journey to the United States, when Syrians, cramped on slippery ship decks, listened for the sounds of their native language. Distinctions in village of origin or religious sect were set aside as passengers searched for something familiar amid the bewildering babble of tongues. Finding someone who spoke Arabic was a source of comfort in a sea of unfamiliar sights, sounds, and smells. The bond of language continued to bring Syrian immigrants together during their first crucial months of transplantation.

From the very beginning of their transatlantic migration, then, Syrians recognized and organized around broad solidarities rooted in language and region of origin. They eventually reconstituted more narrow divisions in ways that reflected homeland patterns. They founded separate places of worship, newspapers, and voluntary associations based on religious sect or village of origin. This history of Syrian immigrant identity formation understood principally in its institutional dimension is complex, and a small but growing body of scholarship explores the

richness of Syrian community life, with its clubs, festivals, religious celebrations, and café culture.[1] This book, however, has approached the
question of identity from a different angle. Specifically, it has explored
the systems of meaning that made possible the development of new self-
understandings among Syrians in the United States as they came into
contact with and interpreted American institutions, laws, and peoples.
The changing significances of race and nation, I have argued, were crucial components of Syrian ethnic group invention.

This book has traced debates around Syrian identity in the Syrian
American press, court records, diplomatic correspondence, and oral histories. It has argued that their vitality and contentiousness cannot be
fully grasped within the assimilation paradigm. Rather, ethnicity and
ethnicization are more useful concepts for understanding the history of
first-wave Syrian immigrants in the United States, for these concepts can
more accurately convey the dialecticity of immigrant adaptation. This
study has demonstrated, in particular, how Syrians asserted their identity as Americans by using preexisting notions of difference. Christian
particularism facilitated the claim of whiteness, while the distinction between those who left and those who stayed behind (represented as a difference between "new" and "old") corresponded with Syrian assertions
that they could be "modern" Americans. Homeland solidarities and cultural attributes were muted, amplified, and given new meaning, but they
were not simply replaced by "American" ones. For this reason, the history of Syrians in the United States from the end of the nineteenth century up until World War II is understood better as the emergence of ethnicity than as the triumph of assimilation.

Proposing ethnicization as a useful concept for the study of Syrian immigrant adaptation does not mean that assimilation did not occur.[2] If we
consider indicators such as the decline in residential segregation, intermarriage, and the adoption of English, it is clear that by the 1920s Syrians were partaking in economic, social, and political networks that
transcended the ethnic group.[3] Indeed, as chapter 5 has argued, Syrians
were conscious of their assimilation and described their integration, particularly that of the second generation, as a successful shift to Americanization. Rather than take these claims at face value, however, this
study has analyzed how they evoked new constructions of the Syrian
homeland and of Syrian culture.

The overarching argument throughout this book has been that Syrians' ethnicity emerged in a U.S. racial order that scrutinized their iden-

tity and repeatedly questioned whether they could become white Americans. Many scholars have argued that Syrians triumphed over this scrutiny and that they emerged on the white side of the color line as they entered the middle class in the United States and in other parts of the Americas. There is indeed evidence to support this interpretation, including, for example, their eventual victory in the naturalization cases, the exclusion of Syria from the Asiatic barred zone, and the myriad experiences where Syrians counted as white—from Costa Najour's win in an Atlanta court in 1909 to Hanneh Joseph's selection as the first runner-up at the International Beauty Pageant in Galveston, Texas, in 1927.[4] All of these moments suggest a consolidation of whiteness. But this interpretation would make the Syrians just another immigrant group that "became white" and benefited from the privileges of whiteness. However, their story is not just like that of the Irish, the Italians, and the Jews because much of the evidence marshaled in this book points away from whiteness and toward a conceptualization of the Syrians as "in between" or "not quite white." The unresolved nature of their racial status can allow us to better understand the racialization of Arabs in the United States in the post-1945 period. The reality is not so much one of rupture—of Syrians going from being white to being people of color—as it is one of continuity with past patterns of racialization. To be sure, there were ebbs and flows in this process, but the not-quite-white status of Syrians lived on. In other words, Syrian encounters with race in the early part of the twentieth century formed the foundation upon which later Arab immigrants were marked as different and potentially threatening to the body politic.

Take, for example, the case of Yemeni immigrant Ahmad Hassan, heard in Detroit, Michigan, in 1942. This case revealed that close to three decades after Syrian Christians had scored a crucial legal victory in favor of their whiteness, other Arabic-speaking groups, particularly Muslim ones, would not fare so well in the courts or in the understanding of the "common man."

Hassan's physical appearance rendered him at a disadvantage from the start. After noting that the petitioner was "an Arab," the presiding judge, Judge Tuttle, declared that he was "undisputedly dark brown in color,"[5] confirming once more that while skin color was not supposed to determine racial eligibility to naturalize, it figured prominently in cases where petitions for citizenship were denied. In the *Hassan* case, darkness of skin definitely did matter, so much so that the judge argued that "a strong burden of proof devolves upon him [Hassan] to establish that he is a white person within the meaning of the [Naturalization] act."[6]

One important argument could have helped establish Hassan's eligibility to naturalize, namely the position of the southwestern part of the Arabian Peninsula outside the Asiatic barred zone. Placement in relation to the barred zone had already been used as a rationale in other racial prerequisite cases, such as the *Basha* case, which affirmed the eligibility of a Syrian immigrant to naturalize, and, more significantly, the *Thind* case, which deemed Indians ineligible for citizenship because India fell within the zone. In the *Hassan* case, however, placement *outside* the zone was declared irrelevant, and the judge resorted to more familiar interpretations of congressional intent and common knowledge. Two factors, in particular, stood out as controlling the decision against Hassan: the fact that he was Muslim and the distance of Yemen from a European border. "Apart from the dark skin of the Arabs," Judge Tuttle opined, "it is well known that they are a part of the Mohammedan world and that a wide gulf separates their culture from that of the predominately Christian peoples of Europe."[7] In addition, and revealing that discussions of race were very often connected to anxieties over sex and marriage, Judge Tuttle argued that (Muslim) Arabs could not be expected to intermarry with "our population and be assimilated into our civilization."[8] It is not clear what evidence, if any, the judge used to make such an assertion. Rates of out-marriage were, in fact, quite high among Muslim Arab immigrants (and even higher among their children), and there was even a perception regarding Muslim men that they were more likely to marry "American" women because they did not immigrate with their wives, or send for them, as was more often the case with Syrian Christians.[9]

Rather than base his argument on the realities of the Arab immigrant experience, Judge Tuttle preferred to rely on suppositions and the old imperialist conviction that closeness to Europe meant closeness to "civilization" and membership in the "white race." In making this argument, he did have the weight of other legal rulings behind him, and he cited the case of an Armenian immigrant, Tatos O. Cartozian, as precedent. Heard in an Oregon district court in 1925, *United States v. Cartozian* had affirmed the whiteness of Armenians, thanks largely to the testimony of noted Columbia University anthropologist Franz Boas. Carefully combining ethnological and common-knowledge rationales, Boas argued that Armenians were white because of their "European origin" and "Alpine stock." The judge placed great weight on Boas's testimony, as well as on the historic "aloofness" of the Armenians from the Turks, their proximity to Europe, their Christian background, and their tendency to "intermarry with white people everywhere."[10] It is worth noting that the judge presiding over the *Cartozian* case was the one who had ruled in favor of Syrian applicant Tom Ellis. Also cited in *United States v. Cartozian* was the *Halladjian* case, which had been used to affirm the eligibility of a Syrian petitioner in 1910 (see chapter 2).[11] While the cases of Armenians and Syrians were frequently used to support each other, they were not mentioned in *In re Ahmad Hassan*, although there were clearly grounds to do so. Why, in this instance, were the Syrian racial prerequisite cases not relevant in the case of a Muslim Arab? The reason appears deceptively simple: in the legal discourse of the 1940s, the term *Arab* did not mean, as it does today in its most general sense, speakers of Arabic, but persons born in the Arabian Peninsula and, increasingly, Arabic-speaking Muslims from Mandate Palestine. The different categorization of Muslim and Christian Arabs was also more complicated, as subsequent debates would show. Establishing the whiteness of both groups would require a new argument—a task taken on by the Immigration and Naturalization Service (INS).

Less than one year after Hassan's case was heard in Michigan, the INS published a lengthy statement on the eligibility of Arabs to naturalize. Strikingly at odds with the ruling in *In re Ahmad Hassan*, the article began by stating that the "Immigration and Naturalization Service and the Board of Immigration Appeals take the view that a person of the Arabian race *is eligible to naturalization*."[12] It then proceeded to link eligibility to the provisions of the *Thind* case and shift the terms of the debate to ones derived from an emerging discourse of anti-Fascism and anti-Nazism. With regard to *Thind*, the INS considered Arabia's exclusion from the barred zone to be "highly significant" and cited Justice Sutherland's now famous opinion that had linked eligibility for immigration into the United States to eligibility to naturalize. But the INS knew that placement in relation to the zone was not enough, and it proceeded (ironically, much as Judge Tuttle had) to link geography to a particular cultural pedigree that, in its view, boosted the eligibility of certain immigrant groups to citizenship. Not surprisingly, compatibility with European civilization was at the top of the list. Here the article did cite the Syrians and Armenians as examples of peoples eligible to naturalization "chiefly because of their European contacts" and added that, by the same logic, "the Arabians . . . would seem the most likely candidates" for citizenship.[13]

The Syrian and Armenian racial prerequisite cases were not directly cited as precedents by the INS, nor were the Syrians viewed as another "Arab" group that had successfully claimed whiteness through the courts and could, therefore, support the claims of Muslim Palestinians and Yemenis. Rather, according to the INS, the history of "European contact" that the Syrians, Armenians, and "Arabians" all shared was the factor that rendered them white. The INS thus returned to the argument that whiteness could be measured in cultural terms and used a yardstick divided, metaphorically, in increments of "contribution to Western civilization." Since the "Semitic races" were situated at the beginning of this yardstick—that is, in the early history of Western civilization (but clearly not in its present)—they could be classed as white. Finally, in an appeal to outdated but still popular theories of ethnology, the INS cited a 1941 decision of the Board of Appeals, which had affirmed the admissibility of a certain Majid Ramsay Sharif to the United States because "Arabians [are] closely related to the Jews . . . whose eligibility to citizenship has never been questioned."[14] All of the components of this INS argument were applied a year later in a Massachusetts court where the petition for naturalization of another Muslim Arab, Mohamed Mohriez, was granted.[15]

To be sure, the desire to include Muslim Arabs in the category of those eligible for naturalization, evident in the INS's article and the *Mohriez* case, was also linked to wartime concern over the devastating effects of European racism. The *Monthly Review,* for example, concluded its statement on Arab eligibility with palpable unease with the ruling against Hassan, noting that "it comes at a time when the evil results of race discrimination are disastrously apparent."[16] In a similar vein, Judge Wyzanski, writing in favor of Mohriez, argued that "we as a country have learned that policies of rigid exclusion are not only false to our profession of democratic liberalism but repugnant to our vital interests as a world power."[17] Granting Mohriez's petition for citizenship was a way to "fulfill the promise that we shall treat all men as created equal."[18]

The controversy over the eligibility of Muslim Arabs to naturalize was interesting in the way it both did and did not revisit the arguments made in the Syrian racial prerequisite cases. The INS position in favor of Arab whiteness was remarkably similar to the argument made for Syrians in the *Dow* case. The main difference was that the INS was willing to incorporate Muslim Arabs into this definition, provided that they were cast as players in the march of Christian, Western civilization. In other words, Muslim Arabs were deemed white when their religious identity was effaced. In this way they became "honorary whites," those accepted into the nation but under suspicion that they did not quite deserve it.[19] Whereas the Christian identity of Syrian applicants in the racial prerequisite cases had been central to their argument for whiteness, Muslim Arabs were at their whitest when stripped of their religious affiliation and rendered part of the Western fantasy of an original "Semitic" race. In both cases race and religion were intertwined, and we see here the development of the idea that there is something oxymoronic about being fully Muslim and fully American at the same time.[20] As the terms *Arab* and *Muslim* became conflated in the post-1945 period, Syrian Christians faced new decisions about defining their ethnic identity.

Finally, while this book has sought to demonstrate how Syrian ethnicity in the United States elucidates patterns of immigrant integration into a host society, it has also stepped outside a U.S.-centric framework of analysis to question how homelands integrated their diasporas into the national community. Chapter 3 has demonstrated how emigrants participated in the development of Arabist thought and how the *mahjar*—because of its modernity—represented the possibilities of a future Arab nation. If we follow Benedict Anderson's argument that the nation is an imagined community based on "deep, horizontal comradeship,"[21] then the horizontal axis of the Arab nation, even in its protonationalist phase, appears very wide indeed.

In the post–World War I period, homeland governments in Syria and Lebanon attempted to strengthen economic and political ties with Syrians abroad.[22] In 1937, for example, the Syrian Foreign Ministry, newly energized after signing the (never-ratified) "Treaty of Friendship and Alliance" with France, issued a communiqué in Arabic, Spanish, French, and Portuguese urging Syrian emigrants to regain their Syrian nationality. The ministry was particularly concerned with reversing the results of the Treaty of Lausanne, which had stipulated that "Ottomans of Syrian origin" residing abroad would automatically become Turkish citizens unless they registered as Syrians before an August 1926 deadline. The independentist government of Syria wanted those citizens back, if not physically at least juridically as part of its program to build the "New Syrian Fatherland."[23] While the success of the directive was mixed, the principle on which it was based—that the nation must retain the citizenship of its emigrants—would become a pillar of Syrian and Lebanese politics.

In the post-Mandate period, particularly under the leadership of the Ba'ath party, the diaspora continued to figure in Syrian nationalist rhetoric and ideology. The Ministry of Culture and National Guidance, for example, published a volume entitled *Arab Emigrants in North America*, which was the third part in its "Nationalist Books" series intended to "enrichen the culture of the Arab citizen."[24] These efforts to cultivate political, economic, and cultural ties between "Arab citizens" at home and abroad echoed themes of the First Arab Congress held in Paris in 1913. What was different about Arab nationalism of the post-1945 period, however, was that its supporters wanted to undo the colonial legacy of the Middle East erected by the French and the British. They sought to do so in a way that balanced the competing influence of the superpowers. Post-1945 Arab nationalism emphasized the unity of the Arabic-speaking peoples and a "third way"—one that would be neither wholly capitalist nor socialist and would be beholden neither to the United States nor to the Soviet Union. While centered in Egypt, this new Arab nationalism, or Pan-Arabism, radiated throughout the Arabic-speaking countries, inculcating in their citizens enthusiasm for a movement that sought to defy the forces of imperialism and chart an independent, nationalist future for the Arab world. Many Arab immigrants to the United States of the post-1945 period were schooled on these tenets of Arab nationalism, and while they objected to the authoritarian turn that nationalist leaders took, they remained attached to the principles of anti-imperialism and Third World solidarity. These immigrants formed the backbone of a more activist and self-consciously "Arab American" population in the United States.

More recently, both Syria and Lebanon have taken a new interest in their diasporas. For Lebanon, this is part of a massive rebuilding effort in the wake of the 1975–90 civil war; for Syria, it is a policy of reversing the brain drain and reconnecting with those whom, interestingly, the government calls *mughtaribun* (those who have left the homeland), not *muhajirun* (emigrants).[25] Under the current president of Syria, Bashar al-Asad, there is a new Ministry of Expatriates (Wizarat al-mughtaribin). While these concerns are obviously linked to recent political developments, they are also connected to a much larger history and problematic that turns on the question of how best to integrate the diaspora into strategies and discourses of national development.

A seminal essay on ethnicity in the United States notes that "representations of the Old Country constitute an important component in the development of ethnic consciousness among immigrants."[26] This book has argued that this assumption also works in reverse: that is, representations of the *mahjar* have been (and will continue to be) influential in the construction of modern national consciousness in the Middle East. More importantly, Syrian migration and ethnicity provide powerful evidence for the reconceptualization of the Middle East as an area with multiple geographies, whose inhabitants shaped a region with boundaries that are far less fixed than standard approaches have made them out to be.[27]

Becoming Arab American

The Arabic-speaking Americans are now in a position to render inestimable service to the land of their adoption, as well as to the lands of their origin. They have become by virtue of their inherited traits and traditions, as well as by their acquired American ways, a logical link between the United States and the Arab world, at a time when the relations between the two have become closer than ever, and when the peace and security of the world will depend partly upon a greater measure of understanding and friendship between them.

Habib Ibrahim Katibah (1946)

If political and economic events had not reactivated Arab immigration and an interest in Arab culture, Syrian-Americans might have Americanized themselves out of existence.

Alixa Naff (1983)

In November 1944, 150 representatives of societies consisting of members of Arabic-speaking origin met in New York City to discuss forming an organization that would advocate an Arab position on issues related to American foreign and domestic policy.[1] The meeting was in large part a response to the Biltmore Conference, which leading Zionist organizations had convened in New York in 1942. Headed by David Ben-Gurion, the future prime minister of Israel, the conference adopted the "Biltmore Program," which supported unrestricted Jewish immigration to Palestine (restricted by the British government's "White Paper" of 1939) and the establishment of a Jewish Commonwealth there. Believing that Americans needed more information on the question of Palestine from an Arab point of view, the group of Arabic-speaking delegates meeting in New York decided to form the Institute of Arab American Affairs (IAA), with

an office located at 160 Broadway Avenue. The active members and officers of the IAA were two Palestinian men, Ismail Khalidi and Ferhat Ziadeh; a Syrian, Habib Katibah; and Philip Hitti, from Lebanon. Khalidi
worked as a broadcaster for the Office of War Information before joining the United Nations, while Ziadeh, trained as a lawyer, taught Arabic at Princeton University in the Army Specialized Training Program.
Katibah was a journalist and a former Near East correspondent for the
Boston Globe. Hitti was professor of Near Eastern studies at Princeton
and served as executive director of the institute.[2] This post was later filled
by Khalil Totah, who had received his PhD from Columbia University in
1926. He then served as the principal at the Quaker school in his native
Ramallah, Palestine, before returning to the United States. The purpose
of the institute, as stated in its constitution, was "to serve as a medium
of good will and mutual understanding between the United States and
the Arabic-speaking countries and peoples."[3] This short-lived organization continued activist trends of an older generation, but it also brought
something new to ethnic institution building, namely the reframing of
Syrian identity in the United States in pan-ethnic terms.[4] Immigrants
from greater Syria were now "Arab American."

The term was by no means widely accepted. Syrians, including those
associated with the newspaper *al-Hoda,* objected to it because they had
embraced a more Lebanese/Phoenician identity. At the urging of Philip
Hitti, who mediated the dispute, the institute titled its publication on
Arabs in the United States *Arabic-Speaking Americans.* It would be two
decades before the term *Arab American* gained much purchase within
Syrian communities in the United States. The story of how some descendants of the first wave of Syrian migration came to identify as Arab
American while others did not is complicated, meriting a book-length
study on its own. This chapter sketches out the broad lines of this development in national and transnational terms and assesses its connections to issues of racial formation and to the central themes of this book.

RENARRATIVIZING SYRIAN IMMIGRATION
AS ARAB IMMIGRATION

Arabic-Speaking Americans, written by Habib Katibah, began with a
brief history of the multiple origins of the Arabs. They had descended
from the Phoenicians, the Nabateans, and the Ghassanids of South Arabia, who were Christianized under the influence of the Byzantine Em-

pire. "It is noteworthy," Katibah writes, "that many of the Christian Arabs of modern Syria claim descent from these proud people."[5] However, the text places special weight on the role of Islam in generating an Arab fluorescence, which was consolidated in a vast Arab-Islamic empire stretching from Spain in the west to China in the east. In the context of this empire, "The Arab power for assimilating others proved to be amazing." Thus, unlike some of the earlier writings by Syrian immigrants that had stressed the exclusively Phoenician origins of the Syrians, Habib Katibah conceived of the Phoenicians as just one of the strands of peoples that produced the original Arabs. "It is from these people," he argues, "that American citizens of Arabic-speaking stock are so proudly descended."[6]

The thirty-page pamphlet then narrates the history of Syrian immigration to the United States and describes the various sectors of American society in which they became participants. In an interesting inversion of the assimilationist language of Hitti's 1924 text, which stressed the ability of Syrians to become model Americans, Katibah notes the role that Syrians played in making *Americans* American. As entrepreneurs, the Syrians "helped materially in creating the American 'house beautiful' by introducing decorative linen into the homes of most of the upper and middle classes."[7]

Katibah's text is also significant in that it situates geographical Syria within the broader topography of the "Arab world." The use of this term in the United States was quite new and was connected to trends in Arab nationalism and to the formation of the Arab League in Cairo in 1945. The league aimed to strengthen the political, economic, and cultural ties among the member states, which at that time included the newly independent states of Syria and Lebanon, as well as Egypt, Iraq, Saudi Arabia, Transjordan, and Yemen. By stressing the Arabness of Syria and Lebanon, the league also attempted to reorient these countries away from their French colonial history. To claim Syrians and Lebanese as Arabs at this point in time was to incorporate them into a revived Arab nationalist discourse that was avowedly anti-imperialist.

Becoming Arab American in the United States in the post-1945 period was thus a political act that signaled affiliation with Arabic-speaking peoples across the lines of nationality. It also signaled a general sympathy with the plight of the Palestinians. Those who were more likely to identify with the term *Arab American* were either politically engaged members of the pre-1945 "Syrian" community, many of whom, like Ismail

Khalidi, were Palestinian, or new immigrants to the United States from the Arab world. Indeed, the post-1945 period witnessed several important shifts in Arab immigration that contributed gradually to the creation of an Arab American identity.

THE NEW ARAB AMERICANS

While the first wave of Arabic-speaking immigrants to the United States were predominantly Christians from geographical Syria (which included present-day Lebanon), the second wave was more diverse in terms of religion and nationality. Regional conflicts and civil wars in the Middle East played an important role in precipitating this change. The establishment of the state of Israel and the first Arab-Israeli war of 1948 displaced close to eight hundred thousand Palestinians from their homes. As refugees, most settled in neighboring Arab countries, although, in what Edward Said aptly called a "paradox of mobility and insecurity"—a simultaneous tendency to migrate but without the protection or citizenship of a home state—many moved again, including to the United States. The post-1945 Arab migration also included a large number of Yemenis who came to the United States in the 1960s and 1970s, the result of disruption by North Yemen's civil war (1962–70).[8] Similarly, the Lebanese civil war between 1975 and 1990 produced another wave of Lebanese emigration, adding to what was an already well-established diaspora. By some accounts, 990,000 persons, or 40 percent of the population, left the country in that fifteen-year period.[9] Unlike the early Lebanese migrants to the United States, a significant percentage of the newer Lebanese migrants were Muslim, both Shiʿa and Sunni from southern and western Lebanon.

Changes to U.S. immigration laws also shaped the new flow of immigrants from the Middle East. The Immigration and Naturalization Act of 1952 ended Asian exclusion and race-based citizenship. It changed the formula for computing quotas and increased slightly the total number of immigrants allowed to enter from each country. In addition, the law introduced a set of preferences by reserving the first 50 percent of the quota for immigrants with skills identified as needed by the United States. The second preference, set at 30 percent, was allocated to parents of adult citizens, and the final 20 percent, or third preference, was for spouses and children of legal resident aliens. If an unused portion of the latter remained, it could be extended to brothers and sisters, as well as to adult sons and daughters of citizens. Finally, the law extended nonquota status to the husbands and spouses of citizens. While on the surface the 1952 act appeared to loosen immigration restrictions by facilitating family reunion and boosting the number of immigrants from the professional classes, it was primarily a retooling of the national-origins system that favored white immigrants. Moreover, the law expanded grounds for exclusion by including new categories for those deemed "immoral" and "subversive" that allowed the immigration service to target communists.[10]

By the early 1960s, considerable opposition to the national-origins system had arisen within the general public and among members of the Kennedy and Johnson administrations. After extensive congressional debate, a new law was passed in 1965 that effectively dismantled the system, although it maintained a distinction between eastern and western hemispheres. The law also preserved a system of preferences based on family ties and personal qualifications deemed of value to the United States. Six percent of the annual quota was set aside for refugees, namely persons deemed to be fleeing persecution from communism, those rendered homeless by wars in the Middle East, and victims of natural disasters.[11] From 1966 to 1981, three-fifths of the refugees admitted were eastern European and the remainder Asian, primarily Chinese and later Vietnamese.[12]

The overall effect of the new law on Middle Eastern migration to the United States was to increase the diversity of the immigrant pool. Thus, while the earlier immigration had consisted mainly of modestly educated and relatively poor Christian immigrants, the post-1945 migration included large numbers of prosperous and highly educated doctors, lawyers, engineers, and teachers from a range of religious backgrounds. These persons made up the 10 percent preference for professionals, scientists, and artists of exceptional ability. To be sure, the new wave of immigration also consisted of a large number of persons engaged in commerce, as well as skilled workers, but the increase in professionals was significant. In addition, many immigrants who became part of the professional class came to the United States originally as college students in the 1950s and 1960s. They excelled in their studies and forged careers here instead of returning to their countries of origin, which were often in political turmoil and lacked economic opportunities.[13] These students formed the backbone of a more activist and self-consciously Arab population in the United States. This more assertive, politically engaged population found inspiration in new ideological currents and social movements both in the Middle East and in the United States. Chief among these were Arab nationalism, Third Worldism, and the civil rights movement. The ways in which Arab immigrants and their descendants connected to these struggles account for the revival of Arab heritage and of "de-assimilation"—that is, a cultural shift away from the Anglo-American core.[14]

The issue that would most radicalize Arab students in the United States and would spark organization and mobilization on a new level was Palestine. The fate of the Palestinians in the face of settlement promoted by the Zionist movement had long been a topic of debate for Arabs in the United States. As noted in chapter 3, Syrians in New York protested the Balfour Declaration in 1917 and launched an educational effort on behalf of the Palestinians. In addition to *Arabic-Speaking Americans,* the IAA published a series entitled "Papers on Palestine" to provide an Arab perspective on the prospects for development in an area then still under British control.[15] The long-standing concern with developments in Palestine among members of the Arabic-speaking community in the United States was energized by the Arab nationalist mood of the 1950s and early 1960s. Arab leaders insisted that Palestine was an Arab issue, not just a Palestinian one. The ideological and military conflict with Israel was at the center of Egypt and Syria's foreign policy, shaping interactions with other states and with their own citizens. The humiliating defeat of Egypt and the other Arab armies by Israel in the 1967 war, along with the international community's reaction to that defeat, galvanized a young generation of Palestinians and their sympathizers into action.[16] George Khoury, from Jerusalem, recalled that he was fired from his job in Detroit for listening to radio reports of the war in one ear. He had told his boss that the war affected his family, to which he replied, "I always wanted the Arabs to lose." In this context, a number of organizations emerged in the United States that linked issues of discrimination and stereotyping of Arabs to the question of Palestine. Those associated with these organizations began to speak of a "political racism" in the United States that targeted persons of Arabic-speaking origin because of their political views. The Association of Arab-American University Graduates (AAUG) was at the forefront of this new wave of national organizing and played a pivotal role in articulating an agenda for Arab American activism. George Khoury, who was trained as an engineer, began to focus most of his time on organizing. He helped found the Arab Student Organization at Wayne State University and then joined the AAUG. Prior to 1967 he had been quite social, proud of his little black book full of telephone numbers. After 1967, expressing his new interest in political engagement, he threw his black book away.[17]

ARAB AMERICAN ORGANIZATIONS

The idea to form an organization consisting of university graduates of "Arab extraction" came out of an informal meeting held on the occasion of the International Congress of Orientalists in Ann Arbor, Michigan, in August 1967. A group of professors and professionals attending the congress met to discuss concerns arising out of recent developments in the Middle East, notably the devastation brought about by the Six-Day War in June 1967. The fourteen persons in attendance passed a resolution affirming "the pressing need for united action to confront certain urgent problems facing our communities in the United States, Canada, and in our land of origin." They charged Rashid Bashshur, a Syrian sociologist at the School of Public Health at the University of Michigan, and Abdeen Jabara, an attorney from Detroit of Lebanese origin, with the task of coordinating a conference, the aim of which was to consider the formation of a permanent organization. This conference was held four months later in Chicago, at which time the AAUG was established. It had forty-three founding members.[18]

Over the following year, the association worked to boost its membership and to clearly define its objectives. These were outlined at the board of directors' meeting in September 1968. Describing itself as "an educational, cultural organization whose purpose is the dissemination of information," the AAUG established three committees—publications, education, and public relations—to produce material "expressive of the Arab point of view."[19] The board agreed on a twofold definition of the association's raison d'être: "1) presentation of a rational point of view with regard to the Arab countries, thus promoting understanding of the Arab case; and 2) solidification of ties amongst Arab-Americans—of potential benefit to the Arab world."[20]

The association's first major public relations effort revolved around injecting an Arab perspective on the Palestinian issue into the mainstream media. This effort took the form of a full-page advertisement in the *New York Times*. With a boldface title that read "Needed, a Nixon Declaration for Five Million Jewish, Christian and Moslem Palestinians," the advertisement appeared in the Sunday paper on November 2, 1969. It contained an open letter to President Nixon and a declaration.

The letter called on the president to earn the title of "Peacemaker" by bringing peace "to the tormented land of Palestine." It stated:

> The Balfour Declaration, issued by the British Government in 1917, "viewed with favor" the dismemberment of Palestine, its mutilation from a land sacred to and inhabited by Moslem, Christian and Jew, to a land which is the exclusive domain of a few. It further "viewed with favor" the transformation of a land in which, historically, men lived on a footing of equality and justice, into an exclusivist, religiously-based state which through no fault of its people, was and is prevented from accommodating the different, and the universal.[21]

The letter then urged President Nixon to reverse the process initiated by the Balfour Declaration through the adoption of what the AAUG called a "Nixon Declaration." This declaration would "commit the Government of the United States to the cause of a lasting peace in Palestine." The text of the AAUG's proposed Nixon Declaration began in this way: "The Government of the United States views with favor the reconstruction of the Palestinian Community in the land of Palestine and its transformation into an independent, free and democratic state in which men and women, regardless of race, national origin, language, creed, will live constructively and peacefully with each other."[22]

The advertisement included the AAUG mailing address to which supporters of the declaration could send donations (the advertisement had cost $8,000). The association received over thirty letters of support containing donations from as little as one dollar to five hundred.[23] These letters came from persons of obvious Arab origin, like Yehia Aossey from Cedar Rapids, Iowa, who wrote that this was the first time he had heard of the AAUG. "I hope you keep up the good work," he continued, "until our People are free." Non-Arabs also expressed their support for the AAUG's position. Sibley Towner of Yale's Divinity School sent a donation and noted that "several of us here at Yale have been aware of your work, and are following it with interest!" Julia Fehler of Northport, New York, wrote simply: "Let's hope your ad helps improve a dreadful, shameful situation."[24]

Along with the letters of support came several critical ones. For example, Alberto Weinberg from New York City objected to the AAUG's use of the term *Palestinian Jews*. "Who authorized you to speak on their behalf, and which countries do you suggest be eliminated (and how) to make room for your proposed 'Palestinian State'?" he asked.[25] Other letters were unsigned and decidedly impolite. While it is perhaps tempting to dismiss these letters as the objections of a few, the terms in which their authors cast their vituperations are worth examining in greater detail, for they are permeated with Cold War concerns. One letter argued that the UN resolutions that the AAUG urged be respected had been passed by "the conniving of the Russians to take advantage of the Arabs and Jews." Moreover, "the Arabs gladly accept arms from anywhere (mainly, communist) and then yelp like dogs when Israel gets arms."[26] Other responses implicitly accused the AAUG of harboring pro-Soviet sympathies. "You hypocrites! Why don't you ask Rusia [sic] to stop shipping arms to the arabs [sic]?" wrote one angry reader. "Try to get this printed in Pravda," wrote another. Enclosed in the latter was a cartoon depicting a beleaguered and bandaged President Nasser accepting boxing gloves from a Soviet general. Inscribed on each glove were the words: "Made in USSR."[27]

Christian anticommunism was another theme in the negative responses to the AAUG advertisement. One letter from a self-described Christian argued that "the Great State of Israel is the only country in the Middle East that stands up to Russia and all that communism stands for. If you Arabs were against communism then it would be different. American [sic] will fight against any country that helps communism and will help any country that fights communism—so go back to your communist country and leave us alone." Finally, drawing on a long-standing homophobic strain in American perceptions of Arabs, one letter began: "Scum. . . . You are not students but paid propagandists. The world cannot respect people who are led by frauds like Hussein and sodomites like Nasser."[28]

These negative responses to the AAUG statement described the organization's effort to bring attention to Palestinian dispossession as a pro-Soviet ploy, deeply threatening to American values. They portrayed members of the association as foreign and told them to go back to some unnamed country to which, it was assumed, they had greater loyalties. These perceptions demonstrate how, as anthropologist Suad Joseph argues, Arabs in America are conceived "against the grain of the nation." There is an enduring representation of Arab as not quite free, not quite white, not quite male, not quite persons in the civil body of the nation. Arabs are thus seen as not quite citizens.[29] They are thought to be un-American because they originate from backward, undemocratic Muslim societies where an obdurate, unyielding religion makes them "un-free." It is worth emphasizing that while contemporary anti-Arab discourse casts Arabs as religious fanatics, likely to be sympathetic to jihadists, this earlier incarnation evident in the letters sent to the association in 1967 elided them with godless communists. The hostility directed at the AAUG did not deter members' efforts to organize and continue their outreach. In 1968, the membership increased by 500 percent.

COALITION BUILDING

By the early 1970s, the AAUG was the leading nonsectarian Arab American organization in the United States. It had pioneered the field of Arab American studies by publishing a series of pathbreaking works on different communities. Its journal, *Arab Studies Quarterly,* featured innovative scholarship on the history and politics of the Arab world, and its series of information papers offered cogent critiques of U.S. Middle Eastern policy at a time when such critiques were few and far between. The membership was active and dynamic. Several members were fast becoming prominent figures in contemporary Arab American thought. Before he became known as a founder of postcolonial studies, for example, Edward Said was vice president of the AAUG. Some of the arguments he developed in his book *Orientalism* were already apparent in his essay "Orientalism and the October War: The Shattered Myths." In this essay, published by the AAUG in 1975, two years after the 1973 Arab-Israeli war, Said identified key tropes used in the Western academic tradition of studying the "Arab people." The Arabs were, for example, represented as irrational, disorganized, overly sensual, and frozen in time. According to Said, "The October [1973] war was a surprise, not because the 'the Arabs' fought well, but because the Arabs were not supposed to fight at all. The war seemed therefore to be a deviation out of context, a violation of a well-established logic."[30]

With its success in reaching members of the Arab American community, the AAUG began to focus on forging alliances with other communities. In his 1972 presidential address, Abdeen Jabara highlighted the need to strengthen ties with "several segments of the American population who are our natural allies." Jabara identified "Black Americans, Chicanos, Oriental Americans, young people and civil libertarians," as natural allies because they had all "felt excluded from any meaningful participation in the American decision process."[31] The prospects for building relations with African Americans were especially promising. As Melani McAlister argues, the 1967 Arab-Israeli War and its aftermath caused black Americans to rethink their relationship to Israel and to the Middle East. A younger, more radical generation of black leaders challenged the long-standing tradition of support for Zionism within their communities. Edward Wilmont Blyden had initiated this tradition of support in 1898 when he described Zionism as "that marvelous movement." W. E. B. Du Bois had argued that "the African movement means to us what the Zionist movement means to the Jews." In 1948, he had written an impassioned defense of the Israeli state in his essay "The Case for the Jews," although he had tempered this support after the 1956 Suez War.[32] Martin Luther King Jr.'s support for Israel was unwavering. After the 1967 war, he gave a speech at the annual convention of the Rabbinical Assembly, where he stated: "I see Israel . . . as one of the great outposts of democracy in the world, and a marvelous example of what can be done, how desert land can be transformed into an oasis of brotherhood and democracy."[33]

But for African Americans who were increasingly drawn to the antiimperialist critiques and to the principles of revolutionary struggle, King's position ignored the violence and exercise of power over the Arab population of Palestine. The motifs of Exodus and delivery from bondage that were so closely tied to the history of the Jews and had served as powerful symbols for early civil rights leaders receded from the discourse of black liberation. Instead, more and more African Americans identified with the dispersion and oppression of the Palestinians and were inspired by the anticolonial movements in the Middle East and North Africa.[34] Decolonization and the struggle against U.S. racism became intrinsically linked. As the boxer Muhammad Ali put it after returning from a tour of the Middle East and Africa, "I am not an American; I'm a black man."[35]

New identifications brought alliances and ruptures. Jewish American and black American relations in particular began to fray over the issue of Israeli policy in the Middle East. Criticism of Israel by black activists caused friction in their relations with Jewish leaders. When, for example, the black caucus demanded a resolution condemning the "imperialist Zionist war" at the 1967 Conference on New Politics in Chicago, a number of Jewish participants walked out.[36] Compounding the problem was the tendency among some black radicals, particularly those associated with the Nation of Islam, to espouse anti-Semitic views.

While the events of 1967 produced tension in black-Jewish relations, it also engendered closer alliances, both real and rhetorical, between African Americans and Arab Americans. A turning point came in 1979 with the so-called "Andrew Young Affair." In July of that year, while serving as U.S. ambassador to the United Nations, Andrew Young met with Zehdi Labib Terzi, the Palestine Liberation Organization's observer at the United Nations. While Young maintained that the State Department knew about this meeting, he submitted his resignation after protests erupted that he had met with a representative of a terrorist organization and had thus violated Carter administration policy.[37] Black leaders expressed dismay at Young's resignation. Joseph Lowery and Walter E. Fauntroy of the Southern Christian Leadership Conference (SCLC) scheduled their own meeting with Terzi, although SCLC spokesman Richard Dunn was quick to note that "we're not taking sides with either party." The organization also scheduled a meeting with the Israeli ambassador.[38] There was considerable debate in the black press on the extent to which Young's resignation would damage black-Jewish relations. G. James Flemming, writing in the *Afro-American,* cautioned readers against assuming that Young had resigned because of pressure from Jewish American groups and Israeli politicians. Rather, he argued, Young had not accurately reported his face-to-face meeting with Terzi to the State Department and had therefore been reprimanded.[39] An unsigned editorial noted that black-Jewish relations had been in a state of uneasiness for some time and that on the question of the Arab-Israeli conflict Jewish leaders had been condescending and paternalistic toward black Americans. "It is as if Jewish leaders are saying that we do not have the intelligence to make up our minds on the issue, or should feel obligated to support them."[40] To be sure, black organizations had different positions on the Middle East, and their tension with Jewish Americans should not be exaggerated. However, there was a general feeling among them that the resignation of Andrew Young revealed the unwillingness of the U.S. and Israeli governments to accept black initiatives in resolving the conflict, particularly if they involved contact with Palestinian representatives. Moreover, as Roy Wilkins of the *Afro-American* argued, the loss of Young from the administration signaled the loss of someone whose leadership had made the United Nations and global affairs take on a fresh and dynamic dimension for the ordinary black citizen. "Those among the U.S. black population who were suspicious of circles of power dominated by whites," wrote Wilkins, "were, through Andy Young, linked with the struggle of African and Third World countries for a new world order."[41]

For members of the AAUG, the fallout from the Andrew Young affair was an opening. In a draft "Proposal for Black and Arab Dialogue in the United States," President Samih Farsoun wrote: "The Andrew Young Affair signaled and confirmed that the Black people and leadership and other minorities (especially the Latinos or Spanish speaking) in the United States are in sympathy with the cause of the Arab, and especially, the Palestinian people."[42] On the basis of this assessment, the AAUG pursued several strategies to increase communication and coordination with black Americans. These strategies were called the "Black America Project." For example, in 1979 the organization sponsored a fact-finding tour in the Middle East that included members of Jesse Jackson's Operation PUSH (People United to Serve Humanity). This tour, and Jackson's subsequent visit to Lebanon, the West Bank, and Israel, helped to refine his thinking on the problems in the region and their relationship to U.S. policy. In his speech at the annual PUSH convention held in 1980 in New Orleans, Jackson argued that "blacks have a vital interest in peace in the Middle East because in a hot war we will die first and in a cold war over oil, we will be unemployed and freeze first."[43] He reiterated PUSH's position that a solution to the Middle East conflict must involve Israeli security within internationally recognized borders as well as the recognition of the Palestinian rights to self-determination and a homeland. AAUG assistant director Penny Johnson attended the PUSH convention to staff the AAUG literature table and to report on its International Affairs Day. She noted that contacts between the two organizations had "so far not resulted in substantial organizational or programmatic links."[44] Still, these contacts were helping to produce alternative political imaginaries in which Arab and African Americans saw themselves as connected in struggle for a "new world order." By 1984 Jackson had a special representative to the Arab American community, Marisa Tamari. In her letter to the AAUG asking for assistance in identifying Arab Americans who would be interested in working with local and state Jackson campaign offices, Tamari wrote: "Our participation in this aspect of the campaign will serve to institutionalize the Arab American element in the Rainbow Coalition across the nation."[45] Arab Americans raised $700,000 for the Jackson campaign.

PROTECTING ARAB AMERICAN CIVIL RIGHTS

In addition to coalition-building efforts, members of the AAUG exposed the stereotypes of Arabs used in school textbooks and challenged the Nixon administration's plan to wiretap and deport Arab American activists.[46] Code named "Operation Boulder," the Nixon directives authorized investigations of individuals of Arabic-speaking origin, allegedly to determine their links to terrorist activities related to the Arab-Israeli conflict.[47] Many leaders of the Arab American community suspected that the real purpose of the directives was to intimidate members, particularly those associated with the Organization of Arab Students and the AAUG, from critiquing U.S. and Israeli policy. According to an Associated Press release dated May 22, 1974, the U.S. Justice Department admitted that it had used electronic devices to eavesdrop on U.S.-born Detroit lawyer and AAUG founding member Abdeen Jabara. Moreover, the Justice Department and FBI had handed over the surveillance to Jewish organizations.[48] During this period the AAUG became, according to Nadia Hijab, its future president, "the midwife to other Arab American organizations."[49]

Three other Arab American organizations formed that were explicitly activist and secular in orientation and that aimed to intervene in the domain of national politics, critique U.S. foreign policy, and combat discrimination against Arab Americans in the educational, media, and employment sectors. In 1972 the National Association of Arab Americans (NAAA) was formed as a political lobby group to advocate for Arab American interests in Washington. In 1980 former congressman James Abourezk founded the American-Arab Anti-Discrimination Committee (ADC) to defend the civil rights of Arab Americans. And in 1985 the Arab American Institute (AAI) was formed, headquartered in Washington, with the aim of encouraging Arab American mobilization in the political arena and of gathering demographic information on the community, principally through the census.[50]

In 1985 these organizations were galvanized into action by the murder of Alex Odeh, West Coast regional director of the ADC, who died as a result of injuries sustained by a bomb that exploded when he opened his Santa Ana office on October 11. Arab American and mainstream Jewish organizations, including B'nai B'rith and the American Jewish Congress, condemned the killing. The FBI released a statement saying that the Jewish Defense League, a small, militantly anti-Arab group based in New York, was the "possible responsible group." However, the group denied any involvement in the murder, and the crime was never officially solved.[51] This lack of resolution continued despite the sworn testimony given by Oliver B. Revell, executive assistant director of the FBI, that "the Alex Odeh murder is the highest priority investigation we have within our domestic terrorist program, and it will continue to be so until it is solved."[52] Revell's comments were made before the Subcommittee on Criminal Justice of the House Committee on the Judiciary. Held in 1986, the "Hearing on Ethnically Motivated Violence against Arab-Americans" consisted of statements from representatives of national Arab American and Muslim organizations, several members of Congress, two members of the American Jewish Committee, and Revell. John Conyers, chairman of the subcommittee, opened the hearings by stating that violence against Arab Americans had become a "national tragedy." Arab Americans were in a "zone of danger" he added, quoting from FBI director Judge Webster. The clearest example of this violence was the murder of Alex Odeh, but Conyers cited numerous other cases of bombings and death threats as evidence of this "zone of danger."[53]

A recurring theme in the testimonies given to the subcommittee was the call for government and public action to protect the civil rights of Arab Americans. The Arab witnesses also conveyed their conviction that they represented an aggrieved collective. As Arab Americans, they demanded fairness from the government, from the media, and from their fellow citizens. This assertion of Arab Americanness by leaders of the community and their organizations represented the interaction of political orientations of the new wave of Middle Eastern immigrants with the conceptions of ethnic and racial identity that had been shaped by older generations of immigrants and their children. Many members of the national Arab American organizations came from countries and educational systems where they had been reared on the tenets of post-1945 Arab nationalism, an ideology that stressed unity across the myriad (and in Arab nationalist rhetoric, "artificial") boundaries of the Middle East. This principle of broad solidarity continued to appeal to them, and it made practical sense in the context of anti-Arab racism in the United States.[54] Many descendents of earlier immigrants, who might have hitherto defined themselves primarily as Americans of Lebanese or Syrian origin, also embraced the term *Arab American* as a more meaningful collective identity, a common bond that transcended national, religious, and cultural differences and served as a basis for organization. Abdeen Jabara, for example, was the son of first-wave Lebanese immigrants. His mother, Mymonie, born in 1906 and the eldest of six children, arrived with her parents in the United States in 1909. The family settled on a farm in North Dakota that had been first homesteaded by her grandfather. Jabara's father, Sam, immigrated first to northern Michigan from the Bekaa Valley in Lebanon around 1910. He worked in a tannery, then a boardinghouse for workers from his village, and eventually opened a grocery business. The couple married in 1923 and settled in Mancelona, northern Michigan.

Though he remembered having been slightly embarrassed by his father's decision to speak Arabic to his sons in his grocery store, as a young college student Abdeen Jabara went twice to the Middle East to study Arabic. During this time he was drawn to civil rights work and used his legal training to found a local chapter of the Civil Rights Research

Council in Detroit, which sent lawyers to the American South to work on cases. Like other second-generation immigrants, the 1967 war caused him to direct his energy into organizing around Arab American concerns. "It was if someone opened a huge floodgate of anti-Arab sentiment in the media," he recalled.[55]

That these affirmations of Arab American identity were often articulated in the context of American Jewish increasing identification with the state Israel after 1967 is hardly surprising. Arthur Herzberg, writing in *Commentary* shortly after the Six-Day War, noted that the crisis had evoked "a sense of belonging to the worldwide Jewish people, of which Israel is the center."[56] Young American Jews volunteered to go to Israel to help with postwar reconstruction, and the United Jewish Appeal's Israel Emergency Fund raised $90 million in one week from U.S. donations.[57] For Jews involved in civil rights and New Left politics, the war was significant for slightly different reasons. Historian Matthew Frye Jacobson argues that 1967 "was a pivotal year in Jewish radical consciousness." Citing Paul Lauter, he adds that 1967 marked the moment that Israel "launched its quite successful effort to convert American-Jewish identity into Israeli nationalism."[58]

In this confluence of events, Arab Americans began to adopt what Ella Shohat (following Gayatri Spivak) calls "strategic essentialism": that is, an insistence on unity in an effort to gain a collective voice and mount an effective civil rights campaign to protect members of "communities of identification."[59] As other movements have done—Black Power and Queer Nation, for example—Arab Americans took the term *Arab* that had been used to defame them and conflate their diversity, and claimed it as a source of pride and a tool of resistance in the face of discrimination.[60] For some this was a profoundly ambivalent process, a painful coming to terms with the destructive power of American racism and a desire not to capitulate to it; for others it was a source of liberation, a coming into their own. These subtle differences are captured in the reflections of Arab American feminists.

ARAB AMERICAN FEMINISM

Leila Ahmed begins a chapter in her memoir with a quote from Zora Neale Hurston: "I remember the very day that I became colored."[61] Ahmed signals here her affinity with African Americans who experienced before her the sting of white racism (including within feminist organizations) and its need to conflate, confine, and control, yet also her discov-

ery in that marginalization of a basis for communication with other
people of color. Poet Lisa Majaj similarly writes of "the discrepancy between the facts of my life and the available categories of inclusion and
exclusion."[62] Her decision to embrace her Arabness is far more celebratory than Ahmed's: "I have grown weary of my silence and paranoia. . . .
I am tired of being afraid to speak who I am. . . . Until one day, retch-
ing, I spat out some unnamable substance. And I attempted to speak."[63]
Claiming her identity as an American, a Palestinian—both at once—
allowed her to "speak who I am."

Arab American feminists were at the forefront of the movement to forge
alliances with people of color outside the institutional framework of the
leading Arab American organizations. They challenged their invisibility in
minority discourses, which had ignored their history of experiencing racist
prejudice. Nada Elia, for example, writes that a student walked out of her
French class because he was not there "to learn Swahili" while others expressed dismay at having her correct their English because she was not a
native speaker of *their* language. She had been directed to the welfare lines
of various government offices and asked if she needed help understanding
the forms—her literacy and PhD clearly a surprise to her interlocutors. "All
of these experiences confirm to me that I am a woman of color," writes
Elia. "But I have not experienced sisterhood. To the dominant discourse,
I am the abject other, demonized without apology, I am 'the white sheep
of the family' someone people of color need not reach out to."[64]

Arab American feminists combined a sophisticated critique of patriarchy within their own communities with activism that challenged the
abuse of power by the state domestically and internationally. They
worked most often at the grassroots level to explore and explain the
specificities and complexities of the Arab American experience, which,
they argued, could not fit neatly into the paradigm of white ethnicity.
This disassociation from whiteness occurred at an experiential level and
was lived through identification with people of color, participation in
progressive antiracist politics, and the crafting of an Arab American minority discourse through poetry, literature, performance, and activism.
Arab American literature in particular "increasingly probes the ways in
which classification as 'white' serves not as a mode of inclusion but as a
form of erasure."[65] The disassociation from whiteness was also occurring at a more institutional level as leading Arab American organizations
began to argue for a separate category for Arabs on the U.S. Census. By
the early 1990s, activism in the Arab American community around questions of racial classification was no longer aimed at securing status as

white, as it had been earlier in the century, but at demonstrating the inadequacy of this designation, disavowing it, and in some cases identifying as black.

LOCATING ARABS ON THE CENSUS

In June of 1993, Helen Samhan, deputy director of the AAI and granddaughter of Salloum Mokarzel (editor of the *Syrian World*) testified before the House Subcommittee on Census, Statistics, and Postal Personnel on the inadequacy of federal methods for classifying Arabs and persons of Middle Eastern descent. According to Samhan, "When viewed in the present paradigm of racial options, immigrants from the Middle East are confused. Their reality resembles that of their recent fellow immigrants from Asia and Latin America—all recognized minorities—more than that of white Europeans who share their racial classification. Immigrants from the Middle East are from the Third World, from societies struggling with development, and yet they find themselves classified as if they were Irish, Italian or French."[66]

Samhan's testimony was part of a broader response by ethnic constituencies to the government's request for comment on the Office of Management and Budget's (OMB) Directive No. 15, "Race and Ethnic Standards for Federal Statistics and Administrative Reporting." The OMB issued the directive in 1977 to codify disparate practices for gathering survey data on race and ethnicity of the U.S. population. Throughout the 1980s and 1990s, the standards came under intense criticism for poorly reflecting the racial and ethnic diversity of the country and for requiring persons to select categories with which they did not identify. Mostafa Hefny, for example, a Detroit schoolteacher of Egyptian origin and a naturalized U.S. citizen, refused to designate himself as "white" on his employer's records, an action that resulted in reprimand and threats of dismissal. Hefny responded by suing the U.S. government over his (mis)classification. "I am a black man at five levels," he argued, "the biological, social, psychological, political and ideological,"[67] and "I would've had more opportunity for advancement and even for hiring had I been considered black. I was prevented from applying and requesting positions and other benefits for minority persons because I knew I was legally white."[68]

Hefny's main objection to the U.S. government's classification of Egyptians as white was that it robbed them of their African identity and, worse, gave others the justification to claim it. Echoing the sentiment of President Nasser and Malcolm X, Hefny argued that "classification as it is done . . .

provides Whites with legal ground to claim Egypt as a White civilization. . . . We are fools if we allow them to take this legacy from us."[69]
While Hefny lost his case, he found sympathetic listeners, including the editors of *Jet* magazine, which ran the story in the November 1990 issue with
the headline "Black 'White' Man Challenges Federal Race Identity Law."

The OMB responded to this dissatisfaction by soliciting public comment, holding hearings, and sponsoring a special workshop on the directive. The House Subcommittee on the Census held four public hearings and heard from twenty-seven witnesses, including Helen Samhan,
on the use of racial categories on the upcoming 2000 census. Samhan
proposed introducing a classification for Americans from the Middle
East on OMB Directive 15. She noted the irony that some arms of the
government—the INS and FBI in particular—did operate as though
Arabs and other Middle Eastern populations formed an identifiable
group to be tracked and monitored, yet the census operated under the fiction that they did not exist separately from white ethnics. In a multitude
of areas, including education, social work, health care, and immigration,
Middle Eastern populations shared the same needs as other recognized
immigrant minorities, yet, as Samhan noted, "There is no statistical
method to measure those needs."[70] She further argued that the lack of
adequate classification led to confusion in the compilation of data. In the
1988 National Education Longitudinal Survey, for example, teachers
listed Iranian, Afghan, Lebanese, and Turkish children as "Asians,"
along with Japanese, Chinese, and other recognizably Asian groups. The
result was that 15 percent of the "Asian" category on the survey consisted of children of Middle Eastern origin or descent. Introducing a new
category for Middle Easterners—based not on race but on region of
origin—she argued, would be consistent with the census's commitment
to refining its measurement criteria and could follow the models used to
categorize Hispanic Americans and Asian Americans.[71] Finally, broad-
ening the categories on the directive to include Middle Easterners would
establish a basis for collecting information on civil rights abuses and hate
crimes against them.

After considering the suggestions of the witnesses and conducting preliminary tests, the OMB revised the standards in a new directive in 1997
called "Standards for Maintaining, Collecting, and Presenting Federal
Data on Race and Ethnicity."[72] These standards defined the questions
for race and ethnicity on the 2000 census. The two most significant
changes were the expansion of the race categories to a minimum of five
(American Indian and Alaska Native, Asian, Black or African American,

Native Hawaiian or other Pacific Islander, and White) and allowing respondents to identify themselves as belonging to one or more races, a
provision advocated by parents in interracial marriages. The directive
contained two categories for data on ethnicity: "Hispanic or Latino" and
"not Hispanic or Latino."[73] Acknowledging the difficulty in defining race
(and leaving open the possibility that these definitions could change), the
OMB wrote in the preamble to the directive that "the categories in this
classification are social-political constructs and should not be interpreted
as being scientific or anthropological in nature."[74] Despite this caveat, the
OMB's reluctance to define race and distinguish it conceptually from ethnicity led to continued criticism, including from the American Anthropological Association, which urged phasing out the category altogether.[75]
Significantly, the directive continued to define as white "a person having
origins in any of the original peoples of Europe, the Middle East, or North
Africa."

The AAI's argument for a new category drew on some of the strategies used previously by other minority groups. The AAI argued, for example, that without adequate representation on the census the needs
of the Arab population would be underserved and the protection of its
civil rights would be undermined. In addition, like Mexican and black
organizations that had mobilized around the census, Arab American
organizations emphasized the problem of an Arab undercount. The
census statistics were one-third those provided by Arab American organizations.

As long as one parent had been born in an Arab country or spoke Arabic, the census could provide information on the size of the population
through questions on place of birth and mother tongue. But with successive generations born in the United States, the decline of Arabic as the
language of the household, and marriage outside the ethnic group, lo-
cating the population of Arab descent became more difficult. In 1980,
the Census Bureau introduced the ancestry question to remedy this problem and capture ethnic self-identification of the third generation and beyond. The new question replaced the parental birthplace question and
gathered data primarily on persons of European American descent, including those who on previous censuses would have been classified simply as "native-born white." The ancestry question was very important
for Arab American organizations because it was the only place on the
census where persons of Arab descent could officially identify themselves. Even here, though, there were problems. To be counted as an an-

cestry group by the census, that group had to meet a certain threshold.[76] This meant that the body of statistics on Arabs in the United States based on the ancestry question consisted mainly of Lebanese, who formed the largest national group within the population and on censuses up to 1950, where they were designated as "Syrian." Arabs from other countries who did not meet the threshold (the Yemenis, for example) were aggregated into a residual "other Arab" category. Moreover, the ancestry question was asked only on the long-form census schedule sent to roughly one-sixth of households.

Because of the limitations of the ancestry question and the fact that there was no way to account for Arab or Middle Eastern ethnicity within the OMB guidelines, the AAI began to focus on the need for a new category for "Middle Easterners" in federal statistics. Shortly thereafter, although it had not done much research on the census, the ADC formally submitted a proposal to the House Subcommittee on the Census urging the use of the category "Arab American." The AAI opposed this idea on grounds that it would yield smaller numbers and argued for a category that would both reflect ties and shared experiences within Middle Eastern communities and establish the largest possible protected class. Using a broad "Middle Eastern" category would allow researchers to break the data down into subsets (Lebanese, Egyptian, Iranian, for example), a task that would be harder to undertake with a smaller "Arab American" group. Because of these competing positions between the AAI and the ADC, the House committee decided that there was no consensus on the issue and put off researching the matter further.[77]

Moreover, while the AAI was drawing attention to the merits of a new category, it received word that the Census Bureau was considering abandoning the ancestry question, which despite its problems had certainly helped increase the visibility of Middle Eastern groups on the census. The news forced the AAI to focus its efforts on preserving the ancestry question and building coalitions with other ethnic groups who opposed its elimination. In this regard, the AAI and its sister organizations in the "Working Group on Preserving the Ancestry Question" were more successful, as census officials decided to keep the question on the 2000 census. The Census Bureau further recognized the work AAI had done around census issues and asked it to become a Census Information Center in 2000, a cooperative program between the bureau and fifty-two national, regional, and local nonprofit organizations. According to the Census Bureau, "This program represents the interest of underserved communities. The centers serve as repositories of census data and reports, making census information and data available to the public and the community they serve."[78]

TOWARD AN ARAB AMERICAN COLLECTIVE SUBJECTIVITY

The mobilization around the census reflected a wider debate on matters of race within Arab American organizations and a number of new developments related to community self-perception. The increased visibility of Arab Americans in the complicated landscape of race and ethnic politics represented what Omi and Winant call the "entrist" model of racial minority movements, a strategy calling for greater participation in existing political organizations and processes.[79] The AAI best typified this model with its argument that "Arab Americans are an ethnic constituency seeking political empowerment. . . . If we want this power, we must go through the process to get it."[80] In terms of the entrist model, the success of the AAI is quite remarkable, since the AAI has grown from a small organization whose members had their donations to political campaigns turned away and its endorsement of a candidate rejected to a nationally recognized lobby group whose annual convention in October 2003 featured speeches from all of the candidates for the Democratic nomination (except Al Sharpton) and a representative of President George W. Bush.[81] Senior political commentator David Broder of the *Washington Post* remarked that "what happened here [in Dearborn, Michigan] . . . was another chapter in one of the unnoticed glories of American life—the entry of yet another immigrant group into the mainstream of the nation's politics."[82]

The emergence of a vibrant Arab American movement also resembled a second pattern that Omi and Winant identify to describe changes in black organization: the rearticulation of collective subjectivity. Black political consciousness, they argue, developed a new vigor in the 1960s because of civil rights leaders' insistence on justice and equality and because of a cultural and ideological intervention, a rearticulation of what it meant to be black in America. This process of rearticulation "produces new subjectivity by making use of information and knowledge already present in the subject's mind. [Social movements] take elements and themes of her/his culture and traditions and infuse them with new meaning."[83]

Over the past two decades, the census has helped increase the visibility of Arab Americans. They have gone from a community whose ethnic identity was relegated to the private sphere to a recognized population whose diversity and growing numbers demand the attention of government statisticians, academics, and community organizers. In December 2003, the Census Bureau released its first ever "Report on Arab Population," thus ending a long period of Arab exclusion from government publications on racial and ethnic groups. The report estimated the Arab population at 1.2 million (considerably less than community estimates of 3.5 million) and provided information on its geographic distribution and considerable growth (38 percent) since the 1990 census.[84] Several Arab American organizations applauded the report, issued as it was at a time when the effects of the post- 9/11 backlash and the invasion of Iraq were still being felt.[85]

Some of the most interesting findings, tucked at the back of the report, concern responses to the race question. Eighty percent of Arabs reported their race as white and no other race, while 17 percent identified as white and another race. Small proportions identified another single race, including 1.1 percent black, and 3.2 percent Hispanic (of any race). Thus, while the Census Bureau reports that the "vast majority" of Arabs identify as white using the census criteria, a considerable portion of the population—one in five—does not see itself as white or exclusively so. A detailed study of the Detroit Arab and Chaldean population conducted by researchers from the University of Michigan found a similar pattern. Nearly two-thirds of respondents identified as "white," while another third identified as "other." While the census provides no figures on religion, the Detroit Arab American Study found that the percentage of those identifying as white was higher among Christians (73 percent) than Muslims (50 percent).[86]

That Muslims were less likely to identify as white is an important development in the post-1945 history of Arab racialization in the United States. In Joan Mandel's engaging documentary film *Tales from Arab Detroit* (1995) a scene shot at a park with two young Arab American women captures this development. The two women begin to discuss issues of identity. One of them describes, in a characteristically midwestern accent, how the school they attend is predominantly Arab although there are some "white people" in it also. To this mention of the "white" minority population at their school, her friend adds as either correction or amplification the term *non-Arab*.

There is also a religious level to their assertion of difference. The two women in the film wear the *hijab* (headscarf) as Muslim/Arab Americans and understand their nonwhiteness as the result of how these categories come together. As in Middle Eastern countries, American Islam in the

1990s was characterized by a heightened religiosity, expressed in increased mosque attendance, participation in Muslim voluntary associations, and the wearing of modest Muslim dress, particularly by young women. While there are obvious and important links between Islamic trends in the Middle East and the United States, it would be a mistake to view the U.S. developments as simply a reflection or appropriation of Middle Eastern constructions of Islam. Changes in the racial identification of American Muslims are rooted in specific American realities, including the growing number of African American converts to Islam, coalition building in response to crisis, and the construction of Islam as a discourse of resistance.[87]

The new affirmation of Arab Muslim (and nonwhite) identity in the United States shares some of the logic of the Black Power movement that decried "passing" as an act of betrayal, a form of collusion with white racism. In a similar vein, the "honorary white" status conferred on Arabs all too often involved their incorporation into broader categories that erased Muslim identity. In the realm of naturalization law, for example, Muslim whiteness was never as stable as Christian Arab whiteness.

The emphasis on "racial equality" in the post-1945 period did not change the more provisional status of Muslim Arab whiteness. Their "not-quite-white" status would become increasingly apparent with the rise in discrimination, hate crimes, and stereotyping. The conflation of Muslim/Arab/Other that lay at the heart of this stereotype was linked to a complex set of factors, including the profusion of anti-Arab imagery in the media in the wake of the 1967 Arab-Israeli war, resentment toward the oil-rich Arab Gulf states, and the concern over Islamic fundamentalism. As Nadine Naber argues, throughout this period film and media used Islam as a device to racialize Arabs as distinct from and inferior to white Americans. The popular films *Not without My Daughter* (set in Iran, not the Arab world) and *Protocol,* for example, repeatedly show Muslim men as corrupt and barbaric—men who refer to their Muslim identity as they enact violence upon women. "Arab Americans," Naber notes, "become racially marked on the assumption that all Arabs are Muslim and that Islam is a cruel, backward and uncivilized religion."[88] Arab Americans are thus racialized primarily through religion rather than by phenotype.

By the 1990s, there had emerged within Arab Muslim communities a movement to counter the vilification of Islam in the United States through education, outreach, and legal campaigns, a program of action made more urgent by the U.S. involvement in the Gulf War and the proliferation of anti-Arab discourse that accompanied it. This movement challenged the racial marking of Muslims as unfree, uncivilized, and cruel and promoted the compatibility of Islam and modernity. In the process, many Arabs—Muslim and non-Muslim—disassociated from whiteness and found affirmation and common ground in identifying as people of color. The race designations that they made on the U.S. Census revealed this disassociation and demonstrated the multiple ways that persons of Arab origin defined their racial and ethnic identity.

Writing on the census in India, anthropologist Bernard Cohn argued that through the asking of questions the British rulers compiled information in categories that they used for the purpose of governing but that the census also "provided an arena for Indians to ask question about themselves."[89] The U.S. Census has allowed Arabs to "ask questions about themselves," specifically around issues of race and ethnicity. The answers to these questions are varied, a phenomenon that can often be seen in the confines of one family, not unlike the splits that occurred in Mexican American families in the sixties, with radicalized children identifying as Chicano/a.[90] In the Coury family of Cleveland, for example, Joseph Coury refers to himself as Lebanese American, while his cousin Rebecca prefers the term *Arab American* because it is more "politically powerful." Her uncle David simply refers to himself as "white."[91]

Indeed, there is still considerable resistance among persons of Arabic-speaking origin to the term *Arab American*. When the AAI was gathering information to compute the size of the Arab American community, it received a barrage of protests from Lebanese Christians and Iraqi Chaldeans who objected to being included in the category "Arab." At the 2006 Southern Federation of Syrian Lebanese American Clubs in San Antonio, Texas, the assertion that the Lebanese are not Arabs was again apparent after the convention chairman gave a cultural presentation on the "Phoenician Discovery of America." In the question-and-answer session that followed, a Lebanese American audience member argued that it is crucial for Lebanese to distinguish themselves from Arabs who "have been co-opting Lebanese achievements and claiming them as their own."[92] The federation is made up of clubs whose members are Christian (predominantly Catholic and Orthodox) and who tend not to identify with the category "Arab" because it is closely associated with Islam in the United States. Moreover, many club members (which often include grandparents, parents, and their children) are very conscious and intensely proud of the role the federation has played in fostering a sense of belonging to a Syrian (and later Lebanese), not Arab, community.

Despite these variations it is significant that on the most recent 2000 census a larger number of Arab Americans (205,822, or one in six) identified themselves of being of Arab or Arabic descent on the ancestry question rather than identifying themselves by country of origin.[93] This suggests a trend toward a pan-ethnic Arab identity or, as I have argued above, a new collective subjectivity. Unlike the dominant historical pattern of other immigrant groups (the Irish, Italians, and Jews), significant segments of the Arab American community resist integration into whiteness and continue to designate themselves, on the census and in their everyday lives, as nonwhites. However, because of the way the Census Bureau has put the data to work (in this case by releasing detailed statistics on the Arab population, but no other ethnic group, to the Department of Homeland Security), new fears have emerged.[94] These fears are connected to the way the government is keeping track of Arab and Muslim immigrants in the post-9/11 climate. The "Special Registration" system, for example, "creates a vast, new legal geography of suspicion for the United States government [and] draws a burdensome zone around Muslim-majority countries."[95] These policies evoke earlier historical moments when geography racialized Syrian immigrants. Unlike earlier patterns, however, the response of many Arab Americans, including the descendants of first-wave Syrian immigrants, is to embrace their inbetweenness rather than to resist it.

Notes

The following are abbreviations used in the notes:

AAUG Records   Association of Arab American University Graduates, Records, Eastern Michigan University, Ypsilanti

IHRC   Immigration History Research Center, University of Minnesota

MAE   Ministère des affaires étrangères, Paris

NAAC   Faris and Yamna Naff Arab-American Collection, Archives Center, National Museum of American History, Smithsonian Institution, Washington, DC

SAF   State Archives of Florida, Tallahassee

SAAC   Syrian-American Archival Collection, Center for Migration Studies, Staten Island, NY

INTRODUCTION

The chapter's epigraph is taken from *In re Halladjian*, 174 Fed. 838 (1909).

1. This was section 2169 of the *Revised Statutes* (1878). The first naturalization law, passed in 1790, provided that to be naturalized an alien must be "a free white person." After the adoption of the Fourteenth Amendment, the act of 1870 extended naturalization "to aliens of African nativity and to persons of African descent." See Luella Gettys, *The Law of Citizenship in the United States* (Chicago: University of Chicago Press, 1934), 70; U.S. House, *Citizenship of the United States, Expatriation, and Protection Abroad*, Report by the Secretary of State to the Committee on Foreign Affairs, 59th Cong., 2nd sess., 1906, H. Doc. 326, 98–99.

2. Costa Najour to Adele Younis (in Arabic), January 1961, SAAC, Gr. II, Series C, folder 203.

3. Ian F. Haney López, *White by Law: The Legal Construction of Race* (New York: New York University Press, 1996), 2.

4. A. H. Keane, *Ethnology* (Cambridge: Cambridge University Press, 1909), 222.

5. Haney López, *White by Law*.

6. "Notes and Comments by the Editor," *Syrian World* 2 (February 1928): 41.

7. On whiteness as performance, see Ariela J. Gross, "Litigating Whiteness: Trials of Racial Determination in the Nineteenth-Century South," *Yale Law Journal* 108 (October 1998): 109–88; John Tehranian, "Performing Whiteness: Naturalization Litigation and the Construction of Racial Identity in America," *Yale Law Journal* 109 (January 2000): 817–48.

8. On this point, see Lisa Suhair Majaj, "Arab-Americans and the Meanings of Race," in *Postcolonial Theory and the United States: Race, Ethnicity, and Literature*, ed. Amritjit Singh and Peter Schmidt (Jackson: University of Mississippi Press, 2000), 323.

9. *New York Times,* October 15, 1909, 10.

10. On the concept of inbetweenness, see David Roediger (with James Barrett), "Inbetween Peoples: Race, Nationality, and the 'New-Immigrant' Working Class," ch. 9 in *Colored White: Transcending the Racial Past,* by David Roediger (Berkeley: University of California Press, 2002).

11. John Higham, *Strangers in the Land: Patterns of American Nativism, 1860–1925* (New York: Atheneum, 1969), 165.

12. Jusserand to Poincaré, "Intervention en faveur des Syriens menacés par les 'Ku Klux,'" January 3, 1923, Levant, 1918–1940, Syrie-Liban, 1918–1929, vol. 407, MAE, 39–40.

13. Roediger and Barrett, "Inbetween Peoples," 141.

14. "Notes and Comments," 41.

15. See Thomas C. Holt, *The Problem of Race in the Twenty-First Century* (Cambridge, MA: Harvard University Press, 2000), 53; Howard Winant, *Racial Conditions: Politics, Theory, Comparisons* (Minneapolis: University of Minnesota Press, 1994), 59; Rohit Barot and John Bird, "Racialization: The Genealogy and Critique of a Concept," *Ethnic and Racial Studies* 24 (July 2001): 601–18. A related concept is that of racial formation, which Michael Omi and Howard Winant define "as the sociohistorical process by which racial categories are created, inhabited, transformed, and destroyed." Michael Omi and Howard Winant, *Racial Formation in the United States: From the 1960s to the 1990s,* 2nd ed. (New York: Routledge, 1994), 55.

16. Cheryl I. Harris, "Whiteness as Property," *Harvard Law Review* 106 (June 1993): 1707–91.

17. Winthrop Jordan, *White over Black: American Attitudes toward the Negro, 1550–1812* (New York: W. W. Norton, 1977).

18. On whiteness as a "psychological wage," see W. E. B. Du Bois, *Black Reconstruction in America: An Essay toward a History of the Part Which Black Folk Played in the Attempt to Reconstruct Democracy in America, 1860–1880* (New York: World Publishing, 1964), 700. The literature on the construction of whiteness

is very extensive. Among the works I have found most useful for this project are David Roediger, *The Wages of Whiteness: Race and the Making of the American Working Class* (London: Verso, 1991); Noel Ignatiev, *How the Irish Became White* (New York: Routledge, 1995); Matthew Frye Jacobson, *Whiteness of a Different Color: European Immigrants and the Alchemy of Race* (Cambridge, MA: Harvard University Press, 1998); Karen Brodkin, *How Jews Became White Folks and What That Says about Race in America* (New Brunswick: Rutgers University Press, 1998); Shelley Fisher Fishkin, "Interrogating 'Whiteness,' Complicating 'Blackness': Remapping American Culture," *American Quarterly* 47 (September 1995): 428–66; George Lipsitz, *The Possessive Investment in Whiteness: How White People Profit from Identity Politics* (Philadelphia: Temple University Press, 1998).

19. Lipsitz, *Possessive Investment in Whiteness*, 1.

20. Roediger, *Colored White*, 23; see also Harris, "Whiteness as Property."

21. *World's Fairs Photographs, 1893* (Chicago: H. W. Hine, 1894), 1.

22. *New York Daily Tribune*, October 2, 1892, 23.

23. Ibid.

24. On the Italians, see Robert Orsi, "The Religious Boundaries of Inbetween People: Street *Feste* and the Problem of the Dark-Skinned Other in Italian Harlem, 1920–1990," *American Quarterly* 44 (September 1992): 314.

25. Marilyn Rashid, "What's Not in a Name," in *Food for Our Grandmothers: Writings by Arab-American and Arab-Canadian Feminists*, ed. Joanna Kadi (Boston: South End Press, 1994), 202.

26. M. C. Bassiouni, ed., *The Civil Rights of Arab Americans: The Special Measures*, AAUG Information Paper No. 10 (Belmont, MA: Association of Arab-American University Graduates, 1974); Mary Ann Fay, "Old Roots—New Soil," in *Taking Root, Bearing Fruit: The Arab-American Experience*, ed. James Zogby (Washington, DC: American-Arab Anti-Discrimination Committee, 1984), 21; American-Arab Anti-Discrimination Committee, New Jersey, "On-line Thesaurus Removes Derogatory Listings for 'Arab,' " press release, August 25, 2006, www.adc.org/Doc/ADC_NJ.doc.

27. Jack G. Shaheen, *Reel Bad Arabs: How Hollywood Vilifies a People* (New York: Olive Branch Press, 2001).

28. I borrow the phrase "tactical appeal to sameness" from Nabeel Abraham and Andrew Shryock's introduction to *Arab Detroit: From Margin to Mainstream*, ed. Nabeel Abraham and Andrew Shryock (Detroit: Wayne State University Press, 2000), 40.

29. Ayad al-Qazzaz, "Images of the Arab in American Social Science Textbooks," in *Arabs in America: Myths and Realities*, ed. Baha Abu-Laban and Faith Zeadey, AAUG Monograph Series no. 5 (Wilmette, IL: Medina University Press International, 1975), 113–32; Fay, "Old Roots," 21; Michael Suleiman, *The Arabs in the Mind of America* (Brattleboro, VT: Amana Press, 1988).

30. Leila Ahmed, "Western Ethnocentrism and Perceptions of the Harem," *Feminist Studies* 8 (Fall 1982): 527.

31. Alixa Naff, *Becoming American: The Early Arab Immigrant Experience* (Carbondale: Southern Illinois Press, 1985), 259. Philip and Joseph Kayal devote two paragraphs to the naturalization cases and attribute the debates over Syrian racial identity to "the general anti-immigrant climate prevalent in the country at

the time." While noting that "legally and politically the question was important," they minimize the participation of Syrians in the debates and add that "socially, the Syrian Christians—often blond and blue-eyed—were not particularly handicapped." See Philip Kayal and Joseph Kayal, *The Syrian-Lebanese in America: A Study in Religion and Assimilation* (Boston: Twayne, 1975), 74. Helen Hatab Samhan, in one of the few studies that problematizes the racial classification of Arabs as "white," concurs with Naff by arguing that "this 'yellow race' crisis, while the most intensely discriminatory experience of the early Arab immigrants, did not have a very penetrating effect on their identity nor on their civic assimilation." See Helen Hatab Samhan, "Not Quite White: Racial Classification and the Arab-American Experience," in *Arabs in America: Building a New Future,* ed. Michael Suleiman (Philadelphia: Temple University Press, 1999), 217.

32. Samhan, "Not-Quite-White"; Therese Saliba, "Resisting Invisibility: Arab Americans in Academia and Activism," in Suleiman, *Arabs in America,* 304–19; Joseph Massad, "Palestinians and the Limits of Racialized Discourse," *Social Text* 11, no. 1 (1993): 94–114.

33. On the rise in hate crimes directed at Arab Muslims, see Kathleen M. Moore, *Al-Mughtaribun: American Law and the Transformation of Muslim Life in the United States* (Albany: State University of New York Press, 1995), ch. 5; Nabeel Abraham, "Anti-Arab Racism and Violence in the United States," in *The Development of Arab-American Identity,* ed. Ernest McCarus (Ann Arbor: University of Michigan Press, 1997), 155–214. On Iraq, see Anne Norton, "Gender, Sexuality and the Iraq of Our Imagination," *Middle East Report,* no. 173 (November/December 1991): 26–28.

34. Holt, *Problem of Race,* 20.

35. Naff, *Becoming American,* 259; Michael W. Suleiman, introduction to *Arabs in America,* 7.

36. Leila Fawaz, *An Occasion for War: Civil Conflict in Lebanon and Damascus in 1860* (Berkeley: University of California Press, 1994), xiv.

37. Ibid., 13.

38. Najib Saliba, *Emigration from Syria and the Syrian-Lebanese Community of Worcester, MA* (Ligonier, PA: Antakya Press, 1992), 1.

39. Ibid., 8; Akram Khater, *Inventing Home, Emigration, Gender and the Middle Class in Lebanon, 1870–1920* (Berkeley: University of California Press, 2001), 14.

40. Naff, *Becoming American,* 330.

41. Alixa Naff, "Arabs in America: A Historical Overview," in *Arabs in the New World: Studies on Arab-American Communities,* ed. Sameer Abraham and Nabeel Abraham (Detroit: Wayne State University, Center for Urban Studies, 1983), 23.

42. On ethnicization, see Kathleen Neils Conzen et al., "The Invention of Ethnicity: A Perspective from the U.S.A.," *Studi emigrazione* 29 (March 1992): 9.

43. See George Sánchez's definition of *ethnicity* in *Becoming Mexican American: Ethnicity, Culture and Identity in Chicano Los Angeles, 1900–1945* (New York: Oxford University Press, 1993), 11.

44. The Arabic word *mahjar* is the noun of place derived from the verb *hajara,* "to emigrate." *Al-mahjar* is the "place of emigration" and in modern usage

connotes diaspora. Albert Hourani noted the importance of European secular education in the thought of Arabists like Négib Azoury. See *Arabic Thought in the Liberal Age, 1798–1939* (1962; repr., Cambridge: Cambridge University Press, 1983), 277–78. See also Bassam Tibi's discussion of Antun Saʿada in *Arab Nationalism: A Critical Enquiry*, trans. Marion Farouk Sluglett and Peter Sluglett (New York: St. Martin's Press, 1971), 165–70; and Kais M. Firro, *Inventing Lebanon: Nationalism and the State under the Mandate* (London: I. B. Tauris, 2003), 18.

45. E. J. Hobsbawm, *The Age of Empire, 1875–1914* (New York: Pantheon Books, 1987), ch. 6, and *Nations and Nationalism since 1780: Programme, Myth, Reality*, 2nd ed. (Cambridge: Cambridge University Press, 1992), 109; Homi K. Bhabha, "DissemiNation: Time, Narrative, and the Margins of the Modern Nation," in *Nation and Narration*, ed. Homi K. Bhabha (London: Routledge, 1990), 315–19.

46. Donna R. Gabaccia, Dirk Hoerder, and Adam Walaszek, "Emigration and Nation-Building during the Mass Migrations from Europe," paper presented at the Association for European Historians, Brisbane, Australia, July 2003. My thanks to Donna Gabaccia for sharing this paper with me.

47. Ibid., 9–11.

48. Hobsbawm, *Age of Empire*, 154; Alejandro Portes, Luis E. Guarnizo, and Patricia Landolt, "The Study of Transnationalism: Pitfalls and Promise of an Emergent Field," *Ethnic and Racial Studies* 22 (March 1999): 226.

49. Khayr al-Din al-Zirikli, *Al-Aʿlam* (Beirut: Dar al-ʿilm lil-malayin, 1995), 3:30 and 6:126. The Ottoman Administrative Decentralization Party was founded in Cairo (a city known for its relative openness and distance from the Ottoman censors) in 1913. Rafiq al-ʿAzm, member of a leading family of Syrian urban notables, was the party president. Rashid Rida, better known for his association with Islamic modernist Muhammad ʿAbduh, was an avid supporter, as was al-Zahrawi, who represented the Decentralization Party at the Arab Congress in Paris in 1913.

50. Hobsbawm describes this as an alternative to territorially based nationality modeled after the French example. Instead, in the "human" theory of the nation, nationality inhered "in the members of such bodies of men and women as considered themselves to belong to a nationality, wherever they happened to live." See *Age of Empire*, 148.

51. This is Matthew Frye Jacobson's term in *Special Sorrows: The Diasporic Imagination of Irish, Polish, and Jewish Immigrants in the United States* (Cambridge, MA: Harvard University Press, 1995), 2. See also a much earlier argument against strictly geographic notions of community in Virginia Yans-McLaughlin, *Family and Community: Italian Immigrants in Buffalo, 1880–1930* (Ithaca: Cornell University Press, 1971), 264. She writes of Italian immigrants that "community was not a place but a spiritual, emotional or blood tie."

52. Kohei Hashimoto, "Lebanese Population Movement 1920–1939: Towards a Study," in *The Lebanese in the World: A Century of Emigration*, ed. Albert Hourani and Nadim Shehadi (London: Centre for Lebanese Studies, 1992), 65.

53. On this point, see Abdelmalek Sayad, *L'immigration ou les paradoxes de l'altérité* (Paris: Éditions universitaires, 1991), 14; Laurie A. Brand, *Citizens*

Abroad: Emigration and the State in the Middle East and North Africa (Cambridge: Cambridge University Press, 2006).

54. On the concept of transnationality, see Shelley Fisher Fishkin, "Crossroads of Cultures: The Transnational Turn in American Studies. Presidential Address to the American Studies Association, Nov. 12, 2004," *American Quarterly* 57 (March 2005): 17–57.

55. Papers of Ahmed Gazal Masud, loaned to author.

56. Letters dated November 29, 1900, and December 1, 1902, respectively, translated from Arabic and excerpted in Afif I. Tannous, "Emigration, a Force of Social Change in an Arab Village," *Rural Sociology* 7, no. 1 (1942): 68.

57. On this point, see Roger Owen, "Lebanese Migration in the Context of World Population Movements," in Hourani and Shehadi, *Lebanese in the World,* 33.

1. FROM INTERNAL TO INTERNATIONAL MIGRATION

1. Phillip K. Hitti, *The Syrians in America* (New York: George Doran, 1924), 56; Kayal and Kayal, *Syrian-Lebanese in America,* 61.

2. El Emir Talal Majid Arslan, "A Word from the Ministry of Emigrants," www.emigrants.gov.lb/opn_ltr.htm, March 9, 1999 (italics added; no longer available online).

3. See, for example, Hitti, *Syrians in America,* 56, and Samir Khalaf's description of this trend in the literature in "The Background and Causes of Lebanese/Syrian Immigration to the United States before World War I," in Hooglund, *Crossing the Waters,* 17.

4. Georges Moanack, "Les libanais de Colombie," paper presented to Cercle Catholique, Beirut, June 1, 1943, Institut français d'études arabes de Damas, 12.

5. José Moya, *Cousins and Strangers: Spanish Immigrants to Buenos Aires, 1850–1930* (Berkeley: University of California Press, 1998), 95.

6. The emphasis on Egypt's pharaonic character gathered support with the excavations carried out after Napoleon's invasion in 1798. See Adid Dawisha, *Arab Nationalism in the Twentieth Century* (Princeton: Princeton University Press, 2003), 98.

7. Exploration in Palestine, with the aim of finding evidence that could authenticate the Bible, was the mainstay of European archeological interest in the area, but philologists like Ernest Renan were drawn to the inscriptions of Phoenicia and were thus, more accurately, engaged in epigraphy, not archeology. See Naomi Shepherd, *The Zealous Intruders: The Western Rediscovery of Palestine* (San Francisco: Harper and Row, 1987), 73–106 and 195.

8. To be sure, the idea that Lebanon possessed a unique national character was already popular in select Maronite circles before World War I and was articulated best in *La question du Liban,* by Bulus Nujaym (a.k.a. M. Jouplain), published in 1908. As Buheiry notes, however, Nujaym did not, at this point, advocate separation from Syria but envisioned Lebanon as playing a vanguard role in the unification of the Syrian nation. Nujaym favored a European analogy: the Lebanese would be "les Piémontais de la Syrie." It was only after World War I in 1919 that Nujaym came out in support of a separate, independent "Grand

Liban." See Marwan Buheiry, "Bulus Nujaym and the Grand Liban Ideal, 1908–1919," in *Intellectual Life in the Arab East, 1890–1939*, ed. Marwan R. Buheiry (Beirut: American University of Beirut, 1981), 62–83.

9. Kamal Salibi, *A House of Many Mansions: The History of Lebanon Reconsidered* (Berkeley: University of California Press, 1988), 172.

10. Michelle Hartman and Alessandro Olsaretti, " 'The First Boat and the First Oar': Inventions of Lebanon in the Writings of Michel Chiha," *Radical History Review* 86 (Spring 2003): 37–65.

11. Salibi, *House of Many Mansions*, 178.

12. Salloum Mokarzel, "History of the Syrians in New York," *Syrian World* 11 (November 1927): 3.

13. On "Mayflowerism," see Rudolph Vecoli, "Problems in Comparative Studies of International Emigrant Communities," in Hourani and Shehadi, *Lebanese in the World*, 721.

14. In "Asl al-hunud wal-ʿarab fi amirka" [The Origin of the Indians and Arabs in America], *al-Hilal* 9, no. 19 (1901): 536–41. Shukri Abu Shaʿr sent an article to *al-Hilal* from Colombia, South America, arguing that the Phoenician imprint was evident in the indigenous American languages. Shukri Abu Shaʿr, "Al-Finiqiyyun wa iktishaf amirka" [The Phoenicians and the Discovery of America], *al-Hilal* 16, no. 9 (1908): 545–48.

15. Personal observation, July 3, 2006, San Antonio, TX.

16. See Leslie Page Moch, *Moving Europeans: Migration in Western Europe since 1650* (Bloomington: Indiana University Press, 1992).

17. Amnon Cohen, "The Receding of the Christian Presence in the Holy Land: A 19th Century Sijill in the Light of 16th Century Tahrirs," in *The Syrian Land in the 18th and 19th Century: The Common and the Specific in the Historical Experience*, ed. Thomas Philipp, Berliner Islamstudien 5 (Stuttgart: Franz Steiner, 1992), 337; Bruce McGowan, "The Age of the Ayans, 1699–1812," in *An Economic and Social History of the Ottoman Empire, 1300–1914*, ed. Halil Inalcik and Donald Quataert (Cambridge: Cambridge University Press, 1994), 647; Zafer Kassimy, "Les mouvements migratoires au départ et à destination de la Syrie," in *Les migrations internationales de la fin du xviiie siècle à nos jours* (Paris: Centre national de la recherche scientifique, 1980), 248.

18. Ismailis are a Shiʿa minority within the Islamic tradition. Norman N. Lewis, *Nomads and Settlers in Syria and Jordan, 1800–1980* (Cambridge: Cambridge University Press, 1987), 61.

19. For a detailed explanation of the decree, see Kemal H. Karpat, *Ottoman Population, 1830–1914* (Madison: University of Wisconsin Press, 1985), 62, and "Ottoman Immigration Policies and Settlement in Palestine," in *Settler Regimes in Africa and the Arab World*, ed. Ibrahim Abu-Lughod and Baha Abu-Laban (Wilmette, IL: Medina University Press International, 1974), 58–62.

20. Karpat, "Ottoman Immigration Policies," 62.

21. Quoted in ibid., 63, 62.

22. An anonymous eyewitness account (possibly by Shahin Makarius) cited 6,000 in Damascus, 12,000 in Lebanon (Hasbayya, Rashayya, Dayr al-Qamar, etc.), and over 150,000 persons displaced. See *Hasr al-litham ʿan nakabat al-Sham* [Unveiling the Calamities of Syria] (Cairo, 1895), 234–35. See also Noël

Verney and George Dambmann, *Les puissances étrangères dans le Levant en Syrie et en Palestine* (Paris: Librairie Guillaumin, 1900), 72.

23. Fawaz, *Occasion for War*. The persecution thesis is still very much part of the official Maronite discourse around migration. When I interviewed the Maronite Patriarch Nasrallah Butros Sfeir in Lebanon in 2004, he began his explanation of the causes of Lebanese migration with a reference to the massacres of 1860. Nasrallah Butros Sfeir, interview, June 14, 2004, Bkerke, Lebanon.

24. Leila Fawaz, *Merchants and Migrants in Nineteenth Century Beirut* (Cambridge, MA: Harvard University Press, 1983), 56, and *Occasion for War*, 168.

25. Fawaz, *Occasion for War*, 75.

26. Linda Schatkowski Schilcher, "The Hauran Conflicts of the 1860s: A Chapter in the Rural History of Modern Syria," *International Journal of Middle East Studies* 13 (1981): 161; Muhammad Kurd ʿAli, *Khitat al-Sham*, 3rd ed. (Beirut: Muʾassasat al-aʿlami lil-matbuʿat, 1983), 3:101–3; Norman Lewis, "The Frontier of Settlement, 1800–1914," reprinted in *Economic History of the Middle East, 1800–1914: A Book of Readings*, ed. Charles Issawi (Chicago: University of Chicago Press, 1966), 261; Jean-Paul Pascual, "La Syria à l'époque ottomane," in *La Syrie d'aujourd'hui*, ed. André Raymond (Paris: CERMOC, 1980), 45.

27. Fawaz, *Merchants and Migrants*, 31.

28. Charles Issawi, "The Historical Background of Lebanese Emigration," in Hourani and Shehadi, *Lebanese in the World*, 23. Stanford Shaw's study of the Ottoman census shows that the province of "Suriyya" (which did not include Mount Lebanon) also had a high rate of growth, particularly between the years 1885 and 1897, when the population went from 400,748 to 701,134 persons. See his "Ottoman Census System, 1831–1914," *International Journal of Middle East Studies* 9 (1978): 338. This period (1878–95) was marked by a concerted effort on the part of the Ottoman government to improve its census-taking system. See Kemal Karpat, "Ottoman Population Records and the Census of 1881/82–1893," *International Journal of Middle East Studies* 9 (1978): 237–74.

29. Louis Charles Lortet, *La Syrie d'aujourd'hui: Voyages dans la Phénicie, le Liban et la Judée, 1875–1880* (Paris: Librairie Hachette, 1884), 47.

30. "Une émigration constante des contrées voisines vient donc sans cesse augmenter l'importance de la ville." Ibid., 66.

31. A concession to build the Beirut-Damascus road was given by the Ottoman government to a French entrepreneur named Compte Edmond de Perthius. Construction of the road began in 1857 and was finished in 1863. See Fawaz, *Merchants and Migrants*, 68.

32. Leila Fawaz, "The Beirut-Damascus Road: Connecting the Syrian Coast to the Interior in the 19th Century," in *The Syrian Land: Processes of Integration and Fragmentation*, ed. Thomas Philipp and Birgit Shaebler, Berliner Islamstudien 6 (Stuttgart: Steiner, 1998), 26.

33. Justin McCarthy, *Death and Exile: The Ethnic Cleansing of Ottoman Muslims* (Princeton, NJ: Darwin Press, 1995); Lewis, "Frontier of Settlement."

34. Estimates on the number of Caucasian emigrants vary. Undercounts in the Russian census, for example, and the high mortality rate of peoples dislocated in war make for statistical difficulties. For a brief discussion of the problem, see

McCarthy, *Death and Exile*, 54 n. 45, and Ehud Toledano, *The Ottoman Slave Trade and Its Suppression, 1840–1890* (Princeton: Princeton University Press, 1982), 150.

35. Toledano, *Ottoman Slave Trade*, 150.

36. McCarthy, *Death and Exile*, 36; Marc Pinson, "Ottoman Colonization of the Circassians in Rumili after the Crimean War," *Études balkaniques* 8, no. 3 (1972): 73.

37. Pinson, "Ottoman Colonization," 80.

38. McCarthy, *Death and Exile*, 62–65.

39. Lewis, "Frontier of Settlement," 263–66.

40. Abdallah Hanna, "Dayr ʿAtiyya," *Annals of the Japan Association for Middle East Studies* 4 (1989): 141–74.

41. Abraham Mitrie Rihbany, *A Far Journey* (Boston: Houghton Mifflin, 1914), 41.

42. Thomas Philipp, *The Syrians in Egypt, 1725–1975* (Stuttgart: Franz Steiner, 1985); Masʿud Dahir, *Al-Hijra al-lubnaniyya ila misr: "Hijrat al-shawam* [The Lebanese Emigration to Egypt: Emigration of the "Shawam"] (Beirut: Manshurat al-jamiʿa al-lubnaniyya, 1986).

43. Boutros Labaki, *Introduction à l'histoire économique du Liban: Soie et commerce extérieur en fin de période ottomane, 1840–1914* (Beirut: Publications de l'Université libanaise, 1984), 77.

44. Ismaʿil Haqqi Bak, *Lubnan, mabahith ʿilmiyya wa-ijtimaʿiyya* [Lebanon: Scientific and Social Studies] (1918; repr., Beirut: Manshurat al-jamiʿa al-lubnaniyya, 1969), 200.

45. Roger Owen, *The Middle East in the World Economy, 1800–1914*, rev. ed. (London: I. B. Tauris, 1993), 249.

46. Gaston Ducousso, *L'industrie de la soie en Syrie et au Liban* (Beirut: Imprimerie Catholique, 1913), ii.

47. Labaki, *Introduction à l'histoire économique*, 398.

48. Ibid., 123–25.

49. Fawaz, *Merchants and Migrants*, 66–67.

50. The Christian protégés of European consuls made especially good use of these courts because in them they held the status of European nationals, not Ottomans. Owen, *Middle East*, 90–91.

51. Cited in Fawaz, *Occasion for War*, 115.

52. Engin Akarli, *The Long Peace: Ottoman Lebanon, 1861–1920* (Berkeley: University of California Press, 1993), 31; Bak, *Lubnan*, 361–62.

53. Preface to the Règlement, cited in Akarli, *Long Peace*, 34.

54. Lortet, *La Syrie d'aujourd'hui*, 75.

55. Labaki, *Introduction à l'histoire économique*, 130–31.

56. Elie Safa, *L'émigration libanaise* (Beirut: Université Saint-Joseph, 1960), 165; E. Pariset, *Les industries de la soie* (Lyon: Publications du Bulletin des soies et des soieries, Imprimerie Pitrat Ainé, 1890), 210.

57. Labaki, *Introduction à l'histoire économique*, 39–40.

58. Kayal and Kayal estimate that in a single eighteen-month period, two thousand out of eighteen thousand inhabitants of Zahle migrated, most of them young men. See *Syrian-Lebanese in America*, 68.

59. Fawaz, *Merchants and Migrants,* 72–73.

60. Cited in Kemal Karpat, "The Ottoman Emigration to America, 1860–1914," *International Journal of Middle East Studies* 17 (1985): 205. On the role of the press in encouraging emigration, see Nadra Jamil al-Sarraj, *Shuʿaraʾ al-rabita al-qalamiyya* (Cairo: Dar al-maʿarif, 1989), 46.

61. Adele Younis, *The Coming of the Arabic-Speaking People to the United States,* ed. Philip M. Kayal (Staten Island, NY: Center for Migration Studies 1995), 166; Naff, *Becoming American,* 77–78.

62. Thomas W. Palmer, "Final Report: The Columbian Exposition of 1893," n.d., cited in Younis, *Coming of the Arabic-Speaking People,* 151.

63. Rossiter Johnson, ed., *A History of the World's Columbia Exposition Held in Chicago in 1893* (New York: D. Appleton, 1898), 440–41.

64. *New York Times,* April 26, 1893, 8.

65. Johnson, *History,* plate 51.

66. Ibid., 441.

67. *Oriental and Occidental Northern and Southern Portrait Types of the Midway Plaisance* (St. Louis: N. D. Thompson, 1894), plate 5.

68. Ibid., plate 6.

69. Mae Ngai, "Response to Presidential Address," *American Quarterly* 57, no. 1 (2005): 59–65.

70. Quoted in Younis, *Coming of the Arabic-Speaking People,* 147.

71. Rustum, Mikhaʾil Asʿad, *Al-Gharib fil-gharb* [The Stranger in the West] (1895; repr., Beirut: Dar al-Hamra, 1992), 21.

72. The Chicago community had already received a Melkite priest from Lebanon to minister to them. St. John the Baptist Melkite Church, Chicago, "Diamond Jubilee Directory of St. John the Baptist Melkite Church," n.d., in my own files; Most Rev. Nicholas J. Samra, auxiliary bishop of Newton, MI, telephone interview, Warren, MI, February 16, 1998.

73. List of names attached to letter from Yusuf (most likely Khairallah), March 13, 1891, Papers of Patriarch Elias Hoyek (1899–1931, no. 73), "Writings from America and Australia," Maronite Patriarchal Archive, Bkerke, Lebanon.

74. Ignacio Klich, "*Criollos* and Arabic Speakers in Argentina: An Uneasy Pas de Deux, 1888–1914," in Hourani and Shehadi, *Lebanese in the World,* 270–71.

75. Moya, *Cousins and Strangers,* 50.

76. Safa, *L'émigration libanaise,* 177; Hasan Hidda, *Tarikh al-mughtaribin al-ʿarab fil-ʿalam* [History of Arab Emigrants in the World] (Damascus: al-ʿArabi, 1974), 66; Claude Fahd Hajjar, *Immigração árabe: Cem anos de reflexão* (Ícone Editora LIDA, 1995), 28. According to one report, the emperor uttered his invitation in perfect Arabic! See Kassimy, "Les mouvements migratoires," 259.

77. Documents from the Ottoman Prime Ministry Archives, Istanbul, Sublime Porte Secretariat, Mt. Lebanon, cited in Klich, "Criollos and Arabic Speakers," 270.

78. On remittances, see Henry Harris Jessup, *Fifty-three Years in Syria* (New York: Fleming H. Revell, 1910), 320; Ministère de la guerre, Commission de géographie du service géographique de l'armée, *Notice sur la Syrie* (Paris: Imprimerie nationale, 1916), 126.

79. Phillip K. Hitti, *Lebanon in History* (London: Macmillan, 1957), 474–76; Jeffrey Lesser, "(Re)Creating Ethnicity: Middle Eastern Immigration to Brazil," *Americas* 53, no. 1 (1996): 54.

80. Fawaz, *Merchants and Migrants,* 35.

81. Elizabeth Beshara, interview by Alixa Naff, Ft. Wayne, IN, 1962, transcript, Series 4/C, NAAC.

82. In the Naff interviews, for example, respondents repeatedly mention that their intention upon leaving was to work hard, save money, return to their villages, and live a more comfortable life. Saliba also makes this point in *Emigration from Syria,* 17.

83. Mike Haddy and Nazira Nicola, interview by Alixa Naff, 1962, transcript, NAAC, Series 4/C.

84. Mikha'il Nu'ayma, *Sab'un,* vol. 1, *1889–1911* (Beirut: Dar Bayrut liltiba'a wal-nashr, 1959), 97.

85. Yusuf Jirjis Zakham, "Al-Suriyyun fi amirka" [The Syrians in America], *Majallat al-Muqtabas* 5, no. 12 (1910): 765–70.

86. See, for example, Sélim Abou, *Immigrés dans l'autre Amérique: Autobiographies de quatre Argentins d'origine libanaise* (Paris: Librairie Plon, 1972), 351; Khater, *Inventing Home,* 10.

87. Labaki, *Introduction à l'histoire économique,* 151.

88. Engin Deniz Akarli, "Ottoman Attitudes towards Lebanese Emigration, 1885–1910," in Hourani and Shehadi, *Lebanese in the World,* 109–38. Akarli notes that the emigrants were referred to as "Jabaliyun" in the documents—that is, from Mount Lebanon—and that a more accurate designation for them would be "Jabalese" (or Mountaineers), not Lebanese.

89. Verney and Dambmann, *Les puissances étrangères,* 148.

90. See Khater, *Inventing Home,* on the fashioning of a Lebanese middle class by return migrants.

91. *Al-Muhadhdhab* 1, no. 50 (1908): 487.

92. Petition printed in *al-Jami'a* 2, no. 2 (1908): 30.

93. While the percentage of Syrian women was much higher, it was still nowhere near that of the earlier Irish migration, in which women represented 52.9 percent of the total. See Hasia R. Diner, *Erin's Daughters in America: Irish Immigrant Women in the Nineteenth Century* (Baltimore: Johns Hopkins University Press, 1983), 31. For the period between 1900 and 1909, women made up 30.4 percent of the total immigration to the United States. See Donna Gabaccia, *From the Other Side: Women, Gender, and Immigrant Life in the U.S., 1820–1990* (Bloomington: Indiana University Press, 1994), 28.

94. U.S. Senate, *Industrial Commission on Immigration,* 1907–10, *Abstracts of Reports,* 61st Cong., 3rd sess., 1911, S. Doc. 747, 1:95; Kayal and Kayal, *Syrian-Lebanese in America,* 70; George Haddad, *Al-Mughtaribun al-suriyyun wa makanatuhum fil-tarikh* [Syrian Emigrants and Their Place in History] (Damascus: al-Jami'a al-Suriyya, 1953), 38.

95. Essa Samara, interview by Alixa Naff, Manchester, NH, 1962, transcript, NAAC, Series 4/C. On marriage arrangements, see also Charles Teebagy, interview by Alixa Naff, Dorchester, MA, 1962, transcript, NAAC, Series 4/C.

96. Dottie Andrake file, NAAC, Series 12, photo 90–4344.

97. Sarah M. A. Gualtieri, "Gendering the Chain Migration Thesis: Women and Syrian Transatlantic Migration," *Comparative Studies of South Asia, Africa and the Middle East* 24 (Spring 2004): 18–28.

98. U.S. Bureau of the Census, *Fifteenth Census of the United States, 1930, Population,* vol. 2, "General Report, Statistics by Subject," Table 31, "Marital Condition of the White Population of Foreign Birth or Parentage," 1060.

99. "The Soffas of Douma, Syria: A Genealogical Record," Near Eastern Misc. Mss., IHRC.

100. Peter Leney, "Annie Midlige, Fur Trader: A Lebanese Widow Defies the HBC," *Beaver,* June/July 1996, 40.

101. Gabaccia, *From the Other Side,* 32.

102. Selma Nimee and Margaret Malooley, interviews by Alixa Naff, Spring Valley, IL, 1962, transcripts, NAAC, Series 4/C.

103. Ibid.

104. Sánchez, *Becoming Mexican American,* 143.

105. A. Ruppin, "Migration from and to Syria, 1860–1914," in Issawi, *Economic History,* 270; Saliba, *Emigration from Syria,* 8.

106. Yusuf Musa Khanashit, *Tara'if al-ams ghara'ib al-yawm* [Curiosities of Yesterday and Marvels of Today], ed. Abdallah Hanna (1936; repr., Damascus: Wizarat al-thaqafah, 1990), 14–15; Munir al-Khuri 'Isa Asa'd, *Tarikh Hims* [The History of Homs] (Homs: Mutraniyya Hims al-urthudhuksiyya, 1984), 507–8; Abdallah Hanna, personal communication, Damascus, June 7, 1997.

107. See Karpat, "Ottoman Emigration to America," 175–209.

108. U.S. Senate, Industrial Commission on Immigration, 1907–10, *Abstract of Reports,* 61st Cong., 3rd sess., 1911, S. Doc. 747, 1:95; U.S. Bureau of the Census, *Thirteenth Census of the United States, 1910,* vol. 1, *Population 1910: General Report and Analysis* (Washington, DC: Government Printing Office, 1913), 963.

109. Basil M. Kherbawi, relying on figures from voluntary associations and churches, estimated that there were two hundred thousand Syrians in the United States in 1913. See his *Tarikh al-wilayat al-muttahida* [History of the United States] (New York: Matba' jarida al-Dalil, 1913), 789. The Cairo-based journal *al-Hilal,* citing the book *Al-Safr al-mufid fil-'alam al-jadid* [The Beneficial Journey to the New World], gave a figure of 122,000 Syrians in the United States in 1911. See *al-Hilal* 19 (April 1911): 418.

110. U.S. Bureau of the Census, *Fourteenth Census of the United States, 1920,* vol. 2, *General Report and Analytical Tables* (Washington, DC: Government Printing Office, 1922), 805.

111. For a discussion of the reports, see Hashimoto, "Lebanese Population Movement," 74–77; Eliane Fersan, "L'émigration libanaise au États-Unis d'après les archives du Ministère des affaires étrangères de France (1920–1931)" (MA thesis, University of the Holy Spirit, Kaslik, Lebanon, 2005).

112. Hashimoto, "Lebanese Population Movement," 95–97; Hitti, *Syrians in America,* 62.

113. Alixa Naff uses this term *mother colony* in "New York: The Mother Colony," in *A Community of Many Worlds: Arab Americans in New York City,* ed. Kathleen Benson and Philip M. Kayal (New York: Museum of the City of New York, 2002), 3–10.

114. I am following Robin Cohen's typology of diasporas here. He defines a trade diaspora as "networks of proactive merchants who transport, buy and sell their goods over long distances." See Robin Cohen, *Global Diasporas: An Introduction* (Seattle: University of Washington Press, 1997), xii.

115. Gregory Orfalea, *The Arab Americans: A History* (Northhampton, MA: Olive Branch Press, 2006), 81; Mokarzel, "History of the Syrians," 8.

116. Lucius Hopkins Miller, *A Study of the Syrian Population of Greater New York* (New York: Federation of Churches, 1904), 22.

117. U.S. Bureau of the Census, *Thirteenth Census of the United States, 1910: Abstract of the Census.* (Washington, DC: Government Printing Office, 1913–14).

118. *New York Times,* August 28, 1898, 14.

119. *New York Times,* September 1895, 16.

120. Cromwell Childe, "New York's Syrian Quarter," *New York Times,* August 20, 1899, IMS4.

121. Ibid.

122. Melani McAlister, *Epic Encounters: Culture, Media, and U.S. Interests in the Middle East, 1945–2000* (Berkeley: University of California Press, 2001), 22.

123. Konrad Bercovici, "Around the World in New York—the Syrian Quarters," *Century Magazine* 108 (July 1924): 348.

124. Quoted in Elizabeth Boosahda, *Arab-American Faces and Voices: The Origins of an Immigrant Community* (Austin: University of Texas Press, 2003), 77.

125. Abraham and Shryock, *Arab Detroit,* 19; Rosina J. Hassoun, *Arab Americans in Michigan* (East Lansing: Michigan State University Press, 2005), 47–48.

126. Saliba, *Emigration from Syria,* 39. In the 1920s, a split occurred within the Syrian Orthodox communities between those who wanted to remain loyal to the Russian Church and those who supported the independence of the See of Antioch, under the jurisdiction of the Patriarchate of Antioch. The latter came to be known as "Antiochian Orthodox."

127. See the report of the consul general of New Orleans to MAE, excerpted in Hashimoto, "Lebanese Population Movement," 97.

128. Safa, *L'émigration libanaise,* 151.

129. Like the English press, the Egyptian paper *al-Hilal* ran an advertisement for this "unsinkable ship." *Al-Hilal* 15, no. 4 (1907): 25. On the Lebanese who perished in the shipwreck of the *Titanic,* see Michel Karam, *Al-Lubnaniyyun fil-taytanik* [The Lebanese on the *Titanic*] (Beirut: Muʻassasa dakash lil-tabaʻa, 2000); Leila Salloum Elias, "The Impact of the Sinking of the *Titanic* on the New York Syrian Community of 1912," *Arab Studies Quarterly* 27 (Winter/Spring 2005): 75–88.

130. *Al-Hoda,* March 8, 1898, 17.

131. Kherbawi, *Tarikh al-wilayat al-muttahida,* 778.

2. CLAIMING "WHITENESS"

Parts of this chapter are drawn from my article "Becoming 'White': Race, Religion and the Foundations of Syrian Ethnicity in the United States," *Journal of American Ethnic History* 20 (Summer 2001): 29–58.

1. Essa Samara, interview, 1962, transcript, NAAC, Series 4/C.

2. Consul of France to MAE, April 20, 1921, Levant, 1918–1940, Syrie-Liban, 1918–1929, vol. 132, MAE, 43b.

3. Costa Najour to Adele Younis (in Arabic), January 1961, SAAC, Gr. II, Series C, folder 203.

4. New York City, for example, had approximately three hundred naturalized Syrians by 1901. U.S. House, Industrial Commission on Immigration, *Reports,* vol. 15, 57th Cong., 1st sess., 1901, H. Doc. 184, 445.

5. Reed Ueda, "Naturalization and Citizenship," in *Harvard Encyclopedia of American Ethnic Groups,* ed. Stephen Thernstrom (Cambridge, MA: Belknap Press, 1980), 740.

6. Higham, *Strangers in the Land,* 165.

7. Ibid., 169.

8. George E. Cunningham, "The Italian, a Hindrance to White Solidarity in Louisiana, 1890–1898," in *Racial Classification and History,* ed. E. Nathaniel Gates (New York: Garland, 1997), 68–82. See also Vincenza Scarpaci, "Walking the Color Line: Italian Immigrants in Rural Louisiana, 1880–1910," in *Are Italians White? How Race Is Made in America,* ed. Jennifer Guglielmo and Salvatore Salerno (New York: Routledge, 2003), 60–76.

9. Higham, *Strangers in the Land,* 165.

10. See Alan M. Kraut, *Silent Travelers: Germs, Genes and the "Immigrant Menace"* (New York: Basic Books, 1994), ch. 4; Nayan Shah, *Contagious Divides: Epidemics and Race in San Francisco's Chinatown* (Berkeley: University of California Press, 2001).

11. Ann R. Gabbert, "El Paso, a Sight for Sore Eyes: Medical and Legal Aspects of Syrian Immigration, 1906–1907," *Historian* 65, no. 1 (2002): 15–42.

12. See Amy Fairchild, "Science at the Borders: Immigrant Medical Inspection and Defense of the Nation, 1891–1930" (PhD diss., Columbia University, 1997).

13. "Nativity and Race of Immigrants Certified for Trachoma," and "Race of Immigrants Deported on Medical Certificates," Records of the Immigration and Naturalization Service (INS), Series A, Part 3, Ellis Island, 1900–1933, microfilm roll 6, Joseph Regenstein Library, University of Chicago.

14. Gabbert, "El Paso," 22.

15. Tafaha Laham al-Tin, interview by Alixa Naff, Alexandria, Ontario, 1961, transcript, NAAC, Series 4/C; Alice Abraham, interview by Alixa Naff, Los Angeles, CA, 1962, transcript, NAAC, Series 4/C.

16. Recollection of Eli A. B., cited in Boosahda, *Arab-American Faces and Voices,* 28–29.

17. Farah S., interview, March 1, 1997, Damascus, Syria; Sarah E. John, "Arabic-Speaking Immigration to the El Paso Area, 1900–1935," in Hooglund, *Crossing the Waters,* 106–7; Alice Abraham, interview by Alixa Naff, Los Angeles, CA, 1962, transcript, NAAC, Series 4/C. On Syrians in Mexico, see Theresa Alfaro Velcamp, *So Far from Allah, So Close to Mexico: Middle Eastern Immigrants in Modern Mexico* (Austin: University of Texas Press, 2008).

18. Alexandra Stern, personal communication based on her research of the U.S. Records of the Immigration and Naturalization Service, Mexican Immigration, 1906–30.

19. Gabbert, "El Paso," 34–35.

20. According to records from the Department of Commerce and Labor, 4,648 Syrians were turned back in the period between 1899 and 1907. Of these, 1,578 persons were debarred on account of trachoma. See Louise Seymour Houghton, "Syrians in the United States," *Survey* 26, no. 14 (1911): 490; "Report of Detained Immigrants," December 17, 1899, and "Race of Immigrants Deported on Medical Certificates during Fiscal Year Ended June 30th, 1909," both in Records of the INS, Series A, Part 3, Ellis Island, 1900–1933, microfilm roll 6, Joseph Regenstein Library, University of Chicago.

21. Kraut, *Silent Travelers,* ch. 4.

22. "Elkourie Takes Burnett to Task," *Birmingham Age-Herald,* October 20, 1907. On Elkourie's leadership of the Cedars/Phoenician Club, see "The Cedars/Phoenician Club of Birmingham," in Southern Federation of Syrian Lebanese American Clubs, *75th Diamond Jubilee Convention, 1931–2006: June 30–July 4, 2006, San Antonio, Texas,* commemorative ed., 2006, in my own files.

23. "Elkourie Takes Burnett to Task." This was the second of two letters written by Elkourie. The first appeared under the title "Dr. El-Kourie Defends Syrian Immigrants" in the *Birmingham Ledger,* September 20, 1907. According to Nancy Faires Conklin, the two letters were collected in a pamphlet and distributed under the title "In Defense of the Semitic and the Syrian Especially." See Nancy Faires Conklin and Nora Faires, " 'Colored' and Catholic: The Lebanese in Birmingham, Alabama," in Hooglund, *Crossing the Waters,* 76.

24. "Elkourie Takes Burnett to Task."

25. Haney López, *White by Law,* 51; *People v. Hall,* 4 Cal. 399 (1854).

26. Joseph R. Haiek, *Arab-American Almanac,* 4th ed. (Glendale, CA: News Circle Publishing House, 1992), 21.

27. "Syrians Admitted," *Los Angeles Times,* November 5, 1909.

28. On the *Shishim* case, see Haiek, *Arab-American Almanac,* 21–23; "Syrian Admitted."

29. Notes of Adele Younis, based on her interview with Costa Najour, August 11–12, 1967, SAAC, Group II, Series A, Box 8, Folder 203.

30. *Atlanta Journal,* November 21, 1909, 10.

31. "Najour's Nativity Still in Doubt," *Atlanta Journal,* December 2, 1909, 5, excerpted in the notes of Adele Younis, SAAC, Group II, Series A, Box 8, folder 203.

32. *In re Najour,* 174 Fed. 735 (1909).

33. Ibid.

34. On this point, see Haney López, *White by Law,* 68.

35. *In re Najour,* 735.

36. *Ex parte Shahid,* 205 Fed. 813 (1913).

37. Costa Najour to Adele Younis (in Arabic), January 1961, SAAC, Gr. II, Series C, Box 8, folder 203.

38. *In re Najour,* 735.

39. *In re Ah Yup,* cited in Haney López, *White by Law,* 210.

40. He was quoting from Thomas H. Huxley's *Methods and Results of Ethnology.* See *In re Dow,* 213 Fed. 358 (1914).

41. Ibid., 366.

42. The classification of Syrians as "Asiatic" could be deduced from the 1910 U.S. Census, which considered Syria part of "Turkey in Asia." However, it is clear from the census that for the purpose of population statistics Syrians were considered white, since immigrants from "Turkey in Asia" were listed in the category "foreign-born white."

43. *In re Dow*, 365.

44. Ibid.

45. *In re Halladjian et al.*, 174 Fed. 838 (1909).

46. *In re Dow*, 367.

47. *In re Ellis*, 179 Fed. 1002 (1910), 1003.

48. U.S. Senate, Industrial Commission on Immigration Commission, *Abstract of Reports*, 2 vols., 61st Cong., 3rd sess., 1911, S. Doc. 747, 1:280.

49. *In re Ellis*, 179 Fed. 1002 (1910), 1003.

50. Jacobson, *Whiteness of a Different Color*, 68–74. See also Souad Joseph's study of how representations of Arabs as "not quite free" has impeded their integration into the category of American citizen: "Against the Grain of the Nation—The Arab-," in Suleiman, *Arabs in America*, 257–71.

51. *In re Najour*, 736.

52. *In re Ellis*, 1004.

53. Ibid.

54. Philip de Tarazi, *Tarikh al-sihafa al-ʿarabiyya* [History of the Arab Press], vol. 2 (Beirut: Dar Sadr, [1913]), 87.

55. Ibid.

56. Jurji Zaydan, *Tabaqat al-umam aw al-salaʾil al-bashariyya* (al-Fajala, Egypt: Matbaʿa al-Hilal, 1912).

57. Ibid., 5.

58. Ibid.

59. Ibid., 7.

60. *Al-Hilal* 22, no. 9 (1914): 705.

61. *Al-Hilal* 22, no. 6 (March 1, 1914): 460.

62. *Al-Muqtabas* 1, no. 10 (1907): 544–45.

63. "Transcript of Court Record," SAAC, Group II, Series C.

64. *In re Dow*, 357.

65. Ibid., 363.

66. Ibid.

67. Eric L. Goldstein, *The Price of Whiteness: Jews, Race, and American Identity* (Princeton: Princeton University Press, 2006), 103.

68. Ibid.

69. *United States v. Balsara*, 180 Fed. 696 (1910). On Syrian involvement in the case, see notes of Adele Younis, SAAC, Group II, Series A, Box 8, Folder 203.

70. Notes of Adele Younis, SAAC, Group II, Series A, Box 8, Folder 203.

71. *In re Dow*, 356.

72. Ibid. See also "Haqiqa qirar al-qadi smith" [The Truth of Judge Smith's Ruling], *Meraat ul-gharb*, April 10, 1914, 1.

73. Cited in Haiek, *Arab-American Almanac*, 22.

74. *Atlanta Constitution*, November 22, 1909, 8.

75. Conklin and Faires, " 'Colored' and Catholic"; William Sherman, *Prairie Peddlers: The Syrian-Lebanese in North Dakota* (Bismarck: University of Mary Press, 2002), 180.

76. *Al-Hoda*, December 4, 1909, 5.

77. Sherman, *Prairie Peddlers*, 181.

78. Ibid., 173.

79. Ibid., 181.

80. Ibid., 173.

81. *Al-Hoda*, March 11, 1914, 3.

82. *Al-Hoda*, April 4, 1914, 3.

83. *Al-Hoda*, April 20, 1914, 5.

84. *Al-Hoda*, March 11, 1914, 3. The same language was used in an article printed in *Meraat ul-gharb*, "On the Syrian Question," April 7, 1914.

85. Ibid.

86. Ibid.

87. See, for example, *al-Hoda*, September 17, 1914, 8. Moore notes that "an important part of the affected community followed the courts' lead in adopting racialist and eugenicist criteria to construct a national identity which in effect denied equal access to citizenship to 'Asiatics.' " In Moore, *Al-Mughtaribun*, xiii.

88. "Haqiqa qirar al-qadi smith."

89. Kalil A. Bishara, *The Origin of the Modern Syrian* (New York: al-Hoda Publishing House, 1914), 5.

90. Kalil A. Bishara, *Asl al-suriy al-hadith* (New York: al-Hoda Publishing House, 1914), 5.

91. Michael Suleiman, "Early Arab-Americans: The Search for Identity," in Hooglund, *Crossing the Waters*, 45. The most common perception was that Islam was an impediment to progress and that its adherents were prone to debauchery. These ideas could be found in the accounts of American missionaries, as well as in enormously popular literary works like Robert Hitchens's *The Garden of Allah* (1904) and Mark Twain's *Innocents Abroad*. See Terry Hammons, " 'A Wild Ass of a Man': American Images of Arabs to 1948" (PhD diss., University of Oklahoma, 1978).

92. *Dow v. United States*, 226 Fed. 147 (1915).

93. Ibid., 148.

94. Ibid.

95. *United States v. Thind*, 261 U.S. 204 (1923).

96. *Takao Ozawa v. United States*, 260 U.S.178 (1922).

97. For a more detailed discussion of the *Thind* and *Ozawa* cases, see Jeff H. Lesser, "Always 'Outsiders': Asians, Naturalization, and the Supreme Court," *Amerasia* 12, no. 1 (1985–86): 83–100.

98. Moore, *Al-Mughtaribun*, 59.

99. Haney López, *White by Law*, 91; David Roediger, "Whiteness and Ethnicity in the History of 'White Ethnics' in the United States," in *Towards the Abolition of Whiteness: Essays on Race, Politics, and Working Class History* (London: Verso, 1994), 182.

100. See "The Comprehensive Immigration Act of 1917," in *Immigration: Select Documents and Case Records,* ed. Edith Abbott (Chicago: University of Chicago Press, 1924), 217.

101. *United States v. Thind,* 215.

102. Joseph Ferris, "Syrian Naturalization Question in the United States," *Syrian World* 2, no. 9 (1928): 22; Samhan, "Not Quite White," 217.

103. Mae M. Ngai, "The Architecture of Race in American Immigration Law: A Re-examination of the Reed Johnson Act of 1924," *Journal of American History* 86, no. 1 (1999): 67–92.

104. See Lesser's discussion of the continuities between naturalization and Japanese internment cases in "Always 'Outsiders,' " 92–93.

105. *United States v. Balsara.* On Syrian involvement in the case, see notes of Adele Younis, SAAC, Group II, Series A, Box 8, Folder 203.

106. *In re Ellis,* 1003; *Dow v. United States,* 148.

107. Sridevi Menon, "Where Is West Asia in Asian America? 'Asia' and the Politics of Space in Asian America," *Social Text* 24 (Spring 2006): 57.

108. Reported in *Syrian World* 3 (June 1929), 47.

109. Jacobson, *Whiteness of a Different Color,* 239. See also Matha Minow, cited in Moore, *Al-Mughtaribun,* 54.

110. N. Mokarzel to Gaston Liébert, September 29, 1920 (contained in dispatch to the French Consul in Panama), Levant, 1918–1940, Syrie-Liban, 1918–1929, vol. 128, MAE, 93.

111. Ignatiev, *How the Irish Became White,* 2.

112. Costa Najour to Adele Younis (in Arabic), January 1961, SAAC, Gr. II, Series C, Box 8, folder 203.

113. Slayman Nimmee, interview by Alixa Naff, Spring Valley, IL 1962, abstract, NAAC, Series 4/C.

114. Mae Ngai, *Impossible Subjects: Illegal Aliens and the Making of Modern America* (Princeton: Princeton University Press, 2004), 237–38.

115. Consul of France in Chicago to MAE, September 17, 1926, Levant, 1918–1940, Syrie-Liban, 1918–1929, vol. 404, MAE, 133.

116. Consul of France in Chicago to MAE, January 19, 1924, Levant, 1918–1940, Syrie-Liban, 1918–1929, vol. 407, MAE, 189.

117. U.S. Bureau of the Census, "Citizenship of the Foreign Born," in *Fifteenth Census of the United States, 1930, Population,* vol. 2, *General Report, Statistics by Subject* (Washington, DC: Government Printing Office, 1933), 411.

118. Ibid., 432.

3. NATION AND MIGRATION

The chapter's epigraphs are taken from Philip Hitti's speech welcoming Emilio Carranza of Mexico to the clubhouse of the American Syrian Federation, printed in *Syrian World* 3 (August 1928): 36, and J. Ray Johnson's "Syrians in America," *Syrian World* 2 (June 1928): 19.

1. For a discussion of these debates, see Rashid Khalidi, "Ottomanism and Arabism in Syria before 1914: A Reassessment," in *The Origins of Arab Na-*

tionalism, ed. R. Khalidi et al. (New York: Columbia University Press, 1991), 50–69; Rashid Khalidi, "Arab Nationalism: Historical Problems in the Literature," *American Historical Review* 96, no. 5 (1991): 1363–73; James Jankowski and Israel Gershoni, eds., *Rethinking Nationalism in the Arab Middle East* (New York: Columbia University Press, 1997).

2. For a summary of the extensive scholarship on early "Arab nationalism" and an argument against a coherent theory of it before World War I, see Dawisha, *Arab Nationalism,* 14–48.

3. By *imaginary* (in French, *imaginaire*), I mean, to use Arjun Appadurai's definition, "a constructed landscape of collective aspirations." See his *Modernity at Large: Cultural Dimensions of Globalization* (Minneapolis: University of Minnesota Press, 1996), 31.

4. By Oswaldo Truzzi, for example, in *Patrícios: Sírios e libaneses em São Paulo* (São Paulo: Editora Hucitec, 1997), 25. On Syrian Christians, Kayal and Kayal write that "sectarian fidelity often replaces nationality" (*Syrian-Lebanese in America,* 37).

5. Hitti, *Syrians in America,* 25.

6. Ibid. Gertrude Bell echoed this sentiment when, as the British Colonial Office representative in Baghdad, she wrote: "There is little or no territorial nationality [among the Syrians]. . . . Syria is merely a geographic term corresponding to no national sentiment in the breasts of the inhabitants." Quoted in Dawisha, *Arab Nationalism,* 33.

7. Rihbany to Hitti, January 2, 1922, Philip Hitti Collection, Box 1, Correspondence 1, IHRC.

8. "Al-Suriyyun fi Amirka" [The Syrians in America], *al-Hilal* 5 (April 1897): 596; Yusuf Zakham, "Amirka al-shamaliyya" [North America], *Majallat al-Muqtabas* 2, no. 4 (1907): 216; "Limaza tuhdam huquq al-suriyyin" [Why Are Syrian Rights Repressed?], *al-Dalil* 8, no. 413 (1912): 1.

9. Jean Fontaine, *La crise religieuse des écrivains syro-libanais chrétiens de 1825 à 1940* (Tunis: Institut des belles lettres arabes, 1996); Michael Suleiman, "The Arab-American Left," in *The Immigrant Left in the United States,* ed. Paul Buhle and Dan Georgakas (Albany: SUNY Press, 1996), 240.

10. *New York Times,* October 24, 1905; "Syrians Stirred Up," *New York Daily Tribune,* August 28, 1905, 5. The *New York Herald* headlined a front-page story of a murder on Washington Street as "Factional War Is Waged between Syrians of New York City. Cutting and Shooting. Brother against Brother. Voices of Women Heard" (October 29, 1905). See Gregory Orfalea's discussion of this coverage in *Before the Flames: A Quest for the History of Arab Americans* (Austin: University of Texas Press, 1988), 78, and Robert Park's account of the 1905 disturbances in *The Immigrant Press and Its Control* (New York: Harper and Brothers, 1922), 345.

11. J. Ray Johnson, "Syrians in America," *Syrian World* 2 (June 1928): 19–24.

12. By *nation,* I do not mean a homogeneous community bounded by set geographical limits, and certainly not a pan-Arab nation-state. It is quite clear from the writings of pre–World War I Arabists that the Arab nation (usually referred to in Arabic as *al-umma al-ʿarabiyya*) was loosely defined in territorial terms but had great cultural resonance. The Arabic-speaking peoples of the

mashriq ("the Arab East") shared an Arab nationality, but it was expected that their national rights could be respected within the political framework of the Ottoman Empire. Many of these points will be elaborated in this chapter.

13. The Committee of Union and Progress (CUP) had backed the overthrow of Sultan Abdülhamid II in 1909 and taken direct control of the government in 1913.

14. Cemal Pasha (wartime governor of Syria) justified his clampdown by citing confiscated documents from the French consulates in Beirut and Damascus that, he claimed, contained evidence of subversive activities on the part of Arabists. See his *Memories of a Turkish Statesman, 1913–1919* (1922; repr., New York: Arno Press, 1973), 197.

15. It is worth mentioning that interpretations of al-Jazzar's rule have undergone substantial revision. A. L. Tibawi, for example, notes that while al-Jazzar was "undoubtedly ruthless" he was an able administrator and, perhaps most importantly, responsible for mounting an effective defense against Napoleon's forces at Acre in 1799. See his *Modern History of Syria* (London: Macmillan, 1969), 32.

16. *As-Sayeh*, August 26, 1915, 5.

17. *As-Sayeh*, May 22, 1916, 1.

18. William I. Cole, *Immigrant Races in Massachusetts: The Syrians* (Boston: Massachusetts Department of Education, n.d. [1921?]), 5. Hitti, citing reports of the provost marshal general and the War Department, gave a figure of 13,965 persons, or 7 percent of the entire Syrian community in the United States. The Syrian-American Club of New York estimated that as many as 15,000 Syrians served in the U.S. Army during World War I. Hitti, *Syrians in America*, 102.

19. Eliezer Tauber, *The Arab Movements in World War I* (London: Frank Cass, 1993), 14.

20. Ibid., 200–201.

21. C. Ernest Dawn was the first scholar to use the term *Ottomanism* to describe an ideology of reform espoused by bureaucrats, religious scholars, and lay intellectuals in the half-century before World War I. Ottomanists were "Westernizers" committed to the reform of the institutions of the Ottoman state, particularly educational ones, along European lines. They held fast to the idea that Islam was in no way incompatible with modernity and was, in its true, unadulterated form, a superior moral, spiritual, and political system. Dawn contrasted Ottomanism with "Arabism," which also arose from a modernist impulse but increasingly insisted on the special character, virtues, and rights of Arab peoples. Arabism became politicized in the second decade of the twentieth century when Ottoman Arabs began forming parties and secret societies that advocated greater autonomy within the Ottoman Empire. Arabism was the intellectual precursor of Arab nationalism and the call for the creation of an independent Arab state. See C. Ernest Dawn, *From Ottomanism to Arabism: Essays on the Origins of Arab Nationalism* (Urbana: University of Illinois Press, 1973), chs. 5 and 6. I am here using *Ottomanism* to designate an identity rooted in the sense of belonging to a multiethnic Ottoman citizenry, where political equality and representative government would, to use Hasan Kayali's words, "foster an imperial allegiance." See his *Arabs and Young Turks: Ottomanism, Arabism, and Islamism in the Ottoman Empire, 1908–1918* (Berkeley: University of California Press, 1997), 15.

22. Quoted in the *New York Times*, January 13, 1899, 12.

23. "Syrian Editor Not Un-American," *New York Times*, January 19, 1899, 12.

24. Ibid.

25. Reported in *al-Hilal* 13, no. 1 (1904): 14.

26. This characterization is due to the fact that immigrants were viewed as being "political" only after they began to participate in the American political process. Hitti, for example, argued that "Syrians cut no figure in the political life of this nation. Very few of them interest themselves in politics or aspire to office." Philip Kayal confirmed this depiction: "Because of confusion about their own identity and because they were few in number, the Syrians remained a politically irrelevant and disorganized social entity. . . . [After the *Dow* case] . . . they became politically and religiously divided and inactive." See his "Arab Christians in the United States," in Abraham and Abraham, *Arabs in the New World*, 49. Michael Suleiman, however, disputes this characterization of the early Arab American community as politically passive in "Arab-American Left," 234.

27. *Al-Ayyam*, no. 132 (1899): 5. The society was enthusiastically supported by the editor of *al-Ayyam*, Yusuf Nuʿman al-Maʿluf (1870–1947), who claimed that the founding of the society marked the beginning of a national awakening *(nahda wataniyya)* in the *mahjar*.

28. On the effects of the CUP's Turkification policies, see Rashid Khalidi, *British Policy towards Syria and Palestine, 1906–1914* (London: Ithaca Press, 1980), 204–5. On the origins of the Young Turk position, see M. Şükrü Hanioğlu, "The Young Turks and the Arabs before the Revolution of 1908," in Khalidi et al., *Origins of Arab Nationalism*, 31–49. Hanioğlu argues that the roots of the Turkification policies lie in the extreme ethnocentrism of the Young Turks, already apparent before the 1908 revolution. Kayali, taking a different approach, argues that the policies of the CUP derived from an interest in centralization, not ethnocentrism. See his *Arabs and Young Turks*, 14.

29. Al-Lajna al-ʿulya li-hizb al-lamarkaziyya bi misr, *Al-Muʾtamar al-ʿarabi al-awwal* [Documents of the First Arab Congress] (Cairo: Matbaʿa al-Busfur, 1913), hereafter *Al-Muʾatamar*, 4–5.

30. *Al-Muʾtamar*, 9.

31. "Decisions of the Arab Congress in Paris," *as-Sayeh*, July 3, 1913, 2.

32. Rufaʾil Yaʿqub, "Kayfa nashaʾat wa ʿashat ʿAfifa Karam," NAAC, Series 1-O.

33. Khalidi, *British Policy*, 311–13.

34. *Al-Muʾtamar*, dal to haʾ; Khalidi, *British Policy*, 315.

35. Kayali, *Arabs and Young Turks*, 193.

36. Al-Tabbara was active in journalism and was the founder of several newspapers, including *al-Ittihad al-ʿUthmani* (1908), *al-Iʾtilaf al-ʿUthmani* (1912), and *Mulhaq al-Islah* (1914). He was accused of treason during the war and was publicly hanged in Beirut on May 6, 1916. See Tarazi, *Tarikh al-sihafa al-ʿarabiyya*, vol. 2, pt. 4, 10; Tauber, *Emergence*, 190.

37. *Al-Muʾtamar*, 86, 88. His speech is the only Arabic source I have found that provides figures for all the countries of the Americas with large Syrian populations.

38. Ibid., 90.

39. Ibid.

40. *Al-Mausu'a al-suhufiyya al-'arabiyya* [Encyclopedia of the Arab Press], vol. 3, *Al-Sihafa al-'arabiyya fi buldan al-mahjar* [The Arab Press in the Countries of the Mahjar] (Tunis: al-Munazama al-'arabiyya lil-tarbiyya wal-thaqafa wal-'ulum, 1991), 89; Tarazi, *Tarikh al-sihafa al-'arabiyya*, vol. 2, pt. 4, 409.

41. *Al-Mu'tamar*, 15; Kherbawi, *Tarikh al-wilayat al-muttahida*, 837.

42. *Al-Mu'tamar*, 68.

43. Ibid., 73.

44. Diab printed several articles in *Meraat ul-gharb* prior to, and during, the congress that conveyed this concern with foreign intervention in Syria. One article, submitted by "one of the influential men of Syria," referred to the "readiness of France and England to swallow up our beloved homeland." *Meraat ul-gharb*, April 14, 1913, 1.

45. See Samir Seikaly's analysis of Shukri al-'Asali's position in "Shukri al-'Asali: A Case Study of a Political Activist," in Khalidi et al., *Origins of Arab Nationalism*, 88.

46. *Al-Mu'tamar*, 69.

47. *Meraat ul-gharb*, April 11, 1913, 1.

48. *Al-Mu'tamar*, 92.

49. Peter van der Veer, "The Diasporic Imagination," in *Nation and Migration: The Politics of Space in the South Asian Diaspora*, ed. Peter van der Veer (Philadelphia: University of Pennsylvania Press, 1995), 6.

50. *Al-Mu'tamar*, 19. On al-Zahrawi, see Ahmed Tarabein, "'Abd al-Hamid Al-Zahrawi: The Career and Thought of an Arab Nationalist," in Khalidi et al., *Origins of Arab Nationalism*, 97–119.

51. Hourani, *Arabic Thought*, 285.

52. Kherbawi, *Tarikh al-wilayat al-muttahida*, 815; Tauber, *Emergence*, 76.

53. Tarazi, *Tarikh al-sihafa al-'arabiyya*, vol. 2, pt. 4, 408. The day after Mokarzel was elected president of the Nahda, he published an editorial in *al-Hoda*, stating that the society would work to achieve three main goals: "the preservation of Lebanon's special status, the opening of a [new] port, and the promotion of Lebanon's civilizational concerns." See al-Hoda, *Al-Hoda, 1898–1968: Hakayat lubnan wa mughtaribihu* [Al-Hoda, 1898–1968: The Story of *al-Hoda* and the Lebanese Emigrants in America] (New York: Mataba' al-Hoda, 1968), 26.

54. *Al-Mu'tamar*, 108.

55. Ibid.

56. Ibid., 109.

57. Al-Hoda, *Al-Hoda, 1898–1968*, 39–40.

58. George Antonius, *The Arab Awakening* (1938; repr., New York: Capricorn Books, 1965).

59. Ibid., 13.

60. Hourani, *Arabic Thought*, 283.

61. Ibid., v.

62. C. Ernest Dawn is a good example. He considered Arabism to be "a reaction against the failure of the Ottoman civilization to keep pace with Europe," in *From Ottomanism to Arabism*, 147. He often resorted to psychological explanations by suggesting that Ottomanism and Arabism arose from an "injured

self-view." See Dawn, *From Ottomanism to Arabism,* 184, and "The Origins of Arab Nationalism," in Khalidi et al., *Origins of Arab Nationalism,* 5.

63. Hourani, *Arabic Thought,* 346.

64. *Al-Mu'tamar,* alif.

65. Ibid., 91. Appeals to past glories had been part of the justification of reform among men like Rifaʿa al-Tahtawi (1801–73) and, later, Butrus al-Bustani. See Tibi, *Arab Nationalism,* 59; Hourani, *Arabic Thought,* 263.

66. *Al-Mu'tamar,* 91.

67. Ibid.

68. Ibid.

69. Ibid., 68.

70. *Al-Hoda,* January 24, 1899, 21.

71. Kherbawi, *Tarikh al-wilayat al-muttahida,* 819.

72. *Majallat al-Muqtabas* 5, no. 12 (1910): 768.

73. Rihbany, *Far Journey,* ix.

74. Axel Havemann, "Between Ottoman Loyalty and Arab 'Independence': Muhammad Kurd ʿAli, Girgi Zaydan, and Sakib Arslan," *Quaderni di studi arabi* 5–6 (1987–88): 346–51.

75. *Majallat al-Muqtabas* 4, no. 8 (1909): 492–501. This article was reprinted in Muhammad Kurd ʿAli, *Gharaʾib al-gharb* [Strange Things of the West] (Cairo: Maktabat al-ahaliyya, 1923). Syrian émigré Farah Antun, owner and editor of the journal *al-Jamiʿa* (published in New York), also warned Syrians that the opportunities in America were exaggerated and that it was not unusual for emigrants to return to Syria after not finding work. See *al-Jamiʿa* 7, no. 1 (1909): 30–38.

76. Jurji Zaydan echoed Kurd ʿAli's concerns in his journal *al-Hilal* 17, no. 10 (1909), in which he railed against the regime of Sultan Abdülhamid II for fostering division and encouraging emigration.

77. *Majallat al-Muqtabas* 1, no. 3 (1907): 184.

78. "Rihla ila Qalamun al-asfal" [A Trip to Lower Qalamun], *Majallat al-Muqtabas* 5, no. 6 (1910): 412.

79. Kurd ʿAli, *Gharaʾib al-gharb,* 31. This complicates the theory that Syrian marriages in the *mahjar* were endogamous—at least for the first generation. Rates of marriage outside the community may have varied according to sect. Muhammad Shaʿban, for example, accused the Druze men of quickly marrying non-Syrians in an article in *al-Hoda* (February 6, 1909, 4).

80. In thinking about this issue, I have been influenced by Joan Scott's work on French workers in " 'L'ouvrière! Mot impie, sordide . . .': Women Workers in the Discourse of French Political Economy, 1840–1860," in *Gender and the Politics of History* (New York: Columbia University Press, 1988), 139–63. On crises in patriarchy in the Middle East, the following works are helpful: Elizabeth Thompson, *Colonial Citizens: Republican Rights, Paternal Privilege, and Gender in French Syria and Lebanon* (New York: Columbia University Press, 2000); Khater, *Inventing Home.*

81. *Al-Mashriq* 5, no. 12 (1902): 572.

82. Anne McClintock, " 'No Longer in a Future Heaven': Nationalism, Gender, and Race," in *Becoming National: A Reader,* ed. Geoff Eley and Ronald Grigor Suny (New York: Oxford University Press, 1996), 263.

83. My understanding of "modernity" is greatly influenced by the work of Lila Abu-Lughod, who, drawing on Paul Rabinow, notes that "it is impossible to define modernity; rather, what one must do is to track the diverse ways the insistent claims to being modern are made." See her introduction to *Remaking Women: Feminism and Modernity in the Middle East,* ed. Lila Abu-Lughod (Princeton: Princeton University Press, 1998), 7.

84. Nadra Moutran, *La Syrie de demain,* 4th ed. (Paris: Librairie Plon, 1916), 46.

85. Khouri to Jusserand, ambassador of France in Washington, May 1, 1921, Levant, 1918–1940, Syrie-Liban, 1918–1929, vol. 126, MAE (in French), 156.

86. Benedict Anderson, *Imagined Communities: Reflections on the Origin and Spread of Nationalism,* rev. ed. (London: Verso, 1991), 195–96.

87. Deniz Kandiyoti, "Identity and Its Discontents: Women and the Nation," *Millennium: Journal of International Studies* 20, no. 3 (1991): 431, cited in McClintock, " 'No Longer,' " 263.

88. Tarazi, *Tarikh al-sihafa al-ʿarabiyya,* vol. 2, pt. 4, 443; *Al-Mausuʿa,* 92.

89. *Al-Mausuʿa,* 60.

90. The U.S. act that in 1924 barred from entry all aliens ineligible for citizenship. Jeff Lesser notes that this restrictive law served as a model for other countries, notably Canada and Argentina. Significantly, Brazil did not adopt similar legislation until a decade later. See Jeff Lesser, *Welcoming the Undesirables: Brazil and the Jewish Question* (Berkeley: University of California Press, 1995), 23.

91. Graham Dawson writes an especially interesting critique of the Lawrence legend and its relationship to British imperial masculinity. See "The Blond Bedouin: Lawrence of Arabia, Imperial Adventure and the Imagining of English-British Masculinity," in *Manful Assertions: Masculinities in Britain since 1800,* ed. Michael Roper and John Tosh (London: Routledge, 1991), 113–44.

92. This was the Sykes-Picot Agreement, which divided the Arab provinces into separate French and British "spheres."

93. Quoted in Elizabeth Monroe, *Britain's Moment in the Middle East, 1914–1956* (Baltimore: Johns Hopkins University Press, 1963), 65.

94. Albert Hourani, *Syria and Lebanon: A Political Essay* (London: Oxford University Press, 1946), 54.

95. Quoted in Philip S. Khoury, *Syria and the French Mandate* (Princeton: Princeton University Press, 1987), 45.

96. Satiʿ al-Husri, *The Day of Maysalun,* trans. Sidney Glazer (Washington, DC: Middle East Institute, 1966), 161.

97. For an excellent analysis of the gendered nature of French colonial rule in Syria and Lebanon, see Thompson, *Colonial Citizens.*

98. Text of the covenant quoted in Hourani, *Syria and Lebanon,* 163.

99. The coastal cities of Tripoli, Tyre, Sidon, and Beirut were added to the territory of the old *mutasarrifiyya,* while the Bekaa Valley to the west was also incorporated into the new Lebanese state.

100. Al-Hoda, *Al-Hoda, 1898–1968,* 45.

101. Ibid.

102. "Les Libanais ont toujours constitué une entité nationale distincte des groupements voisins par sa langue, ses moeurs, ses affinités, sa culture occiden-

tale." "Les revendications du Liban: Mémoire de la délégation libanaise à la conférence de la paix," in *The Mufakkira of Bishop Abdallah Khoury,* ed. Sami Salameh (Lebanon: Notre Dame University Press, 2001), 195.

103. Translated and excerpted in the *New York Times,* October 6, 1918, 48.

104. *As-Sayeh,* June 21, 1920, 1.

105. *Meraat ul-gharb,* January 2, 1919, 3. The editor of *al-Dalil* also shared this view and had expressed fears over religious fanaticism in an independent Syria as early as 1913. See Motaz Abdullah Alhourani, "The Arab-American Press and the Arab World: News Coverage in *al-Bayan* and *al-Dalil*" (MA thesis abstract, Kansas State University, 1992), 15.

106. *Meraat ul-gharb,* January 2, 1919, 3, and January 30, 1919, 4.

107. Nadine Méouchy, "Les formes de conscience politique et communautaire au Liban et en Syrie à l'époque du mandat français, 1920–1939" (PhD diss., Université de Paris, Sorbonne, 1989), 107.

108. Tauber, *Arab Movements,* 226.

109. Ibid., 229.

110. Bearn to MAE, October 23, 1920, Levant, 1918–1940, Syrie-Liban, 1918–1929, vol. 126, MAE, 26.

111. Michael W. Suleiman, "The Mokarzels' Contributions to the Arabic-Speaking Community in the United States," *Arab Studies Quarterly* 21 (Spring 1999): 73–74.

112. De Caix to MAE, December 28, 1920, Levant, 1918–1940, Syrie-Liban, 1918–1929, vol. 128, MAE, 105–6.

113. Hederi to Consul General of France, New York, June 17, 1922, Levant, 1918–1940, Syrie-Liban, 1918–1929, vol. 126, MAE, 3–5.

114. "Syrian American Society of the U.S," summary of memorandum, NAAC, Series I, M-1.

115. Lawrence Davidson, "Debating Palestine: Arab-American Challenges to Zionism, 1917–1932," in Suleiman, *Arabs in America,* 227–40.

116. *New York Times,* November 9, 1917.

117. Davidson, "Debating Palestine," 231. See also Khalil Babun, "Al-Khatar al-sahyuni" [The Zionist Danger], *Meraat ul-gharb,* January 9, 1919, 5. In addition to Shatara, Amin al-Rihani, a poet and essayist from Lebanon, also became an outspoken advocate of Palestinian national rights and debated with American Zionists in his frequent submissions to newspapers and popular magazines. In 1929, he was part of a delegation that met with Secretary of State Stimson in an effort to persuade the U.S. government to help solve the conflict in Palestine. See Davidson, "Debating Palestine," 234–36; Jurj Saydah, *Adabuna wa udaba'una fil-mahajir al-amrikiyya* [Our Literature and Writers in the American Diaspora], 3rd ed. (Beirut: Dar al-ʿilm lil-malayin, 1964), 238–39.

118. Davidson, "Debating Palestine," 233.

119. Clausse to MAE, November 16, 1920, Levant, 1918–1929, Syrie-Liban, 1918–1929, vol. 126, MAE, 30. French authorities were especially alarmed by the actions of the "Ligue de la Syrie," which had strong bases of support among Syrian Muslims in New York and Rio de Janeiro. See "Bordereau d'envoi," March 25, 1921, Levant, 1918–1940, Syrie-Liban, 1918–1929, vol. 128, MAE, 150. It would be a mistake, however, to assume that opinions on French rule in Syria can

be easily classified along religious lines. As the example of Amin Rihani and others such as George Atlas in Brazil show, there was active opposition to the Mandate in Christian circles. France accused some of her detractors of harboring "des sentiments germanophiles." See dispatch from Brillouin to Cavallace, April 24, 1920, Levant, 1918–1940, Syrie-Liban, 1918–1929, vol. 128, MAE, 7.

120. *Syrian World* 1 (July 1926): 2.

121. She called the *Syrian World* a "beautiful and useful magazine." *Syrian World* 3, no. 7 (January 1929): 46.

122. *Syrian World* 1 (July 1926): 2.

123. Michael A. Shadid, *A Doctor for the People* (New York: Vanguard Press, 1939), 35.

124. Ibid., 40.

125. Ibid., 43–46; Raouf J. Halaby, "Dr. Michael Shadid and the Debate over Identity in The Syrian World," in Hooglund, *Crossing the Waters,* 58; Salom Rizk, *Syrian Yankee* (Garden City, NY: Doubleday, 1943), 316.

126. *Syrian World* 1 (February 1927): 22.

127. Ibid., 48.

128. Ibid., 23.

129. "Readers' Forum," *Syrian World* 1 (March 1927): 56.

130. *Syrian World* 1 (April 1927): 50.

131. *Syrian World* 1 (May 1927): 56.

132. "Echoes of the Syrian Revolution in America," *Syrian World* 1 (February 1927): 25–29; "Our Stand in the Controversy," excerpt from *al-Bayan* in *Syrian World* 2 (March 1928): 45–46.

133. Telegrams dated July 7 and 12, 1927, collected and sent to MAE. File compiled and stored in the Lebanese Emigration Research Center, Notre Dame University, Lebanon.

134. Excerpt from the Beirut newspaper *Lisan al-hal,* in *Syrian World* 2 (May 1928): 55.

135. *Syrian World* 2 (February 1928): 48–49.

136. *Syrian World* 2 (October 1928): 11. Suleiman points out that this was not the first time the Mokarzels had accused the clergy of corruption. Naoum had accused Maronite priests of inappropriate use of funds as early as 1902. See "Mokarzels' Contributions," 74.

137. Excerpted in *Syrian World* 2 (May 1928): 55.

138. Rihbany to Hitti, May 3, 1921, Philip Hitti Papers, Box 4, Correspondence 1, IHRC.

139. Ferris to Hitti, April 28, 1921, Philip Hitti Papers, Box 4, Correspondence 1, IHRC.

140. *Syrian World* 3 (October 1928): 25. In his memoir *A Doctor for the People,* Shadid added that his daughter's "violent" reaction to the prospect of living in the Middle East had also discouraged him from returning (94–95).

141. *Congressional Record* 71, pt. 1 (April 29, 1929): 638. Senator Reed included other groups besides the Syrians in his description of the "trash" [that] "came here in large numbers from Syria and the Turkish Provinces and from different countries of the Balkan peninsula and from all that part of southeastern Europe."

142. *Syrian World* 3 (June 1929): 44.

143. Ibid., 50.

144. *Congressional Record* 71 (June 7, 1929): 2501–2. Portions of Burton's and Reed's speeches were excerpted in the *Syrian World* 3 (June 1929): 49.

4. THE LYNCHING OF NOLA ROMEY

Parts of this chapter are drawn from my article "Strange Fruit? Syrian Immigrants, Extralegal Violence and Racial Formation in the Jim Crow South," *Arab Studies Quarterly* 26 (Spring/Summer 2004): 63–88. The chapter's epigraphs are taken from Richard Wright, *Black Boy*, quoted in Jacquelyn Dowd Hall, *Revolt against Chivalry: Jessie Daniel Ames and the Women's Campaign against Lynching* (New York: Columbia University Press, 1979), 136, and W. E. B. Du Bois, "Race Relations in the United States, 1917–1947," *Phylon* 9, no. 3 (1948): 236.

1. *Tampa Tribune*, May 18, 1929, 1.

2. *Chicago Defender*, May 25, 1929, 1; *New York Times*, May 18, 1929, 18; *Los Angeles Times*, May 18, 1929, 2.

3. *Meraat ul-gharb* [Mirror of the West], May 23, 1929. See also *Miami Herald*, May 18, 1929, 1; *Florida Union Times*, May 19, 1929, 19.

4. Although the *Lake City Reporter* of May 24, 1929, erroneously described them as "native born Assyrians" (1). Romey's name was most probably an anglicized version of the Arabic Rumi or Rumia, while his first name, Nola, was anglicized from Niqula (Nicholas in English). The Arabic name of his Syrian wife, Fannie, was Famia.

5. *Syrian World* 3 (June 1929): 46; *Miami Herald*, May 18, 1929; *New York Times*, May 18, 1929.

6. *Syrian World* 3 (June 1929): 45.

7. James Elbert Cutler, *Lynch-Law: An Investigation into the History of Lynching in the United States* (1905; repr., New York: Negro Universities Press, 1969), 10.

8. W. Fitzhugh Brundage, *Lynching in the New South Georgia and Virginia, 1880–1930* (Urbana: University of Illinois Press, 1993), 3–4; Christopher Waldrep, "Word and Deed: The Language of Lynching, 1820–1953," in *Lethal Imagination: Violence and Brutality in American History*, ed. Michael A. Bellesiles (New York: New York University Press, 1999), 229–58; Ken Gonzales-Day, *Lynching in the West, 1850–1935* (Durham: Duke University Press, 2006), 12–14.

9. Jacquelyn Dowd Hall, *Revolt against Chivalry: Jessie Daniel Ames and the Women's Campaign against Lynching* (New York: Columbia University Press, 1979), 132.

10. James R. McGovern, *Anatomy of a Lynching: The Killing of Claude Neal* (Baton Rouge: Louisiana State University Press, 1982), x.

11. Paul Ortiz, *Emancipation Betrayed: The Hidden History of Black Organizing and White Violence in Florida* (Berkeley: University of California Press, 2005), xiv; Brundage, *Lynching*, 8. For statistics outside the South (and superb analysis of how race and gender came together in the practice of lynching), see Hall, *Revolt against Chivalry*, 134.

12. Brundage, *Lynching*, 2.

13. Mississippi had the highest number at eighty-eight. See U.S. Senate, Committee on the Judiciary, *Crime of Lynching,* 80th Cong., 2nd sess., 1948, 100; Ortiz, *Emancipation Betrayed,* xiv.

14. Between 1880 and 1930, 3,220 of those lynched in the South were black, while 723 were white. Brundage, *Lynching,* 8; Jonathan Markovitz, *Legacies of Lynching* (Minneapolis: University of Minnesota Press, 2004), xxiv.

15. Brundage, *Lynching,* 6.

16. Orlando Patterson calls the "human sacrifice of the lynch mob" the central ritual of southern civil religion. See the chapter "Feast of Blood: Race, Religion, and Human Sacrifice in the Postbellum South," in his *Rituals of Blood: Consequences of Slavery in Two American Centuries* (Washington, DC: Civitas Counterpoint, 1998), 222.

17. Walter T. Howard, *Lynchings: Extralegal Violence in Florida during the 1930s* (Selsingrove: Susquehanna University Press, 1995), 27.

18. The song was written by Abel Meeropol, a schoolteacher and union activist from the Bronx.

19. Thomas C. Holt, "Marking: Race, Race-Making, and the Writing of History," *American Historical Review* 100, no. 1 (1995): 3; Grace E. Hale, *Making Whiteness: The Culture of Segregation in the South, 1890–1940* (New York: Pantheon Books, 1998), 214.

20. Brundage, *Lynching,* 43.

21. Hale, *Making Whiteness,* 201.

22. Edward Keuchel, *A History of Columbia County* (Tallahassee, FL: Sentry Press, 1981), 166.

23. Florida Tobacco Fair Association, *Facts Concerning Lake City and Columbia County, Florida* (Lake City, October 1897), SAF, Special Collections, 5.

24. Ibid.

25. Quoted in Keuchel, *History of Columbia County,* 173.

26. Ibid.

27. See entry for Ellis Moses and family, line 38, Enumeration District 89, Lake City, Columbia County, FL, Manuscript Census of Population, Fourteenth Census of the United States, 1920, National Archives Microfilm Publication, Los Angeles Public Library.

28. See entry for Nola Romey, line 32, Enumeration District 129, Valdosta City, Lowndes County, Georgia, Manuscript Census of Population, Fourteenth Census of the United States, 1920, National Archives Microfilm Publication, Los Angeles Public Library.

29. Ibid.

30. *The State v. N. G. Romey,* "Indictment for Misdemeanor," December 2, 1916, and August 25, 1922, Superior Court Criminal Disposed of Docket *[sic],* County Court, Valdosta, Georgia.

31. *Valdosta Daily Times,* May 17, 1929, 6.

32. Cited in Christopher C. Meyers, " 'Killing Them by the Wholesale': A Lynching Rampage in South Georgia," *Georgia Historical Quarterly* 90 (Summer 2006): 226.

33. Howard, *Lynchings,* 194.

34. Robert P. Ingalls, "Lynching and Establishment Violence in Tampa, 1858–1935," *Journal of Southern History* 53, no. 4 (1987): 615.

35. U.S. Bureau of the Census, *Fifteenth Census of the United States: 1930. Population [Reports by States]*, vol. 3, pt. 1 (Washington, DC: Government Printing Office, 1932), 437.

36. Howard, *Lynchings*, 24.

37. "Dragged from the Pulpit and Lynched," *New York Times*, July 5, 1895, 5.

38. "Negro Shot to Pieces by Mob," *New York Times*, November 28, 1900, 6.

39. NAACP, *Thirty Years of Lynching in the United States, 1889–1918* (1919; repr., New York: Negro Universities Press, 1969), 18; *Los Angeles Times*, May 22, 1911, 15.

40. "Six Negroes Are Lynched by Fake Florida Officials," *Los Angeles Times*, May 22, 1911, 15.

41. *New York Times*, October 7, 1920, 2.

42. Ibid.

43. Excerpted in *Lake City Reporter*, August 3, 1928.

44. *Lake City Reporter*, November 9, 1928.

45. On the history of how Syrian immigrants occupied this particular economic niche, see Naff, *Becoming American*, and Oswaldo Truzzi, "The Right Place at the Right Time: Syrians and Lebanese in Brazil and the United States: A Comparative Approach," *Journal of American Ethnic History* 16, no. 2 (1997): 1–34. On the ordinance, see the transcript of the testimony by Arthur Hall (Police Sergeant) in *Lake City Reporter*, May 24, 1929.

46. *Lake City Reporter*, May 23, 1929.

47. *Miami Herald*, May 18, 1929. It was most likely this report that was translated and printed in the popular New York Arabic-language newspaper *Meraat ul-gharb* [Mirror of the West]. See *Meraat ul-gharb*, May 23, 1929.

48. *Syrian World* 3 (June 1929): 46.

49. *Syrian World* listed his name as Esau, a transliteration of the Arabic name 'Isa. He is enumerated in the 1920 census as Icer, and this name was used in several of the English-language reports.

50. *Syrian World* 3 (June 1929): 47.

51. *Valdosta Times*, May 20, 1929, 2.

52. *Syrian World* 3 (June 1929): 4; see also *Valdosta Daily Times*, May 20, 1929, 5.

53. *Florida Times Union* (Jacksonville), May 17, 1929, 5

54. *Lake City Reporter*, May 24, 1929.

55. *Lake City Reporter*, May 23, 1929, 1.

56. *Miami Herald*, May 18, 1929, 22; *Lake City Reporter*, May 24, 1929.

57. *Miami Herald*, May 18, 1929, 22; *Florida Times Union*, May 19, 1929, 19.

58. *Lake City Reporter*, May 24, 1929.

59. Brundage, *Lynching*, 76.

60. *Valdosta Daily Times*, May 17, 1929, 1.

61. *Miami Herald*, May 18, 1929, 22.

62. Administrative Correspondence of Governor Doyle E. Carlton, 1929–1932, Series 204, Box 16, Folder 5, SAF. Reprinted with slight changes in *Miami Herald*,

May 19, 1929, 22. Esau is closer to the English transliteration of the name 'Isa—Icer's name in Arabic.

63. *Valdosta Daily Times,* May 18, 1929, 2.

64. NAACP, *Thirty Years of Lynching,* 23.

65. Telegram to Sheriff W. B. Douglass, May 17, 1929, Administrative Correspondence of Governor Doyle E. Carlton, 1929–1932, Series 204, Box 16, Folder 5, SAF.

66. Telegram to Governor Carlton from Sheriff W. B. Douglass, May 18, 1929, Administrative Correspondence of Governor Doyle E. Carlton, 1929–1932, Series 204, Box 16, Folder 5, SAF.

67. Charlton W. Tebeau, *A History of Florida* (Coral Gables: University of Miami Press, 1971), 395.

68. Joe M. Joseph to Carlton, June 25, 1929, Administrative Correspondence of Governor Doyle E. Carlton, 1929–1932, Series 204, Box 16, Folder 5, SAF.

69. *Syrian World* 4 (September 1929): 53.

70. "Suriy yuqtalu bi-aidi al-jumhur" [Syrian Killed at the Hands of a Mob], *Meraat ul-gharb,* May 23, 1929, 2.

71. *Syrian World* 3 (June 1929): 48.

72. Unsigned letter to Governor Carlton, May 18, 1929, Administrative Correspondence of Governor Doyle E. Carlton, 1929–1932, Series 204, Box 16, Folder 5, SAF.

73. Unsigned, undated letter to Governor Carlton, Administrative Correspondence of Governor Doyle E. Carlton, 1929–1932, Series 204, Box 16, Folder 5, SAF.

74. Unsigned letter to Governor Carlton, May 20, 1929, Administrative Correspondence of Governor Doyle E. Carlton, 1929–1932, Series 204, Box 16, Folder 5, SAF.

75. Phone conversation with Philip Moses, Lake City, Florida, July 10, 2006. Confirmed in phone conversation with Sally Barnes (née Moses), Atlanta, GA, July 17, 2006.

76. Unsigned letter to Governor Carlton, May 20, 1929, Administrative Correspondence of Governor Doyle E. Carlton, 1929–1932, Series 204, Box 16, Folder 5, SAF.

77. Arthur F. Raper, *The Tragedy of Lynching* (Chapel Hill: University of North Carolina Press, 1933), 14.

78. Unsigned, undated letter to Carlton, Administrative Correspondence of Governor Doyle E. Carlton, 1929–1932, Series 204, Box 16, Folder 5, SAF.

79. *Valdosta Daily Times,* May 20, 1929, 5.

80. Ibid.

81. *Lake City Reporter,* May 24, 1929, 1.

82. Ibid.

83. "Application for Letters," June 6, 1929, Book H, Lake City County Court House.

84. Entry for Ellis Moses and family, line 33, Enumeration District 37–77, Birmingham City, Jefferson County, AL, Manuscript Census of Population, Fifteenth Census of the United States, 1930, AncestryLibrary.com.

85. NAACP, *Thirty Years of Lynching*, 5.

86. Hall, *Revolt against Chivalry*, 64; Mitchell F. Ducey, *The Commission on Interracial Cooperation Papers, 1919–1944 and the Association of Southern Women for the Prevention of Lynching Papers, 1930–1942* (Ann Arbor, MI: University Microfilms International, 1984), 3.

87. Hall, *Revolt against Chivalry*, 61.

88. Quoted in Ducey, *Commission on Interracial Cooperation*, 4.

89. Hall, *Revolt against Chivalry*, 163.

90. "Committee on Women's Work," *Commission on Interracial Cooperation Papers, 1919–1944* (New York: NYT Microfilming Corporation of America, 1983), (hereafter *CIC Papers*), Series VI, Reel 43, #185.

91. Ibid.

92. Hall, *Revolt against Chivalry*, 302.

93. "State Interracial Committees, 1918–1945," *CIC Papers*, Series VII, Reel 45, #31.

94. Quoted in Hall, *Revolt against Chivalry*, 181.

95. Howard, *Lynchings*, 42.

96. "Committee on Women's Work."

97. Brundage, *Lynching*, 32.

98. Phone conversation with Philip Moses, Lake City, FL, July 10, 2006.

99. Name withheld by request.

100. Cited in Conklin and Faires, " 'Colored' and Catholic," 77.

101. Jusserand to Poincaré, January 3, 1923, Levant, 1918–1940, Syrie-Liban, 1918–1929, vol. 407, MAE.

102. *Congressional Record* 71, pt. 1 (April 29, 1929): 638. Senator Reed included other groups in addition to the Syrians in his description of the "trash" [that] "came here in large numbers from Syria and the Turkish Provinces and from different countries of the Balkan peninsula and from all that part of southeastern Europe." He did, however, single out "Arabs" when he linked fitness for immigration to self-government.

103. Ingalls, for example, in "Lynching and Establishment Violence," noted the connection between outsiderness and vulnerability to mob violence in his study of lynching in Tampa, Florida. Roberta Senechal de la Roche argues that "lynching varies directly with cultural difference" expressed in symbolic aspects of social life such as language, religion, cuisine, clothing and entertainment. See Roberta Senechal de la Roche, "The Sociogenesis of Lynching," in *Under Sentence of Death: Lynching in the South*, ed. W. Fitzhugh Brundage (Durham: University of North Carolina Press, 1997), 58.

104. Based on my viewing of a photograph of Nola and Fannie in the possession of a family member who does not want the photograph reproduced.

105. *Chicago Defender*, May 25, 1929, 1.

106. J. Alexander Karlin, *New Orleans Lynchings of 1891 and the American Press* (n.p.: "s.n.," 1941), 7, reprinted as a pamphlet from *Louisiana Historical Quarterly* 24 (January 1941): 187–204.

107. Ibid.

108. Eugene Levy, " 'Is the Jew a White Man?': Press Reaction to the Leo Frank Case, 1913–1915," *Phylon* 35, no. 2 (1974): 212–22.

109. For an especially interesting analysis of the Leo Frank case, see Nancy MacLean, "The Leo Frank Case Reconsidered: Gender and Sexual Politics in the Making of Reactionary Populism," *Journal of American History* 78, no. 3 (1991): 917–48.

110. Quoted in *Syrian World* 3 (June 1929): 42.

111. David Roediger, "Whiteness and Ethnicity," 190.

112. Ignatiev, *How the Irish Became White*, 2.

113. Evidence can be found in Paula Maria Stathakis, "Almost White: Greek and Lebanese-Syrian Immigrants in North and South Carolina, 1900–1940" (PhD diss., University of South Carolina, 1996), 213–17.

114. Syrians in New York helped Bhicaji Franyi Balsara become naturalized in 1910. His petition for naturalization had originally been turned down on the grounds that he was an "alien-other than white." See *United States v. Balsara*, 180 Fed. 696 (1910). On the NAACP campaign, see Robert L. Zangrando, *The NAACP Crusade against Lynching, 1909–1950* (Philadelphia: Temple University Press, 1980).

115. Goldstein, *Price of Whiteness*, 55.

5. MARRIAGE AND RESPECTABILITY

This chapter's epigraphs are taken from A. Hakim, "The Sage of Washington Street on the Marriage Problem among Syrians," *Syrian World* 3, no. 5 (1928): 31, and an interview with "Catherine" in Evelyn Shakir's *Bint Arab* (Westport, CT: Praeger, 1997), 113.

1. In classical Arabic, America is *Amrika*. However, in colloquial usage it is often rendered as *Amirka*.

2. Najib Masha'lani, "Al-Ilitqa' al-faj'" [The Surprise Encounter], *al-Mashriq* 5, no. 12 (1902): 569–72.

3. *Al-Ni'ma* 2, no. 8 (1911): 505.

4. Wadih Safady, *Cenas y cenários dos caminhos de minha vida*, vol. 1 (São Paulo: Penna Editora, 1966), 220.

5. Cited in Naff, *Becoming American*, 234.

6. Khater, *Inventing Home*, 31–38.

7. *Al-Ni'ma* 3, no. 1 (1911): 75–76.

8. Letters contained in the folder "Writings of South America and Australia," Papers of Patriarch Elias Hoyek, Maronite Patriarchal Archive, Bkerke, Lebanon.

9. Lawrence Oschinsky, "Islam in Chicago: Being a Study of the Acculturation of Muslim Palestinian Community in That City" (MA thesis, University of Chicago, 1947), 27.

10. Khater, *Inventing Home*, 66.

11. Ministère de la guerre, *Notice sur la Syrie*, 126.

12. Khater, *Inventing Home*, 141–43.

13. U.S. Bureau of the Census, *Thirteenth Census, 1910*, vol. 1, *Population 1910: General Report and Analysis* (Washington, DC: Government Printing Office, 1913), 963.

14. Oschinsky, "Islam in Chicago"; Abdo Elkholy, *Arab Moslems in the United States: Religion and Assimilation* (New Haven: College and University Press, 1966), 29–33; Evelyn Shakir, *Bint Arab: Arab and Arab American Women in the United States* (Westport, CT: Praeger, 1997), 114.

15. "Muhajara al-mara' al-durziyya" [The Emigration of the Druze Woman], *al-Bayan*, March 31, 1914; see also *al-Bayan*, April 7, 1914; *al-Bayan*, April 14, 1914.

16. *Al-Hoda*, February 6, 1909, 4.

17. Ibid. (italics added).

18. U.S. Bureau of the Census, *Fourteenth Census, 1920*, vol. 2, *General Report and Analytical Tables* (Washington, DC: Government Printing Office, 1922), 973. Naff tracked rates of out-marriage using the 1910 and 1920 census figures for "white stock of foreign or mixed parentage." See Naff, *Becoming American*, 237. Other studies of out-marriage can be found in Kayal and Kayal, *Syrian-Lebanese in America*, and Elkholy, *Arab Moslems*. Paula Hajar offers an interesting example based on her own family in "Changes and Continuities in the Code of Honor, among Syrian Lebanese Immigrants to the United States," unpublished manuscript, New York, 65.

19. Khater, *Inventing Home*, 142–43.

20. Harry C. Ford, "Why I Wrote a Syrian Play," *Syrian World* 2 (July 1927): 33–34.

21. Shaheen, *Reel Bad Arabs*, 23.

22. Quoted in *New York Times*, September 27, 1920, 23.

23. "Anna Ascends," *Syrian World* 2 (July 1927): 35.

24. Ibid., 40.

25. This is James Baldwin's term in "On Being White and Other Lies," *Essence*, April 1984, 90–92.

26. For discussions of this issue, see Roderick A. Ferguson, *Aberrations in Black: Toward a Queer of Color Critique* (Minneapolis: University of Minnesota Press, 2004), 14–16; Shah, *Contagious Divides*, 13–15.

27. Hitti, *Syrians in America*, 31.

28. U.S. House, Industrial Commission on Immigration, *Reports*, vol. 15, 57th Cong., 1st sess., 1901, H. Doc. 184, 444.

29. Tahafa Laham al-Tin, interview by Alixa Naff, 1962, transcript, NAAC, Series 4/C.

30. *Syrian World* 2 (April 1928): 9; Truzzi, *Patrícios*, 72; Safady, *Cenas e cenários*, 225. In Safady's version, the women were abandoned by their husbands at the Port of Beirut.

31. *Syrian World* 2 (April 1928): 9.

32. "Argentinean Women Married to Syrians," *Syrian World* 2 (June 1927): 57.

33. Ibid.

34. *Syrian World* 3 (November 1928): 27–32; 3 (December 1928): 20–25; 3 (January 1929): 18–23.

35. Washington Street in New York City was at the center of Syrian community and business life, although by this time many Syrian-owned businesses were thriving on Brooklyn's Atlantic Avenue.

36. *Syrian World* 3 (January 1929): 20.

37. *Syrian World* 1 (February 1927): 52.

38. U.S. Senate, Industrial Commission on Immigration, 1907–10, *Abstracts of Reports,* 2 vols., 61st Cong., 3rd sess., 1911, S. Doc. 747, 1:17.

39. Naff, *Becoming American,* 236.

40. Kayal and Kayal, *Syrian-Lebanese in America,* 198.

41. *Syrian World* 3 (December 1928): 21.

42. Ibid., 22.

43. Ibid., 46–47.

44. *Syrian World* 3 (March 1929): 48.

45. Ibid., 47–49.

46. "Readers' Forum," *Syrian World* 3 (February 1929): 45–47.

47. Ibid., 45. See also comments of Anna Shire in "Readers' Forum," *Syrian World* 3 (May 1929): 40–42.

48. Ibid., 49.

49. See *Al-Mausu'a,* 81; Alixa Naff, "The Arabic-Language Press," in *The Ethnic Press in the United States,* ed. Sally Miller (New York: Greenwood Press, 1987), 11.

50. Quoted in Shakir, *Bint Arab,* 68.

51. "Bayn al-rajulayn" [Between Two Men], *al-Hoda,* December 4, 1908, 4.

52. *As-Sayeh,* September 12, 1912, 4. See also ʿAfifa Karam's "Radd ʿala iʿtirad" [Reply to a Rebuttal], in which she writes, "We hear words but see no action." In *al-Hoda,* January 9, 1909, 4.

53. "The women's awakening" (*al-nahda al-nisaʾiyya*) was the phrase used to describe the late nineteenth-century female literary culture. It also described the expansion in education and the formation of new associations that were the institutional precursors of women's movements in Syria and Egypt. See Beth Baron, *The Women's Awakening in Egypt: Culture, Society and the Press* (New Haven: Yale University Press, 1994). On the construction of women as "managers of the house," see Afsaneh Najmabadi, "Crafting an Educated Housewife in Iran," in Abu-Lughod, *Remaking Women,* 91–125.

54. Baron, *Women's Awakening,* 125; Najmabadi notes that this construction was also true for late nineteenth-century Persian texts, in "Crafting an Educated Housewife," 92. For an interesting parallel in France, where women were closely linked to the reproduction of national culture but not to the politics of the state, see Leora Auslander, *Taste and Power: Furnishing Modern France* (Berkeley: University of California Press, 1996), 413.

55. Deniz Kandiyoti notes that nineteenth-century "male reformers of the time found the plight of women a powerful vehicle for the expression of their own restiveness with social conventions they found particularly stultifying and archaic." "End of Empire: Islam, Nationalism, and Women in Turkey," in *Women, Islam and the State,* ed. Deniz Kandiyoti (Philadelphia: Temple University Press, 1991), 26.

56. Cited in Suleiman, "Mokarzels' Contribution," 75.

57. Ibid., 76.

58. Leila Ahmed, *Women and Gender in Islam: Historical Roots of a Modern Debate* (New Haven: Yale University Press, 1992), 152–53.

59. *Syrian World* 3 (January 1929): 48.

60. Phone conversation with surviving daughter, full name withheld by request, July 26, 2006.

61. *Al-Dalil,* July 6, 1912.

62. Kayal and Kayal, *Syrian-Lebanese in America,* 193.

63. Naff, *Becoming American,* 292.

64. Southern Federation, *75th Diamond Jubilee Convention.*

65. Helen Hatab, "Syrian-American Ethnicity: Structure and Ideology in Transition" (MA thesis, American University of Beirut, 1975), 127.

CONCLUSION

1. A good example is Hooglund, *Crossing the Waters.*

2. The concept of assimilation has been understood differently in historical and sociological literature over the last century. From early notions of a "melting pot" to integration into an "Anglo-American core," assimilation (after falling out of fashion among many historians in the 1960s and 1970s) has been reexamined and found useful for describing processes that result in greater homogeneity within a society. Russell A. Kazal argues, for example, that questions of assimilation are important to three areas of historical scholarship: (a) research on how ethnic enclaves fit together in a larger pluralistic model; (b) the study of homogenization along class lines; and (c) reinterpretations of Americanization as a process of claiming "whiteness." See his analysis of the literature in "Revisiting Assimilation: The Rise, Fall, and Reappraisal of a Concept in American Ethnic History," *American Historical Review* 100 (April 1995): 437–71.

3. This view of assimilation is based on two working definitions found, respectively, in Ewa Morawska, "Ethnicity," in *Encyclopedia of Social History,* ed. Peter Stearns (New York: Garland, 1994), 241, and Harold J. Abramson, "Assimilation and Pluralism," in Thernstrom, *Harvard Encyclopedia,* 150.

4. Southern Federation, *75th Diamond Jubilee Convention,* n.p.

5. *In re Ahmad Hassan,* 48 F. Supp. 843 (1942).

6. Ibid., 845.

7. Ibid.

8. Ibid.

9. Oschinsky, "Islam in Chicago," 27; Elkholy, *Arab Moslems,* 29–33.

10. *United States v. Cartozian,* 6 F. 2d. 919 (1925).

11. *In re Halladjian,* 174 Fed. 834 (1909). The case involved four Armenian applicants and was heard in the circuit court of the District of Massachusetts. It was cited in *In re Mudarri* 176 Fed. 465.

12. U.S. INS, "The Eligibility of Arabs to Naturalization," *Monthly Review* 1 (October 1943): 12 (italics in original).

13. Ibid.

14. Ibid. Both the INS and the naturalization courts appeared oblivious to the power of institutionalized anti-Semitism to construct Jews as nonwhite. As Karen Brodkin argues, the systematic exclusion of Jews from professional, educational and social spaces reserved for "authentic" (usually Protestant) whites, contributed to their racialization. Not until after the Second World War, with the rise in philo-Semitism and the ascendancy of Jews into the American middle

class, did Jews become, in her estimation, fully "white." See Brodkin, *How Jews Became White Folks*.

15. *Ex parte Mohriez*, 54 F. Supp. 941 (1944).

16. U.S. INS, "Eligibility of Arabs," 12.

17. *Ex parte Mohriez*, 943.

18. Ibid.

19. Massad, "Palestinians." Massad argues that "honorary white" status was first conferred on European Jews, who became objects of Gentile white support and sympathy in the post-Holocaust era. It has, in his opinion, only recently been conferred on Palestinians as *objects* of Israeli human rights violations. I am suggesting that naturalization law defined Muslim Arabs as "honorary whites" much earlier but that their whiteness was not considered as legitimate as that of the Syrian Christians, who claimed it earlier and more successfully.

· 20. On this point, see Moustafa Bayoumi, "Racing Religion," *CR: The New Centennial Review* 6, no. 2 (2006): 267–93.

21. B. Anderson, *Imagined Communities*, 7.

22. Brand, *Citizens Abroad*.   ·

23. "A Call to the Syrians Abroad to Regain Their Syrian Nationality," September 21, 1937, Murasalat al-mughtaribin [Correspondence of Emigrants], al-Qism al-khass, Da'irat al-watha'iq al-tarikhiyya, Damascus.

24. Jurj Tu'ama, *Al-Mughtaribun al-'arab fi amrika al-shamaliyya* [Arab Emigrants in North America] (Damascus: Wizarat al-thaqafah wal-irshad al-qawmi, 1965). See also Hizb al-Ba'th al-Ishtiraki, al-Qiadat al-Qawmiyya, *Al-Mughtaribun al-'arab bayn al-madi wal-hadir wa tumuhat al-mustaqbal* [Arab Emigrants: Between the Past and the Present, and Future Aspirations] (Damascus: Maktab al-i'lam wal-nashr, 1984).

25. The word *mughtaribun* actually comes from the root *gharb,* meaning "west." The literal translation is thus "those who have gone west."

26. Conzen et al., "Invention of Ethnicity," 21.

27. I have taken the concept of "multiple geographies" from the authors of the white paper for the Regional Worlds program at the University of Chicago. The program endeavored to rethink area studies by proposing alternative approaches to the study of regions that emphasize processes, not traits. As the authors of the white paper write, "Regions, in our approach, are taken to be initial contexts for themes which generate variable geographies, rather than as fixed geographies marked by set themes." See Arjun Appadurai et al., *Area Studies, Regional Worlds: A White Paper for the Ford Foundation* (Chicago: Globalization Project of the University of Chicago, June 1997), 2.

EPILOGUE

This chapter's epigraphs are taken from Habib Ibrahim Katibah, *Arabic-Speaking Americans* (New York: Institute of Arab American Affairs, 1946), 28, and Alixa Naff, "Arabs in America: A Historical Overview," in *Arabs in the New World: Studies on Arab-American Communities,* ed. Sameer Abraham and Nabeel Abraham (Detroit: Wayne State University, Center for Urban Studies, 1983), 23.

1. *New York Times,* November 28, 1944, 17.

2. Ferhat Ziadeh, phone interview, August 6, 2006; Ferhat Ziadeh, "Winds Blow Where Ships Do Not Wish to Go," in *Paths to the Middle East: Ten Scholars Look Back,* ed. Thomas Naff (Albany: State University of New York Press, 1993), 293–324.

3. Habib Ibrahim Katibah, preface to Katibah, *Arabic-Speaking Americans.*

4. Katibah had been a member of an organization called the Arab League, headed by Palestinian American surgeon Fu'ad Shatara and located next to the New York offices of *as-Sayeh.* See Ziadeh, "Winds Blow," 300.

5. Katibah, *Arabic-Speaking Americans,* 3.

6. Ibid., 4.

7. Ibid., 8.

8. Michael Suleiman, "Arab-Americans and the Political Process," in McCarus, *Development of Arab-American Identity,* 46.

9. Boutros Labaki, "Lebanese Emigration during the War (1975–1989)," in Hourani and Shehadi, *Lebanese in the World,* 609.

10. Aristide R. Zolberg, *A Nation by Design: Immigration Policy in the Fashioning of America* (Cambridge, MA: Harvard University Press, 2006), 316–17.

11. Ibid., 333.

12. Ibid., 338.

13. Michael Suleiman, introduction to *Arabs in America,* 9.

14. Ibid.; Naff, "Arabs in America," 23; Elaine C. Hagopian, "Minority Rights in a Nation-State: The Nixon Administration's Campaign against Arab-Americans," *Journal of Palestine Studies* 5, nos. 1–2 (1975): 104.

15. Telephone conversation with Ferhat Ziadeh, August 6, 2006, Seattle, WA.

16. Janice J. Terry, "Community and Political Activism among Arab Americans in Detroit," in Suleiman, *Arabs in America,* 241–54.

17. George Khoury, interview, April 29, 2006, Dearborn, MI.

18. Letters of the Ad Hoc Conference Committee, Association of Arab American University Graduates (AAUG), Eastern Michigan University, Ypsilanti, Michigan, Box 16, Archives 1967, AAUG Records. My thanks to Janice J. Terry for facilitating my access to these archives.

19. Minutes of the meeting of the AAUG Board of Directors, AAUG Records, Box 14, Board of Directors 1968.

20. Ibid., 6.

21. *New York Times,* November 2, 1969, E9.

22. Ibid.

23. Folder "NYT Positive Responses," AAUG Records, Box 49.

24. Ibid.

25. Letter to AAUG, November 2, 1969, Folder "NYT Negative Responses," AAUG Records, Box 49.

26. Unsigned postcard to AAUG, November 9, 1969, Folder "NYT Negative Responses," AAUG Records, Box 49.

27. Unsigned letters to AAUG, Folder "NYT Negative Responses," AAUG Records, Box 49.

28. Ibid.

29. Joseph, "Against the Grain," 257.

30. Edward Said, "Orientalism and the October War: The Shattered Myths," in Abu-Laban and Zeadey, *Arabs in America,* 84. Unlike in the 1967 war, the Arab armies experienced several early military successes in 1973, notably the Egyptian army's rapid crossing of the Suez Canal, which overwhelmed Israeli positions.

31. Presidential address by Abdeen Jabara, Berkeley, CA, November 11, 1972, AAUG Records, Box 10, "Presidential Addresses."

32. Both Du Bois and Blyden are quoted in Robert G. Weisbord and Richard Kazarian Jr., *Israel in the Black American Perspective* (Westport, CT: Greenwood Press, 1985), 22; see also McAlister, *Epic Encounters,* ch. 2.

33. Quoted in Weisbord and Kazarian, *Israel,* 40.

34. McAlister, *Epic Encounters,* 88–91.

35. Quoted in ibid., 92; Nikhil Pal Singh, *Black Is a Country: Race and the Unfinished Struggle for Democracy* (Cambridge, MA: Harvard University Press, 2004), 184–85.

36. Weisbord and Kazarian, *Israel,* 37; Matthew Frye Jacobson, *Roots Too: White Ethnic Revival in Post-Civil Rights America* (Cambridge, MA: Harvard University Press, 2006), 222.

37. "Andrew Young and the State Department," *Christian Science Monitor,* August 31, 1979, Folder "Black Press on Arab Issues," AAUG Records, Box 33.

38. *Christian Science Monitor,* August 21, 1979, Folder "Black Press on Arab Issues," AAUG Records, Box 33.

39. G. James Flemming, "Unfortunate: The Making of a Black-Jewish 'Rift,'" *Afro-American,* August 28–September 1, 1979, Folder "Black Press on Arab Issues," AAUG Records, Box 33.

40. "Black-Jewish Relations," Folder "Black Press on Arab Issues," AAUG Records, Box 33.

41. Roy Wilkins, "Young Stood Up for Justice," *Afro-American,* August 28–September 1, 1979, 4, Folder "Black Press on Arab Issues," AAUG Records, Box 33.

42. Samih Farsoun, "Proposal for Black and Arab Dialogue in the United States," August 1979, Folder "Proposal for Black-Arab Dialogue," AAUG Records, Box 33.

43. Jesse Jackson's speech to the annual PUSH (People United to Save Humanity) convention, July 19, 1980, New Orleans, LA, Folder "Black America Project 1980," AAUG Records, Box 33.

44. Memo from Penny Johnson to the AAUG Board, July 30, 1980, Folder "Black America Project 1980," AAUG Records, Box 33.

45. Marisa Tamari to AAUG, February 15, 1984, Folder "Jesse Jackson Presidential Campaign," AAUG Records, Box 33.

46. Abu-Laban and Zeadey, *Arabs in America;* Baha Abu-Laban and Michael Suleiman, eds., *Arab Americans: Continuity and Change* (Belmont, MA: Association of Arab-American University Graduates, 1989); James Zogby, ed. *Taking Root, Bearing Fruit: The Arab-American Experience* (Washington, DC: American-Arab Anti-Discrimination Committee, 1984).

47. Hagopian, "Minority Rights," 101.

48. Ibid.

49. Nadia Hijab, "AAUG in the 1990s: In Search of Purpose, Resources, and Good Organizational Culture," *Arab Studies Quarterly* 29, nos. 3 and 4 (2007): 155.

50. Ibid., 110.

51. "F.B.I. Says Jewish Defense League May Have Planted Fatal Bombs," *New York Times,* November 9, 1985, 1. Members of the Jewish Defense League continue to deny involvement in the death of Alex Odeh. See Jewish Defense League, "JDL Reiterates No Connection to Odeh Death," press release, October 11, 2007, www.jdl.org/misc/odeh_reiteration.shtml.

52. U.S. House, *Ethnically Motivated Violence against Arab-Americans,* hearing before the Subcommittee on Criminal Justice of the Committee on the Judiciary, 99th Cong., 2nd sess., 1986, 11.

53. See "F.B.I. Chief Warns Arabs of Danger," *New York Times,* December 11, 1985, A13.

54. Michael Suleiman, "The Arab Community in the United States: A Comparison of Lebanese and Non-Lebanese," in Hourani and Shehadi, *Lebanese in the World,* 194; Yvonne Yazbeck Haddad, "Maintaining the Faith of the Fathers: Dilemmas of Religious Identity in the Christian and Muslim Arab-American Communities," in McCarus, *Development of Arab-American Identity,* 80.

55. "Abdeen Jabara: A Champion from and of the Heartland," interview, *Café Arabica,* November 1996, at www.cafearabica.com/people/people12/peoabdeen8x1.html.

56. Quoted in McAlister, *Epic Encounters,* 111.

57. Ibid.

58. Jacobson, *Roots Too,* 222.

59. T. Saliba, "Resisting Invisibility," 306.

60. Nadine Naber, "Ambiguous Insiders: An Investigation of Arab American Invisibility," *Ethnic and Racial Studies* 23 (January 2000): 51.

61. Leila Ahmed, *A Border Passage* (New York: Penguin Books, 1999), 243.

62. Lisa Suhair Majaj, "Boundaries: Arab/American," in Kadi, *Food for Our Grandmothers,* 66. On Arab American feminist positioning, see also Mervat Hatem, "The Invisible American Half: Arab American Hybridity and Feminist Discourse in the 1990s," 1998, www.haussite.net/haus.o/SCRIPT/txt2001/01/hatem.HTML.

63. Majaj, "Boundaries," 80.

64. Nada Elia, "The 'White' Sheep of the Family: But Bleaching Is like Starvation," in *This Bridge We Call Home: Radical Visions for Transformation,* ed. Gloria Anzaldua and Analouise Keating (New York: Routledge, 2002), 226, 223–31. See also T. Saliba, "Resisting Invisibility," 304–19.

65. Majaj, "Arab-Americans," 331.

66. Helen Samhan, "Statement to the House Subcommittee on Census, Statistics and Postal Personnel," June 30, 1993, in U.S. House, *Review the Status of Planning for the 2000 Census,* Hearing before the Subcommittee on Census, Statistics, and Postal Personnel of the Committee on Post Office and Civil Service, 103rd Cong., 1st sess., 1993. My thanks to Helen Samhan for sharing a copy of her testimony with me.

67. Excerpts of Hefny's letter to his employer, cited in Asa G. Hilliard, "What Do We Need to Know Now? Race, Identity, Hegemony, and Education," *Rethinking Schools* 14 (Winter 1999): 2.

68. Joan MacFarlane, "Black or White? Egyptian Immigrant Fights for Black Classification," July 16, 1997, *CNN News*, www.cnn.com/US/9707/16/racial.suit/index.html.

69. Hefny was interviewed in the November 1990 issue of *Jet*, which ran the story under the headline "Black 'White' Man Challenges Federal Race Identity Law." The citations above are taken from Soheir A. Morsy, "Beyond the Honorary 'White' Classification of Egyptians: Societal Identity in Historical Context," in *Race*, ed. Steven Gregory and Roger Sanjek (New Brunswick: Rutgers University Press, 1994), 175–76.

70. Samhan, "Statement"; AAI, "Talking Points on 'Middle Eastern' Ethnic Classification," in my own files.

71. Samhan, "Statement," 3.

72. Margo Anderson and Stephen Fienberg, *Who Counts: The Politics of Census-Taking in Contemporary America* (New York: Russell Sage Foundation, 1999), 3.

73. Ibid., 170.

74. "Revisions to the Standards for the Classification of Federal Data on Race and Ethnicity," *Federal Register* 62, no. 210 (October 30, 1997): 58782–90, reprinted in appendix of *Encyclopedia of the U.S. Census*, ed. Margo Anderson (Washington, DC: Congressional Quarterly Press, 2000), 400–402.

75. American Anthropological Association, "Response to IMB Directive 15: Race and Ethnic Standards for Federal Statistics and Administrative Reporting," September 1997, www.aaanet.org/gvt/ombdraft.htm.

76. I have been unsuccessful in securing accurate information on what this threshold was. A member of the Census Statistical Information Staff informed me that she didn't think there was a certain number but that the census just chose the largest groups. Phone conversation, May 21, 2004.

77. Phone conversation with Helen Samhan, deputy director of the AAI, April 8, 2004.

78. Presentation to AAI Census Information Board meeting by Aref Dajani, principal researcher, Computing Applications, U.S. Census Bureau, Dearborn, MI, October 18, 2003, in my own files.

79. Omi and Winant, *Racial Formation*, 107.

80. AAI, "Back to Basics Politics: Papers of the Arab American Institute, 1985–1989," distributed at the AAI Annual Convention, Dearborn, MI, 2003.

81. Personal observation of the AAI's National Leadership Conference (October 17–19, 2003), Dearborn, MI. See also Lynette Clemetson, "Arab-Americans Gain a Higher Political Profile," *New York Times*, October 19, 2003.

82. David S. Broder, "Mobilizing Arab Americans," *Washington Post*, October 22, 2003, A29.

83. Omi and Winant, *Racial Formation*, 99.

84. G. Patricia de la Cruz and Angela Brittingham, "The Arab Population: 2000," Census 2000 Brief, U.S. Bureau of the Census, December 2003. See also U.S. Bureau of the Census, "Report on Arab Population Released by Census Bureau,"

press release, December 3, 2003, www.census.gov/Press-Release/www/releases/archives/census_2000/001576.html.

85. In the period between September 11, 2001, and October 11, 2002, there were seven hundred violent incidents targeting Arab Americans or those perceived as such. See ADC, *Report on Hate Crimes and Discrimination against Arab Americans: The Post-September 11 Backlash* (Washington, DC: ADC Research Institute, 2003), www.adc.org/hatecrimes/pdf/2003_report_web.pdf.

86. Detroit Arab American Study, "Preliminary Findings from the Detroit Arab American Study: Executive Summary," July 2004, www.umich.edu/news/Releases/2004/Jul04/daas.pdf. The Detroit Arab American Study was sponsored by the Center for Arab American Studies at the University of Michigan, Dearborn, and the University of Michigan's Institute for Social Research.

87. Hisham Aidi notes that "Islam has provided an anti-imperial idiom for many subordinate groups in the West." See his "Let Us Be Moors: Islam, Race and 'Connected Histories,'" *Middle East Report,* no. 229 (Winter 2003): 42–53.

88. Naber, "Ambiguous Insiders," 52.

89. Bernard S. Cohn, *An Anthropologist among the Historians and Other Essays* (New York: Oxford University Press, 1987), 230.

90. Ian F. Haney López, *Racism on Trial: The Chicano Fight for Justice* (Cambridge, MA: Harvard University Press, 2003), 206.

91. Lynette Clemetson, "Some Younger U.S. Arabs Reassert Ethnicity," *New York Times,* January 11, 2004.

92. Personal observation, July 3, 2006, San Antonio, TX.

93. This is up from less than 10 percent on the 1990 census. Helen Samhan, "By the Numbers," *Arab American Business,* October 2003, 27. See also U.S. Bureau of the Census, American Fact Finder, "Ancestry," http://factfinder.census.gov.

94. "Homeland Security Given Data on Arab-Americans," *New York Times,* July 30, 2004; Electronic Privacy Information Center, "Department of Homeland Security Obtained Data on Arab Americans from Census Bureau," http://epic.org/privacy/census/foia/default.html. The ADC and the AAI coordinated a formal response to the release of this information, endorsed by twenty-four civil liberties, faith-based, and human rights groups.

95. Bayoumi, "Racing Religion," 277.

Bibliography

ARCHIVES

Association of Arab American University Graduates. Records. Eastern Michigan University, Ypsilanti, Michigan.

Board of Lady Managers. World's Columbian Exhibition, 1893. Vols. 28–30. Chicago Historical Society.

Carlton, Governor Doyle. Correspondence. RG 000102. State Archives of Florida, Tallahassee, FL.

Faris and Yamna Naff Arab-American Collection. National Museum of American History, Archives Center. Smithsonian Institution, Behring Center, Washington, DC

Hitti, Philip. Papers. Near Eastern American Collection. Immigration History Research Center, University of Minnesota.

Hoyek, Patriarch Elias. Papers. Maronite Patriarchal Archive, Bkerke, Lebanon.

Kayal, Philip M. Papers. Syrian American Archival Collection, Group I. Coll. No. 090. Center for Migration Studies, Staten Island, NY.

Levant, 1918–1940. Syrie-Liban, 1918–1929. Vols. 126–407. Ministère des affaires étrangères, Archives diplomatiques, Paris.

Murasalat al-mughtaribin [Correspondence of Emigrants]. Al-Qism al-khass. Da'irat al-watha'iq al-tarikhiyya [Center for Historical Documents], Damascus, Syria.

Sholtz, Governor David. Correspondence. RG 000102. State Archives of Florida, Tallahassee, FL.

Soffa Family. Papers. Near Eastern American Collection. Immigration History Research Center, University of Minnesota.

Younis, Adele L. Papers. Center for Migration Studies, Staten Island, New York. Syrian American Archival Collection, Group II. Coll. No. 090. Center for Migration Studies, Staten Island, NY.

MICROFILM COLLECTIONS

Commission on Interracial Cooperation. *Commission on Interracial Cooperation Papers, 1919–1944.* New York: NYT Microfilming Corporation of America, 1983. Series VI.

National Association for the Advancement of Colored People. *NAACP Papers.* Part 7. *The Anti-Lynching Campaign, 1912–1955.* Series A: *Anti-Lynching Investigative Files, 1912–1953.* Frederick, MD: University Publications of America, 1987.

Records of the Immigration and Naturalization Service (INS), Series A. Part 3. Ellis Island, 1900–1933. Joseph Regenstein Library, University of Chicago.

JOURNALS AND NEWSPAPERS

al-Ayyam, New York
al-Bayan, New York
al-Dalil, New York
al-Hilal, Cairo
al-Hoda, Philadelphia and New York
al-Jamia. Alexandria and New York
al-Kalima, New York
Kawkab Amirka, New York
al-Kawn, New York
Majallat al-Muqtabas, Damascus
al-Mashriq, Beirut
Meraat ul-gharb, New York
al-Muqtabas, Damascus
al-Nima, Damascus
as-Sayeh, New York
Syrian World, New York

PRIMARY SOURCES

Abbott, Edith, ed. *Immigration: Select Documents and Case Records.* Chicago: University of Chicago Press, 1924.

American-Arab Anti-Discrimination Committee. *Report on Hate Crimes and Discrimination against Arab Americans: The Post-September 11 Backlash.* Washington, DC: ADC Research Institute, 2003. www.adc.org/hatecrimes/pdf/2003_report_web.pdf.

Bak, Isma'il Haqqi. *Lubnan, mabahith 'ilmiyya wa-ijtima'iyya* [Lebanon: Scientific and Social Studies]. 1918. Reprint, Beirut: Manshurat al-jami'a al-lubnaniyya, 1969.

Barakat, Leyyah. *A Message from Mount Lebanon.* Philadelphia: Sunday School Times, 1912.

Benough, W. "The Syrian Colony." *Harpers Weekly,* August 3, 1895, 746.

Bercovici, Konrad. "Around the World in New York—the Syrian Quarters." *Century Magazine* 108 (July 1924): 348.

Bishara, Khalil A. *Asl al-suriy al-hadith*. New York: al-Hoda Publishing House, 1914. Simultaneously published by al-Hoda in English as *The Origin of the Modern Syrian*.

Burton, Isabel. *The Inner Life of Syria, Palestine, and the Holy Land*. London: Kegan Paul, 1884.

Cole, William I. *Immigrant Races in Massachusetts: The Syrians*. Boston: Massachusetts Department of Education, n.d. [1921?].

Detroit Arab American Survey. "Preliminary Findings from the Detroit Arab American Study: Executive Summary." Center for Arab American Studies, University of Michigan, Dearborn, and University of Michigan's Institute for Social Research, July 2004. www.umich.edu/news/Releases/2004/Jul04/daas.pdf.

"Dr. El-Kourie Defends Syrian Immigrants." *Birmingham Ledger,* September 20, 1907.

Ducousso, Gaston. *L'industrie de la soie en Syrie et au Liban*. Beirut: Imprimerie Catholique, 1913.

Duncan, Norman. "A People from the East." *Harper's Monthly,* March 1903, 553–62.

"Elkourie Takes Burnett to Task." *Birmingham Age-Herald,* October 20, 1907.

Hasr al-litham'an nakabat al-Sham [Unveiling the Calamities of Syria]. Cairo, 1895.

Hitti, Phillip K. *Lebanon in History*. London: Macmillan, 1957.

———. *The Syrians in America*. New York: George Doran, 1924.

al-Hoda. *Al-Hoda, 1898–1968: Hakayat lubnan wa mughtaribihu* [*Al-Hoda, 1898–1968: The Story of Lebanon and Its Emigrants*]. New York: al-Hoda Publishing House, 1968.

Houghton, Louise Seymour. "The Syrians in the United States." Parts 1–3. *Survey* 26, nos. 14 (1911): 481–95, 16 (1911): 647–65, 23 (1911): 787–803.

al-Husri, Sati'. *The Day of Maysalun*. Translated by Sidney Glazer. Washington, DC: Middle East Institute, 1966.

Jessup, Henry Harris. *Fifty-three Years in Syria*. New York: Fleming H. Revell, 1910.

Johnson, Rossiter, ed. *A History of the World's Columbia Exposition Held in Chicago in 1893*. New York: D. Appleton, 1898.

Keane, A. H. *Ethnology*. Cambridge: Cambridge University Press, 1909.

Khanashat, Yusuf Musa. *Tara'if al-ams ghara'ib al-yawm* [Curiosities of Yesterday and Marvels of Today]. Edited by Abdallah Hanna. 1936. Reprint, Damascus: Wizarat al-thaqafa, 1990.

Kherbawi, Basil M. *Tarikh al-wilayat al-muttahida* [History of the United States]. New York: Matba' jarida al-Dalil, 1913.

al-Khuri, Jurji Tuma. *Al-Dalil ila al-barazil* [A Guide to Brazil]. Lebanon: Matba'at al-sharqiyya, 1906.

Kurd 'Ali, Muhammad. *Ghara'ib al-gharb* [Strange Things of the West]. Cairo: Maktabat al-ahaliyya, 1923.

———. *Khitat al-Sham*. 3rd ed. Beirut: Mu'assasat al-a'lami lil-matbu'at, 1983.

al-Lajna al-'ulya li-hizb al-lamarkaziyya bi misr. *Al-Mu'tamar al-'arabi al-awwal* [Documents of the First Arab Congress]. Cairo: Matba'a al-Busfur, 1913.

Lortet, Louis Charles. *La Syrie d'aujourd'hui: Voyages dans la Phénicie, le Liban et la Judée, 1875–1880*. Paris: Librairie Hachette, 1884.

Ma'luf, 'Isa Iskandar. *Tarikh madinat zahla* [The History of the City of Zahle]. Zahle, Lebanon: Zahle al-Fatat Press, 1911.

Ma'luf, Yusuf Nu'man. *Khizanat al-ayyam fi tarajim al-'izam* [Treasures of the Ages in the Biographies of Great Men]. New York: Matba' jarida al-Ayyam, 1899.

Ministère de la guerre. Commission de géographie du service géographique de l'armée. *Notice sur la Syrie.* Paris: Imprimerie nationale, 1916.

Miller, Lucius Hopkins. *Our Syrian Population: Study of the Syrian Population of Greater New York.* New York: Federation of Churches, 1904.

Mishaqa, M. *Kitab mashad al-i'yan bi-hawadith suriya wa lubnan* [An Eyewitness Account of the Events in Syria and Lebanon]. Cairo, 1908.

Mokarzel, Salloum, and Habib Otash. *Dalil al-tijari al-suriy* [A Guide to Syrian Commerce]. New York: Matba' jarida al-Hoda, 1908.

Moutran, Nadra. *La Syrie de demain.* 4th ed. Paris: Librairie Plon, 1916.

National Association for the Advancement of Colored People. *Thirty Years of Lynching in the United States, 1889–1918.* 1919. Reprint, New York: Negro Universities Press, 1969.

Oriental and Occidental Northern and Southern Portrait Types of the Midway Plaisance. St. Louis: N. D. Thompson, 1894.

Pariset, E. *Les industries de la soie.* Lyon: Publications du Bulletin des soies et des soieries, Imprimerie Pitrat Ainé, 1890.

Park, Robert E. *The Immigrant Press and Its Control.* Americanization Series. New York: Harper and Brothers, 1922.

Pasha, Cemal. *Memories of a Turkish Statesman, 1913–1919.* New York: Arno Press, 1973. Originally published as *Hatirat* (Istanbul, 1922).

"A Picturesque Colony." *New York Herald Tribune,* October 2, 1892.

Rihbany, Abraham Mitrie. *A Far Journey.* Boston: Houghton Mifflin, 1914.

al-Rishani, Yusuf. "Al-Suriyyun fi amrika" [The Syrians in America]. In *Al-Gharib fil-gharb* [The Stranger in the West], by Mikha'il As'ad Rustum, edited by Yusuf Qazma Khuri. 1905. Reprint, Beirut: Dar al-Hamra', 1992.

Rizk, Salom. *Syrian Yankee.* Garden City, NY: Doubleday, 1943.

Rustum, Mikha'il As'ad. *Al-Gharib fil-gharb* [The Stranger in the West]. 1895. Reprint, Beirut: Dar al-Hamra', 1992.

Salameh, Sami, ed. *The Mufakkira of Bishop Abdallah Khoury.* Zouk Mosbeh, Lebanon: Notre Dame University Press, 2001.

Shadid, Michael A. *A Doctor for the People.* New York: Vanguard Press, 1939.

Southern Federation of Syrian Lebanese American Clubs. *75th Diamond Jubilee Convention, 1931–2006: June 30–July 4, 2006, San Antonio, Texas.* Commemorative ed. 2006.

U.S. Bureau of the Census. *Thirteenth Census of the United States, 1910.* Vol. 1. *Population 1910: General Report and Analysis.* Washington, DC: Government Printing Office, 1913.

———. *Thirteenth Census of the United States, 1910. Abstract of the Census.* Washington, DC: Government Printing Office, 1913–1914.

———. *Fourteenth Census of the United States, 1920.* Vol. 2. *General Report and Analytical Tables.* Washington, DC: Government Printing Office, 1922.

————. *Fifteenth Census of the United States. Reports by States [Florida], 1930.* Washington, DC: Government Printing Office, 1933.

————. *Fifteenth Census of the United States, 1930, Population.* Vol. 2. *General Report, Statistics by Subject.* Washington, DC: Government Printing Office, 1933.

————. *Fifteenth Census of the United States: 1930. Population [Reports by States].* Vol. 3, pt. 1. Washington, DC: Government Printing Office, 1933.

————. *1990 Census of Population, Social and Economic Characteristics.* Washington, DC: GPO, 1990.

U.S. Congress. *Congressional Record.*70th Cong., 1st sess., 1928. Vol. 69, pts. 3 and 6.

U.S. Department of the Interior. *Eleventh Census of the United States, 1890: Population Statistics.* Vol. 1. Washington, DC: GPO, 1895.

U.S. House. *Citizenship of the United States, Expatriation, and Protection Abroad.* Report by the Secretary of State to the Committee on Foreign Affairs. 59th Cong., 2nd sess., 1906, H. Doc. 326.

————. *Ethnically Motivated Violence against Arab-Americans.* Hearing before the Subcommittee on Criminal Justice of the Committee on the Judiciary, 99th Cong., 2nd sess., 1986.

————. *Review the Status of Planning for the 2000 Census.* Hearing before the Subcommittee on Census, Statistics, and Postal Personnel of the Committee on Post Office and Civil Service, 103rd Cong., 1st sess., 1993.

U.S. House. Industrial Commission on Immigration. *Reports,* vol. 15. 57th Cong., 1st sess., 1901, H. Doc. 184.

U.S. Immigration and Naturalization Service. "The Eligibility of Arabs to Naturalization." *Monthly Review* 1 (October 1943).

U.S. Senate. Committee on the Judiciary. *Crime of Lynching.* 80th Cong., 2nd sess., 1948.

U.S. Senate. Industrial Commission on Immigration. *Abstracts of Reports.* 2 vols. 61st Cong., 3rd sess., 1911, S. Doc. 747.

Verney, Noël, and Dambmann, George. *Les puissances étrangères dans le Levant en Syrie et en Palestine.* Paris: Librairie Guillaumin, 1900.

World's Fair Photographs, 1893. Chicago: H. W. Hine, 1894.

Zaydan, Jurji. *Tabaqat al-umam aw al-salaïl al-bashariyya.* Al-Fajala, Egypt: Matbaʿa al-Hilal, 1912.

SECONDARY SOURCES

"Abdeen Jabara: A Champion from and of the Heartland." Interview, *Café Arabica,* November 1996. www.cafearabica.com/people/people12/peoabdeen8x1 .html.

Abou, Sélim. *Immigrés dans l'autre Amérique: Autobiographies de quatre Argentins d'origine libanaise.* Paris: Librairie Plon, 1972.

Abraham, Nabeel. "Anti-Arab Racism and Violence in the United States." In *The Development of Arab-American Identity,* edited by Ernest McCarus, 155–214. Ann Arbor: University of Michigan Press, 1997.

Abraham, Sameer, and Nabeel Abraham, eds. *Arabs in the New World: Studies on Arab-American Communities.* Detroit: Wayne State University, Center for Urban Studies, 1983.

———. Introduction to *Arabs in the New World: Studies on Arab-American Communities,* edited by Sameer Abraham and Nabeel Abraham. Detroit: Wayne State University, Center for Urban Studies, 1983.

Abraham, Nabeel, and Andrew Shryock, eds. *Arab Detroit: From Margin to Mainstream.* Detroit: Wayne State University Press, 2000.

Abramson, Harold J. "Assimilation and Pluralism." In *Harvard Encyclopedia of American Ethnic Groups,* edited by Stephen Thernstrom. Cambridge, MA: Belknap Press, 1980.

Abu-Laban, Baha, and Michael Suleiman, eds. *Arab Americans: Continuity and Change.* Belmont, MA: Association of Arab-American University Graduates, 1989.

Abu-Laban, Baha, and Faith Zeadey, eds. *Arabs in America: Myths and Realities.* AAUG Monograph Series, no. 5. Wilmette, IL: Medina University Press International, 1975.

Abu-Lughod, Lila. Introduction to *Remaking Women: Feminism and Modernity in the Middle East,* edited by Lila Abu-Lughod. Princeton: Princeton University Press, 1998.

———, ed. *Remaking Women: Feminism and Modernity in the Middle East.* Princeton: Princeton University Press, 1998.

———. *Veiled Sentiments: Honor and Poetry in a Bedouin Society.* Berkeley: University of California Press, 1986.

"Action Alert." *ADC Times* 18, no. 8, 1997.

Ahmed, Leila. *A Border Passage.* New York: Penguin Books, 1999.

———. "Western Ethnocentrism and Perceptions of the Harem." *Feminist Studies* 8 (Fall 1982): 521–34.

———. *Women and Gender in Islam: Historical Roots of a Modern Debate.* New Haven: Yale University Press, 1992.

Aidi, Hisham. "Let Us Be Moors: Islam, Race and 'Connected Histories.'" *Middle East Report,* no. 229 (Winter 2003): 42–53.

Akarli, Engin Deniz. *The Long Peace: Ottoman Lebanon, 1861–1920.* Berkeley: University of California Press, 1993.

———. "Ottoman Attitudes towards Lebanese Emigration, 1885–1910." In *The Lebanese in the World,* edited by Albert Hourani and Nadim Shehadi, 109–38. London: Centre for Lebanese Studies, 1992.

Alhourani, Motaz Abdullah. "The Arab-American Press and the Arab World: News Coverage in *al-Bayan* and *al-Dalil.*" MA thesis abstract, Kansas State University, 1992.

American Anthropological Association. "Response to IMB Directive 15: Race and Ethnic Standards for Federal Statistics and Administrative Reporting." September 1997. www.aaanet.org/gvt/ombdraft.htm.

American-Arab Anti-Discrimination Committee. "Census 2000 and the Arab American Census Initiative." March 16, 2000. Received from Media@adc.org.

American-Arab Anti-Discrimination Committee, New Jersey. "Online Thesaurus Removes Derogatory Listings for 'Arab.'" Press release, August 25,
2006. www.adc.org/Doc/ADC_NJ.doc.

Anderson, Benedict. *Imagined Communities: Reflections on the Origin and
Spread of Nationalism.* Rev. ed. London: Verso, 1991.

Anderson, Margo J. *The American Census: A Social History.* New Haven: Yale
University Press, 1988.

——, ed. *Encyclopedia of the U.S. Census.* Washington, DC: Congressional
Quarterly Press, 2000.

Anderson, Margo, and Stephen Fienberg. *Who Counts: The Politics of Census-
Taking in Contemporary America.* New York: Russell Sage Foundation,
1999.

Antonius, George. *The Arab Awakening.* 1938. Reprint, New York: Capricorn
Books, 1965.

Appadurai, Arjun. *Modernity at Large: Cultural Dimensions of Globalization.*
Minneapolis: University of Minnesota Press, 1996.

Appadurai, Arjun, Jacqueline Bhabha, Steven Collins, and Arjun Guneratne.
Area Studies, Regional Worlds: A White Paper for the Ford Foundation.
Chicago: Globalization Project of the University of Chicago, June 1997.

Asaʿd, Munir al-Khuri ʿIsa. *Tarikh Hims* [The History of Homs]. Homs: Mutraniyya Hims al-urthudhuksiyya, 1984.

Aswad, Barbara C., ed. *Arabic-Speaking Communities in American Cities.* New
York: Center for Migration Studies and Association of Arab-American University Graduates, 1974.

Auslander, Leora. *Taste and Power: Furnishing Modern France.* Berkeley: University of California Press, 1996.

Baily, Samuel L. *Immigrants in the Land of Promise: Italians in Buenos Aires and
New York City, 1870–1914.* Ithaca: Cornell University Press, 1999.

Baldwin, James. "On Being White and Other Lies." *Essence,* April 1984, 90–92.

Baron, Beth. *The Women's Awakening in Egypt: Culture, Society and the Press.*
New Haven: Yale University Press, 1994.

Barot, Rohit, and John Bird. "Racialization: The Genealogy and Critique of a
Concept." *Ethnic and Racial Studies* 24 (July 2001): 601–18.

Barot, Rohit, Harriet Bradley, and Steve Fenton. "Rethinking Ethnicity and Gender." In *Ethnicity, Gender and Social Change,* edited by Barot Rohit, Harriet
Bradley, and Steve Fenton, 1–25. New York: St. Martin's Press, 1999.

Barth, Fredrik. *Ethnic Groups and Boundaries: The Social Organization of Cultural
Difference.* Boston: Little, Brown, 1969.

Bassiouni, M. C., ed. *The Civil Rights of Arab Americans: The Special Measures.*
AAUG Information Paper No. 10. Belmont, MA: Association of Arab-
American University Graduates, 1974.

Bayoumi, Moustafa. "Racing Religion." *CR: The New Centennial Review* 6, no.
2 (2006): 267–93.

Benson, Kathleen, and Philip M. Kayal, eds. *A Community of Many Worlds: Arab
Americans in New York City.* New York: Museum of the City of New York,
2002.

Bernard, William S. "Immigration: History of U.S. Policy." In *Harvard Encyclopedia of American Ethnic Groups,* edited by Stephen Thernstrom. Cambridge, MA: Belknap Press, 1980.

Bhabha, Homi K. "DissemiNation: Time, Narrative, and the Margins of the Modern Nation." In *Nation and Narration,* edited by Homi K. Bhabha, 291–322. London: Routledge, 1990.

Bodnar, John. *The Transplanted: A History of Immigrants in Urban America.* Bloomington: Indiana University Press, 1985.

Boosahda, Elizabeth. *Arab-American Faces and Voices: The Origins of an Immigrant Community.* Austin: University of Texas Press, 2003.

Brand, A. Laurie. *Citizens Abroad: Emigration and the State in the Middle East and North Africa.* Cambridge: Cambridge University Press, 2006.

Braude, Benjamin. "Foundation Myths of the *Millet* System." In *Christians and Jews in the Ottoman Empire: The Functioning of a Plural Society,* vol. 1, *The Central Lands,* edited by Benjamin Braude and Bernard Lewis, 69–88. New York: Holmes and Meier, 1982.

Brodkin, Karen. *How Jews Became White Folks and What That Says about Race in America.* New Brunswick: Rutgers University Press, 1998.

Brundage, W. Fitzhugh. *Lynching in the New South Georgia and Virginia, 1880–1930.* Urbana: University of Illinois Press, 1993.

Buheiry, Marwan. "Bulus Nujaym and the Grand Liban Ideal, 1908–1919." In *Intellectual Life in the Arab East, 1890–1939,* edited by Marwan R. Buheiry, 62–83. Beirut: American University of Beirut, 1981.

———, ed. *Intellectual Life in the Arab East, 1890–1939.* Beirut: American University of Beirut, 1981.

Chéhab, Maurice. *Dawr Lubnan fi tarikh al-harir* [The Role of Lebanon in the History of Silk]. Beirut: Manshurat al-Jamiʿa al-Lubnaniyya, 1968.

Chevallier, Dominique. "Lyon et la Syrie en 1919: Les bases d'une intervention." In *Villes et travail en Syrie du XIXe au XXe siècle,* 41–52. Paris: G. P. Maisonneuve et Larose, 1982.

Cleveland, William L. *The Making of an Arab Nationalist: Ottomanism and Arabism in the Life and Thought of Satiʾ al-Husri.* Princeton: Princeton University Press, 1971.

Cohen, Amnon. "The Receding of the Christian Presence in the Holy Land: A 19th Century Sijill in the Light of 16th Century Tahrirs." In *The Syrian Land in the 18th and 19th Century: The Common and the Specific in the Historical Experience,* edited by Thomas Philipp, 333–40. Berliner Islamstudien 5. Stuttgart: Franz Steiner, 1992.

Cohen, Robin. *Global Diasporas: An Introduction.* Seattle: University of Washington Press, 1997.

Cohn, Bernard S. *An Anthropologist among the Historians and Other Essays.* New York: Oxford University Press, 1987.

Commins, David Dean. *Islamic Reform: Politics and Social Change in Late Ottoman Syria.* New York: Oxford University Press, 1990.

Conklin, Nancy Faires, and Nora Faires. " 'Colored' and Catholic: The Lebanese in Birmingham, Alabama." In *Crossing the Waters: Arabic-Speaking Immi-*

grants to the United States before 1940, edited by Eric J. Hooglund, 69–84. Washington, DC: Smithsonian Institution Press, 1987.

Conzen, Kathleen Neils. "Ethnicity as Festive Culture: Nineteenth-Century German America on Parade." In The Invention of Ethnicity, edited by Werner Sollors, 44–76. New York, 1989.

Conzen, Kathleen Neils, et al. "The Invention of Ethnicity: A Perspective from the U.S.A." Studi emigrazione 29 (March 1992): 3–41.

Cunningham, George E. "The Italian, a Hindrance to White Solidarity in Louisiana, 1890–1898." in Racial Classification and History, edited by E. Nathaniel Gates, 68–82. New York: Garland, 1997.

Cutler, James Elbert. Lynch-Law: An Investigation into the History of Lynching in the United States. 1905. Reprint, New York: Negro Universities Press, 1969.

Dahbany-Miraglia, Dina. "Random Thoughts on the Position of Women among Early Arab Immigrants." Unpublished manuscript, n.d.

Dahir, Mas'ud. Al-Hijra al-lubnaniyya ila misr: Hijrat al-shawam [The Lebanese Emigration to Egypt: Emigration of the "Shawam"]. Beirut: Manshurat al-jami'a al-lubnaniyya, 1986.

Davidson, Lawrence. "Debating Palestine: Arab-American Challenges to Zionism, 1917–1932." In Arabs in America: Building a New Future, edited by Michael Suleiman, 227–40. Philadelphia: Temple University Press, 1999.

Dawisha, Adid. Arab Nationalism in the Twentieth Century. Princeton: Princeton University Press, 2003.

Dawn, C. Ernest. From Ottomanism to Arabism: Essays on the Origins of Arab Nationalism. Urbana: University of Illinois Press, 1973.

———. "The Origins of Arab Nationalism." In The Origins of Arab Nationalism: A Reassessment, edited by Rashid Khalidi, Lisa Anderson, Muhammad Muslih, and Reeva S. Simon, 3–30. New York: Columbia University Press, 1991.

Dawson, Graham. "The Blond Bedouin: Lawrence of Arabia, Imperial Adventure and the Imagining of English-British Masculinity." In Manful Assertions: Masculinities in Britain since 1800, edited by Michael Roper and John Tosh, 113–44. London: Routledge, 1991.

Diner, Hasia R. Erin's Daughters in America: Irish Immigrant Women in the Nineteenth Century. Baltimore: Johns Hopkins University Press, 1983.

Du Bois, W. E. B. Black Reconstruction in America: An Essay toward a History of the Part Which Black Folk Played in the Attempt to Reconstruct Democracy in America, 1860–1880. New York: World Publishing, 1964.

———. "Race Relations in the United States, 1917–1947," Phylon 9, no. 3 (1948): 234–47.

Ducey, Mitchell F. The Commission on Interracial Cooperation Papers, 1919–1944 and the Association of Southern Women for the Prevention of Lynching Papers, 1930–1942. Ann Arbor, MI: University Microfilms International, 1984.

El Emir Talal Majid Arslan. "A Word from the Ministry of Emigrants." March 9, 1999. www.emigrants.gov.lb/opn_ltr.htm.

Electronic Privacy Information Center. "Department of Homeland Security Obtained Data on Arab Americans from Census Bureau." http://epic.org/privacy/census/foia/default.html.

Elia, Nada. "The 'White' Sheep of the Family: But Bleaching Is Like Starvation."
    In *This Bridge We Call Home: Radical Visions for Transformation*, edited by
    Gloria Anzaldua and Analouise Keating, 223–31. New York: Routledge,
    2002.
Elias, Leila Salloum. "The Impact of the Sinking of the Titanic on the New York
    Syrian Community of 1912." *Arab Studies Quarterly* 27 (Winter/Spring
    2005): 75–88.
Elkholy, Abdo A. "The Arab-Americans: Nationalism and Traditional Preser-
    vations." In *The Arab-Americans: Studies in Assimilation*, edited by Elaine C.
    Hagopian and Ann Paden, 3–17. AAUG Monograph Series, no. 1. Wilmette,
    IL: Medina University Press International, 1969.
———. *The Arab Moslems in the United States: Religion and Assimilation*. New
    Haven: College and University Press, 1966.
Fairchild, Amy. "Science at the Borders: Immigrant Medical Inspection and De-
    fense of the Nation, 1891–1930." PhD diss., Columbia University, 1997.
Fawaz, Leila Tarazi. "The Beirut-Damascus Road: Connecting the Syrian Coast
    to the Interior in the 19th Century." In *The Syrian Land: Processes of Inte-
    gration and Fragmentation*, edited by Thomas Philipp and Birgit Shaebler,
    19–28. Berliner Islamstudien 6. Stuttgart: Steiner, 1998.
———. *Merchants and Migrants in Nineteenth-Century Beirut*. Cambridge,
    MA: Harvard University Press, 1983.
———. *An Occasion for War: Civil Conflict in Lebanon and Damascus in 1860*.
    Berkeley: University of California Press, 1994.
———. "Zahle and Dayr al-Qamar: Two Market Towns of Mount Lebanon
    during the Civil War of 1860." In *Lebanon: A History of Conflict and Con-
    sensus*, edited by Nadim Shehadi and Dana Haffar Mills, 49–63. London:
    Centre for Lebanese Studies, 1988.
Fay, Mary Ann. "Old Roots—New Soil." In *Taking Root, Bearing Fruit: The
    Arab-American Experience*, edited by James Zogby, 17–23. Washington, DC:
    American-Arab Anti-Discrimination Committee, 1984.
Ferguson, Roderick A. *Aberrations in Black: Toward a Queer of Color Critique*.
    Minneapolis: University of Minnesota Press, 2004.
Fersan, Eliane. "L'émigration libanaise au États-Unis d'après les archives du
    Ministère des affaires étrangères de France (1920–1931)." MA thesis, Uni-
    versity of the Holy Spirit, Kaslik, Lebanon, 2005.
Firro, Kais M. *Inventing Lebanon: Nationalism and the State under the Man-
    date*. London: I. B. Tauris, 2003.
Fishkin, Shelley Fisher. "Crossroads of Cultures: The Transnational Turn in
    American Studies. Presidential Address to the American Studies Association,
    Nov. 12, 2004." *American Quarterly* 57 (March 2005): 17–57.
———. "Interrogating 'Whiteness,' Complicating 'Blackness': Remapping
    American Culture." *American Quarterly* 47 (September 1995): 428–66.
Fontaine, Jean. *La crise religieuse des écrivains Syro-Libanais chrétiens de 1825
    à 1940*. Tunis: Institut des belles lettres arabes, 1996.
Friedman-Kasaba, Kathie. *Memories of Migration: Gender, Ethnicity, and Work
    in the Lives of Jewish and Italian Women in New York, 1870–1924*. Albany:
    SUNY Press, 1996.

Gabaccia, Donna. *From the Other Side: Women, Gender, and Immigrant Life in the U.S., 1820–1990*. Bloomington: Indiana University Press, 1994.

Gabaccia, Donna R., Dirk Hoerder, and Adam Walaszek. "Emigration and Nation-Building during the Mass Migrations from Europe." Paper presented at the Association for European Historians, Brisbane, Australia, July 2003.

Gabbert, Ann R. "El Paso, a Sight for Sore Eyes: Medical and Legal Aspects of Syrian Immigration, 1906–1907." *Historian* 65, no. 1 (2002): 15–42.

Gettys, Luella. *The Law of Citizenship in the United States*. Chicago: University of Chicago Press, 1934.

Gibran, Jean, and Kahlil Gibran. *Kahlil Gibran: His Life and World*. Boston: New York Graphic Society, 1974.

Goldberg, David Theo, ed. *Anatomy of Racism*. Minneapolis: University of Minnesota Press, 1990.

———. *Racial Subjects: Writing on Race in America*. New York: Routledge, 1997.

Goldstein, Eric L. *The Price of Whiteness: Jews, Race, and American Identity*. Princeton: Princeton University Press, 2006.

Gonzales-Day, Ken. *Lynching in the West, 1850–1935*. Durham: Duke University Press, 2006.

Gosset, Thomas F. *Race: The History of an Idea in America*. New ed. New York: Oxford University Press, 1968.

Gross, Ariela J. "Litigating Whiteness: Trials of Racial Determination in the Nineteenth-Century South." *Yale Law Journal* 108 (October 1998): 109–88.

Gualtieri, Antonio R. "Religious Elements in the Canadian Perception of Arabs." In *Canada and the Arab World*, edited by Tareq Y. Ismael, 69–84. Alberta: University of Alberta Press, 1985.

Gualtieri, Sarah M. A. "Gendering the Chain Migration Thesis: Women and Syrian Transatlantic Migration." *Comparative Studies of South Asia, Africa and the Middle East* 24 (Spring 2004): 18–28.

———. "Strange Fruit? Syrian Immigrants, Extralegal Violence and Racial Formation in the Jim Crow South." *Arab Studies Quarterly* 26 (Spring/Summer 2004): 63–88.

Haddad, George. *Al-Mughtaribun al-suriyyun wa makanatuhum fil-tarikh* [Syrian Emigrants and Their Place in History]. Damascus: al-Jami'a al-Suriyya, 1953.

Haddad, Safia. "The Woman's Role in Socialization of Syrian-Americans in Chicago." PhD diss., University of Chicago, 1964.

———. "The Woman's Role in Socialization of Syrian-Americans in Chicago." In *The Arab-Americans: Studies in Assimilation*, edited by Elaine C. Hagopian and Ann Paden, 84–101. AAUG Monograph Series, no. 1. Wilmette, IL: Medina University Press International, 1969.

Haddad, Yvonne Yazbeck. "American Foreign Policy in the Middle East and Its Impact on the Identity of Arab Muslims in the United States." In *The Muslims of America*, edited by Yvonne Yazbeck Haddad, 217–35. New York: Oxford University Press, 1991.

———. "Maintaining the Faith of the Fathers: Dilemmas of Religious Identity in the Christian and Muslim Arab-American Communities." In *The Development of Arab-American Identity,* ed. Ernest McCarus, 61–84. Ann Arbor: University of Michigan Press, 1997.

Hagopian, Elaine C. "Minority Rights in a Nation-State: The Nixon Administration's Campaign against Arab-Americans." *Journal of Palestine Studies* 5, nos. 1–2 (1975): 97–114.

Hagopian, Elaine C., and Ann Paden, eds. *The Arab-Americans: Studies in Assimilation.* AAUG Monograph Series, no. 1. Wilmette, IL: Medina University Press International, 1969.

Haiek, Joseph. *Arab-American Almanac.* 4th ed. Glendale, CA: News Circle Publishing House, 1992.

Haim, Sylvia G. *Arab Nationalism: An Anthology.* Berkeley: University of California Press, 1962.

Hajar, Paula. "Changes and Continuities in the Code of Honor among Syrian Lebanese Immigrants to the United States." Unpublished manuscript, New York, 1989.

Hajjar, Claude Fahd. *Immigração árabe: Cem anos de reflexão.* São Paulo: Ícone Editora LIDA, 1995.

Halaby, Raouf J. "Dr. Michael Shadid and the Debate over Identity in *The Syrian World.*" In *Crossing the Waters: Arabic-Speaking Immigrants to the United States before 1940,* edited by Eric J. Hooglund, 55–65. Washington, DC: Smithsonian Institution Press, 1987.

Hale, Grace E. *Making Whiteness: The Culture of Segregation in the South, 1890–1940.* New York: Pantheon Books, 1998.

Hall, Jacquelyn Dowd. *Revolt against Chivalry: Jessie Daniel Ames and the Women's Campaign against Lynching.* New York: Columbia University Press, 1979.

Hammons, Terry B. "'A Wild Ass of a Man': American Images of Arabs to 1948." PhD diss., University of Oklahoma, 1978.

Haney López, Ian F. *Racism on Trial: The Chicano Fight for Justice.* Cambridge, MA: Belknap Press, 2003.

———. *White by Law: The Legal Construction of Race.* New York: New York University Press, 1996.

Hanioğlu, M. Şükrü. "The Young Turks and the Arabs before the Revolution of 1908." In *The Origins of Arab Nationalism,* edited by Rashid Khalidi, Lisa Anderson, Muhammad Muslih, and Reeva S. Simon, 31–49. New York: Columbia University Press, 1991.

Hanna, ʿAbdallah. "Dayr ʿAtiyya." *Annals of the Japan Association for Middle East Studies* 4 (1989): 141–74.

Harris, Cheryl I. "Whiteness as Property." *Harvard Law Review* 106 (June 1993): 1707–91.

Hartman, Michelle, and Alessandro Olsaretti. "'The First Boat and the First Oar': Inventions of Lebanon in the Writings of Michel Chiha." *Radical History Review* 86 (Spring 2003): 37–65.

Harzig, Christiane. Introduction to *Peasant Maids, City Women: From the European Countryside to Urban America,* edited by Christiane Harzig, Maria Anna Knothe, Margareta Matovic, Deirdre Mageean, and Monika Blaschke, 1–21. Ithaca: Cornell University Press, 1997.

Hashimoto, Kohei. "Lebanese Population Movement, 1920–1939: Towards a Study." In *The Lebanese in the World: A Century of Emigration,* edited by Albert Hourani and Nadim Shehadi, 65–107. London: Centre for Lebanese Studies, 1992.

Hassoun, Rosina J. *Arab Americans in Michigan.* East Lansing: Michigan State University Press, 2005.

Hatab, Helena Regina. "Syrian-American Ethnicity: Structure and Ideology in Transition." MA thesis, American University of Beirut, 1975.

Hatem, Mervat. "The Invisible American Half: Arab American Hybridity and Feminist Discourse in the 1990s." 1998. www.haussite.net/haus.o/SCRIPT/txt2001/o1/hatem.HTML.

Havemann, Axel. "Between Ottoman Loyalty and Arab 'Independence': Muhammad Kurd ʿAli, Girgi Zaydan, and Sakib Arslan." *Quaderni di studi arabi* 5–6 (1987–88): 347–56.

Hidda, Hasan. *Tarikh al-mughtaribin al-ʿarab fil-ʿalam* [History of Arab Emigrants in the World]. Damascus: al-ʿArabi, 1974.

Higham, John. *Strangers in the Land: Patterns of American Nativism, 1860–1925.* New York: Atheneum, 1965.

Hijab, Nadia. "AAUG in the 1990s: In Search of Purpose, Resources, and Good Organizational Culture." *Arab Studies Quarterly* 29, nos. 3 and 4 (2007): 155–64.

Hilliard, Asa G. "What Do We Need to Know Now? Race, Identity, Hegemony, and Education." *Rethinking Schools* 14 (Winter 1999): 2–6.

Hizb al-Baʿth al-ʿArabi al-Ishtiraki, al-Qiyada al-Qawmiyya. *Al-Mughtaribun al-ʿarab bayn al-madi wal-hadir wa tumuhat al-mustaqbal* [Arab Emigrants: Between the Past and the Present, and Future Aspirations]. Damascus: Maktab al-iʿlam wal-nashr, 1984.

Hobsbawm, Eric. *The Age of Empire, 1875–1914.* New York: Pantheon Books, 1987.

———. *Nations and Nationalism since 1780: Programme, Myth, Reality.* 2nd ed. Cambridge: Cambridge University Press, 1992.

Holt, Thomas C. "Marking: Race, Race-Making, and the Writing of History." *American Historical Review* 100, no. 1 (1995): 1–20.

———. *The Problem of Race in the Twenty-first Century.* Cambridge, MA: Harvard University Press, 2000.

Hooglund, Eric J., ed. *Crossing the Waters: Arabic-Speaking Immigrants to the United States before 1940.* Washington, DC: Smithsonian Institution Press, 1987.

Hourani, Albert. *Arabic Thought in the Liberal Age, 1739–1939.* 1962. Reprint, Cambridge: Cambridge University Press, 1983.

———. "Lebanese and Syrians in Egypt." In *The Lebanese in the World: A Century of Emigration,* edited by Albert Hourani and Nadim Shehadi, 497–507. London: Centre for Lebanese Studies, 1992.

———. "Ottoman Reform and the Politics of Notables." In *The Modern Middle East: A Reader,* edited by Albert Hourani, Philip Khoury, and Mary C. Wilson, 83–110. Berkeley: University of California Press, 1993.

———. *Syria and Lebanon: A Political Essay.* London: Oxford University Press, 1954.

Hourani, Albert, Philip Khoury, and Mary C. Wilson, eds. *The Modern Middle East: A Reader.* Berkeley: University of California Press, 1993.

Hourani, Albert, and Nadim Shehadi, eds. *The Lebanese in the World.* London: Centre for Lebanese Studies, 1992.

Howard, Walter T. *Lynchings: Extralegal Violence in Florida during the 1930s.* Selsingrove: Susquehanna University Press, 1995.

Ignatiev, Noel. *How the Irish Became White.* New York: Routledge, 1995.

Ingalls, Robert P. "Lynching and Establishment Violence in Tampa, 1858–1935." *Journal of Southern History* 53, no. 4 (1987): 613–44.

Issawi, Charles, ed. *Economic History of the Middle East, 1800–1914: A Book of Readings.* Chicago: University of Chicago Press, 1966.

———. "The Historical Background of Lebanese Emigration, 1800–1914." In *The Lebanese in the World: A Century of Emigration,* edited by Albert Hourani and Nadim Shehadi, 13–31. London: Centre for Lebanese Studies, 1992.

Jacobson, Matthew Frye. *Roots Too: White Ethnic Revival in Post–Civil Rights America.* Cambridge, MA: Harvard University Press, 2006).

———. *Special Sorrows: The Diasporic Imagination of Irish, Polish, and Jewish Immigrants in the United States.* Cambridge, MA: Harvard University Press, 1995.

———. *Whiteness of a Different Color: European Immigrants and the Alchemy of Race.* Cambridge, MA: Harvard University Press, 1998.

Jankowski, James, and Israel Gershoni, eds. *Rethinking Nationalism in the Arab Middle East.* New York: Columbia University Press, 1997.

John, Sarah E. "Arabic-Speaking Immigration to the El Paso Area, 1900–1935." In *Crossing the Waters: Arabic-Speaking Immigrants to the United States before 1940,* edited by Eric J. Hooglund, 105–18. Washington, DC: Smithsonian Institution Press, 1987.

Jordan, Winthrop. *White over Black: American Attitudes toward the Negro, 1550–1812.* New York: W. W. Norton, 1977.

Joseph, Souad. "Against the Grain of the Nation—The Arab-." In *Arabs in America: Building a New Future,* edited by Michael Suleiman, 257–71. Philadelphia: Temple University Press, 1999.

Kadi, Joanna, ed. *Food for Our Grandmothers: Writings by Arab-American and Arab-Canadian Feminists.* Boston: South End Press, 1994.

Kandiyoti, Deniz. "End of Empire: Islam, Nationalism, and Women in Turkey." In *Women, Islam and the State,* edited by Deniz Kandiyoti, 22–47. Philadelphia: Temple University Press, 1991.

Karam, Michel. *Al-Lubnaniyyun fil-taytanik* [The Lebanese on the *Titanic*]. Beirut: Mu'assasa dakash lil-tabaa, 2000.

Karpat, Kemal. "Jewish Population Movements in the Ottoman Empire, 1862–1914." In *The Jews of the Ottoman Empire,* edited by Avigdor Levy, 399–415. Princeton: Darwin Press, 1994.

———. "The Ottoman Emigration to America, 1860–1914." *International Journal of Middle East Studies* 17 (1985): 175–209.

———. "Ottoman Immigration Policies and Settlement in Palestine." In *Settler Regimes in Africa and the Arab World,* edited by Ibrahim Abu-Lughod and Baha Abu-Laban, 58–62. Wilmette, IL: Medina University Press International, 1974.

———. *Ottoman Population, 1830–1914.* Madison: University of Wisconsin Press, 1985.

———. "Ottoman Population Records and the Census of 1881/82–1893." *International Journal of Middle East Studies* 9 (1978): 237–74.

Kassimy, Zafer. "Les mouvements migratoires au départ et à destination de la Syrie." In *Les migrations internationales de la fin du XVIIIe siècle à nos jours.* Paris: Centre national de la recherche scientifique, 1980.

Katibah, Habib Ibrahim. *Arabic-Speaking Americans.* New York: Institute of Arab American Affairs, 1946.

Kayal, Philip. "Arab Christians in the United States." In *Arabs in the New World: Studies on Arab-American Communities,* edited by Sameer Abraham and Nabeel Abraham, 45–61. Detroit: Wayne State University, Center for Urban Studies, 1983.

Kayal, Philip, and Joseph Kayal. *The Syrian-Lebanese in America: A Study in Religion and Assimilation.* Boston: Twayne, 1975.

Kayali, Hasan. *Arabs and Young Turks: Ottomanism, Arabism, and Islamism in the Ottoman Empire, 1908–1918.* Berkeley: University of California Press, 1997.

Kazal, Russell A. "Revisiting Assimilation: The Rise, Fall, and Reappraisal of a Concept in American Ethnic History." *American Historical Review* 100 (April 1995): 437–71.

Keuchel, Edward. *A History of Columbia County.* Tallahassee, FL: Sentry Press, 1981.

Khalaf, Samir. "The Background and Causes of Lebanese/Syrian Immigration to the United States before World War I." In *Crossing the Waters: Arabic-Speaking Immigrants to the United States before 1940,* edited by Eric J. Hooglund, 17–36. Washington, DC: Smithsonian Institution Press, 1987.

Khalidi, Rashid. "'Abd al-Ghani al-'Uraisi and *al-Mufid:* The Press and Arab Nationalism before 1914." In *Intellectual Life in the Arab East, 1890–1939,* edited by Marwan R. Buheiry, 38–61. Beirut: American University of Beirut, 1981.

———. "Arab Nationalism: Historical Problems in the Literature." *American Historical Review* 96, no. 5 (1991): 1363–73.

———. *British Policy towards Syria and Palestine, 1906–1914.* London: Ithaca Press, 1980.

———. "Ottoman Notables in Jerusalem: Nationalism and Other Options." *Muslim World* 84, no. 1–2 (1994): 1–18.

———. "Ottomanism and Arabism in Syria before 1914: A Reassessment." In *The Origins of Arab Nationalism,* edited by Rashid Khalidi, Lisa Anderson, Muhammad Muslih, and Reeva S. Simon, 50–69. New York: Columbia University Press, 1991.

———. *Palestinian Identity: The Construction of Modern National Consciousness.* New York: Columbia University Press, 1997.

Khalidi, Rashid, Lisa Anderson, Muhammad Muslih, and Reeva S. Simon, eds. *The Origins of Arab Nationalism: A Reassessment.* New York: Columbia University Press, 1991

Khater, Akram. "House to 'Goddess of the House': Gender, Class, and Silk in 19th Century Mount Lebanon." *International Journal of Middle East Studies* 28 (1996): 325–48.

————. *Inventing Home: Emigration, Gender and the Middle Class in Lebanon, 1870–1920*. Berkeley: University of California Press, 2001.

————. "She Married Silk: A Rewriting of Peasant History in 19th Century Mount Lebanon." PhD diss., University of California, Berkeley, 1993.

Khoury, Philip S. *Syria and the French Mandate*. Princeton: Princeton University Press, 1987.

Kivisto, Peter. "The Transplanted Then and Now: The Reorientation of Immigration Studies from the Chicago School to the New Social History." *Ethnic and Racial Studies* 13, no. 4 (1990): 455–81.

Klich, Ignacio. "*Criollos* and Arabic Speakers in Argentina: An Uneasy *Pas de Deux*, 1888–1914." In *The Lebanese in the World*, edited by Albert Hourani and Nadim Shehadi, 243–84. London: Centre for Lebanese Studies, 1992.

Kraut, Alan M. *Silent Travellers: Germs, Genes and the "Immigrant Menace."* New York: Basic Books, 1994.

Labaki, Boutros. *Introduction à l'histoire économique du Liban: Soie et commerce extérieur en fin de période ottomane, 1840–1914*. Beirut: Publications de l'Université libanaise, 1984.

————. "Lebanese Emigration during the War (1975–1989)." In *The Lebanese in the World: A Century of Emigration*, edited by Albert Hourani and Nadim Shehadi, 605–26. London: Centre for Lebanese Studies, 1992.

Leney, Peter. "Annie Midlige, Fur Trader: A Lebanese Widow Defies the HBC." *Beaver*, June/July 1996, 37–41.

Lesser, Jeff. "Always 'Outsiders': Asians, Naturalization, and the Supreme Court." *Amerasia* 12, no. 1 (1985–86): 83–100.

————. "From Pedlars to Proprietors: Lebanese, Syrian and Jewish Immigrants in Brazil." In *The Lebanese in the World: A Century of Emigration*, edited by Albert Hourani and Nadim Shehadi, 398–410. London: Centre for Lebanese Studies, 1992.

————. "(Re)Creating Ethnicity: Middle Eastern Immigration to Brazil." *Americas* 53, no. 1 (1996): 45–65.

————. *Welcoming the Undesirables: Brazil and the Jewish Question*. Berkeley: University of California Press, 1995.

Levy, Eugene. " 'Is the Jew a White Man?': Press Reaction to the Leo Frank Case, 1913–1915." *Phylon* 35, no. 2 (1974): 212–22.

Lewis, Norman. "The Frontier of Settlement, 1800–1914." Reprinted in *Economic History of the Middle East, 1800–1914: A Book of Readings*, edited by Charles Issawi, 258–68. Chicago: University of Chicago Press, 1966.

————. *Nomads and Settlers in Syria and Jordan, 1800–1980*. Cambridge: Cambridge University Press, 1987.

Lipsitz, George. *The Possessive Investment in Whiteness: How White People Profit from Identity Politics*. Philadelphia: Temple University Press, 1998.

MacFarlane, Joan. "Black or White? Egyptian Immigrant Fights for Black Classification." July 16, 1997. www.cnn.com/US/9707/16/racial.suit/index.html.

MacLean, Nancy. "The Leo Frank Case Reconsidered: Gender and Sexual Politics in the Making of Reactionary Populism." *Journal of American History* 78, no. 3 (1991): 917–48.

Majaj, Lisa Suhair. "Arab-Americans and the Meanings of Race." In *Postcolonial Theory and the United States: Race, Ethnicity, and Literature,* edited by Amritjit Singh and Peter Schmidt, 320–37. Jackson: University of Mississippi Press, 2000.

——. "Boundaries: Arab/American." In *Food for Our Grandmothers: Writings by Arab-American and Arab-Canadian Feminist's,* edited by Joanna Kadi, 65–86. Boston: South End Press, 1994.

Makdisi, Ussama Samir. "Fantasies of the Possible: Community, History and Violence in the Nineteenth-Century Ottoman Empire." PhD diss., Princeton University, 1997.

——. "Reclaiming the Land of the Bible: Missionaries, Secularism, and Evangelical Modernity." *American Historical Review* 102 (June 1997): 680–713.

Mandel, Neville, and Mim Kemal Oke. "The Ottoman Empire, Zionism and the Question of Palestine (1880–1908)." *International Journal of Middle East Studies* 14, no. 3 (1982): 329–41.

Markovitz, Jonathan. *Legacies of Lynching.* Minneapolis: University of Minnesota Press, 2004.

Massad, Joseph. "Palestinians and the Limits of Racialized Discourse." *Social Text* 11, no. 1 (1993): 94–114.

Al-Mausu'a al-suhufiyya al-'arabiyya [Encyclopedia of the Arab Press]. Vol. 3, *al-Sihafa al-arabiyya fi buldan al-mahjar* [The Arab Press in the Countries of the Mahjar]. Tunis: al-Munazama al-'arabiyya lil-tarbiyya wal-thaqafa wal-'ulum, 1991.

McAlister, Melani. *Epic Encounters: Culture, Media, and U.S. Interests in the Middle East, 1945–2000.* Berkeley: University of California Press, 2001.

McCarthy, Justin. *Death and Exile: The Ethnic Cleansing of Ottoman Muslims.* Princeton, NJ: Darwin Press, 1995.

McCarus, Ernest, ed. *The Development of Arab-American Identity.* Ann Arbor: University of Michigan Press, 1997.

McClintock, Ann. " 'No Longer in a Future Heaven': Nationalism, Gender, and Race." In *Becoming National: A Reader,* edited by Geoff Eley and Ronald Grigor Suny, 260–84. New York: Oxford University Press, 1996.

McGovern, James R. *Anatomy of a Lynching: The Killing of Claude Neal.* Baton Rouge: Louisiana State University Press, 1982.

McGowan, Bruce. "The Age of the Ayans, 1699–1812." In *An Economic and Social History of the Ottoman Empire, 1300–1914,* edited by Halil Inalcik and Donald Quataert, 637–758. Cambridge: Cambridge University Press, 1994.

Mehdi, Beverlee Turner. *The Arabs in America, 1492–1977: A Chronology and Fact Book.* Ethnic Chronology Series 31. New York: Oceana Publications, 1969.

Menon, Sridevi. "Where Is West Asia in Asian America? 'Asia' and the Politics of Space in Asian America." *Social Text* 24 (Spring 2006): 55–79.

Méouchy, Nadine. "Les formes de conscience politique et communautaire au Liban et en Syrie à l'époque du mandat français, 1920–1939." PhD diss., Université de Paris, Sorbonne, 1989.

Meyers, Christopher C. " 'Killing Them by the Wholesale': A Lynching Rampage in South Georgia." *Georgia Historical Quarterly* vol. 90 (Summer 2006): 214–35.

Miller, Randall M., and Thomas D. Marzik, eds. *Immigrants and Religion in Urban America.* Philadelphia: Temple University Press, 1977.

Moanack, Georges. "Les libanais de Colombie." Paper presented to Cercle Catholique, Beirut, June 1, 1943, Institut français d'études arabes de Damas.

Moch, Leslie Page. *Moving Europeans: Migration in Western Europe since 1650.* Bloomington: Indiana University Press, 1992.

Monroe, Elizabeth. *Britain's Moment in the Middle East, 1914–1956.* Baltimore: Johns Hopkins University Press, 1963.

Moore, Kathleen M. *Al-Mughtaribun: American Law and the Transformation of Muslim Life in the United States.* Albany: State University of New York Press, 1995.

Morawska, Ewa. "Ethnicity." In *Encyclopedia of Social History,* edited by Peter Stearns. New York: Garland, 1994.

Morsy, Soheir A. "Beyond the Honorary 'White' Classification of Egyptians: Societal Identity in Historical Context." In *Race,* edited by Steven Gregory and Roger Sanjek, 175–98. New Brunswick: Rutgers University Press, 1994.

Moya, José. *Cousins and Strangers: Spanish Immigrants to Buenos Aires, 1850–1930.* Berkeley: University of California Press, 1998.

Naber, Nadine. "Ambiguous Insiders: An Investigation of Arab American Invisibility." *Ethnic and Racial Studies* 23 (January 2000): 37–61.

Naff, Alixa. "The Arab Immigrant Experience." In *The First One Hundred Years: A Centennial Anthology Celebrating Antiochian Orthodoxy in North America,* edited by George S. Corey et al., 51–77. Englewood, NJ: Antakya Press, 1995.

———. "The Arabic-Language Press." In *The Ethnic Press in the United States: A Historical Analysis and Handbook,* edited by Sally Miller, 1–14. New York: Greenwood Press, 1987.

———. "Arabs." In *Harvard Encyclopedia of American Ethnic Groups,* edited by Stephen Thernstrom. Cambridge, MA: Belknap Press, 1980.

———. "Arabs in America: A Historical Overview." In *Arabs in the New World: Studies on Arab-American Communities,* edited by Sameer Abraham and Nabeel Abraham, 8–29. Detroit: Wayne State University, Center for Urban Studies, 1983.

———. *Becoming American: The Early Arab Immigrant Experience.* Carbondale: Southern Illinois Press, 1985.

———. "New York: The Mother Colony." In *A Community of Many Worlds: Arab Americans in New York City,* ed. Kathleen Benson and Philip M. Kayal, 3–10. New York: Museum of the City of New York, 2002.

———. "The Social History of Zahle, the Principal Market Town in Nineteenth-Century Lebanon." PhD diss., University of California, Los Angeles, 1972.

Najmabadi, Afsaneh. "Crafting an Educated Housewife in Iran." In *Remaking Women: Feminism and Modernity in the Middle East,* edited by Lila Abu-Lughod, 91–125. Princeton: Princeton University Press, 1998.

Ngai, Mae M. "The Architecture of Race in American Immigration Law: A Reexamination of the Reed Johnson Act of 1924." *Journal of American History* 86, no. 1 (1999): 67–92.

———. *Impossible Subjects: Illegal Aliens and the Making of Modern America.* Princeton: Princeton University Press, 2004.

———. "Response to Presidential Address." *American Quarterly* 57, no. 1 (2005): 59–65.

Norton, Anne. "Gender, Sexuality and the Iraq of Our Imagination." *Middle East Report*, no. 173 (November/December 1991): 26–28.

Nuʿayma, Mikhaʾil. *Jubran Khalil Jubran*. Beirut: Muʾassasat Nawfal, 1974.

———. *Sabʿun*. Vol. 1. *1889–1911*. Beirut: Dar Bayrut lil-tibaʿa wal-nashr, 1959.

Omi, Michael, and Howard Winant. *Racial Formation in the United States: From the 1960s to the 1990s*. 2nd ed. New York: Routledge, 1994.

Orfalea, Gregory. *The Arab Americans: A History*. Northhampton, MA: Olive Branch Press, 2006.

———. *Before the Flames: A Quest for the History of Arab Americans*. Austin: University of Texas Press, 1988.

Orsi, Robert. "The Religious Boundaries of Inbetween People: Street *Feste* and the Problem of the Dark-Skinned Other in Italian Harlem, 1920–1990." *American Quarterly* 44 (September 1992): 313–47.

Ortiz, Paul. *Emancipation Betrayed: The Hidden History of Black Organizing and White Violence in Florida*. Berkeley: University of California Press, 2005.

Oschinsky, Lawrence. "Islam in Chicago: Being a Study of the Acculturation of Muslim Palestinian Community in That City." MA thesis, University of Chicago, 1947.

Otto, Annie Salem, ed. *The Letters of Kahlil Gibran and Mary Haskell*. Houston: Smith, 1970.

Owen, Roger. "Lebanese Migration in the Context of World Population Movements." In *The Lebanese in the World: A Century of Emigration*, edited by Albert Hourani and Nadim Shehadi, 33–39. London: Centre for Lebanese Studies, 1992.

———. "The Middle East in the Eighteenth Century—An 'Islamic' Society in Decline? A Critique of Gibb and Bowen's Islamic Society in the West." *Review of Middle East Studies* 1 (1975): 101–12.

———. *The Middle East in the World Economy, 1800–1914*. Rev. ed. London: I. B. Tauris, 1993.

Pascual, Jean-Paul. "La Syrie à l'époque ottomane." In *La Syrie d'aujourd'hui*, edited by André Raymond, 31–53. Paris: CERMOC, 1980.

Patterson, Orlando. *Rituals of Blood: Consequences of Slavery in Two American Centuries*. Washington, DC: Civitas Counterpoint, 1998.

Philipp, Thomas. *The Syrians in Egypt, 1725–1975*. Stuttgart: Franz Steiner, 1985.

Pinson, Mark. "Ottoman Colonization of the Circassians in Rumili after the Crimean War." *Études balkaniques* 8, no. 3 (1972): 71–85.

Portes, Alejandro, Luis E. Guarnizo, and Patricia Landolt. "The Study of Transnationalism: Pitfalls and Promise of an Emergent Field." *Ethnic and Racial Studies* 22 (March 1999): 217–37.

al-Qazzaz, Ayad. "Images of the Arab in American Social Science Textbooks." In *Arabs in America: Myths and Realities*, edited by Baha Abu-Laban and Faith Zeadey, 113–32. AAUG Monograph Series, no. 5. Wilmette, IL: Medina University Press International, 1975.

Quataert, Donald. "Ottoman Women, Households, and Textile Manufacturing, 1800–1914." In *The Modern Middle East: A Reader*, edited by Albert

Hourani, Philip S. Khoury, and Mary C. Wilson, 161–76. Berkeley: University of California Press, 1993.

Raper, Arthur F. *The Tragedy of Lynching*. Chapel Hill: University of North Carolina Press, 1933.

Rashid, Marilyn. "What's Not in a Name." In *Food for Our Grandmothers: Writings by Arab-American and Arab-Canadian Feminists,* edited by Joanna Kadi, 197–203. Boston: South End Press, 1994.

Reed, Ueda. "Naturalization and Citizenship." In *Harvard Encyclopedia of American Ethnic Groups,* edited by Stephen Thernstrom. Cambridge, MA: Belknap Press, 1980.

Roediger, David. *Colored White: Transcending the Racial Past*. Berkeley: University of California Press, 2002.

———. *The Wages of Whiteness: Race and the Making of the American Working Class*. London: Verso, 1991.

———. "Whiteness and Ethnicity in the History of 'White Ethnics' in the United States." Chapter 11 in *Towards the Abolition of Whiteness: Essays on Race, Politics, and Working Class History*. London: Verso, 1994.

Roediger, David, with James R. Barrett. "Inbetween Peoples: Race, Nationality, and the 'New Immigrant' Working Class." *Journal of American Ethnic History* 16.3 (Spring/1997): 1–44. Chapter 9 in *Colored White: Transcending the Racial Past,* by David Roediger. Berkeley: University of California Press, 2002.

Roper, Michael, and John Tosh, eds. *Manful Assertions: Masculinities in Britain since 1800*. London: Routledge, 1991.

Ruppin, A. "Migration from and to Syria, 1860–1914." Chapter 6 in *The Economic History of the Middle East, 1800–1914: A Book of Readings,* edited by Charles Issawi. Chicago: University of Chicago Press, 1966.

Safa, Elie. *L'émigration libanaise*. Beirut: Université Saint-Joseph, 1960.

Safady, Wadih. *Cenas e cenários dos caminhos de minha vida*. Vol. 1. São Paulo: Penna Editora, 1966.

Said, Edward W. *Covering Islam: How the Media and Experts Determine How We See the Rest of the World*. New York: Pantheon Books, 1981.

———. *Orientalism*. New York: Vintage Books, 19791978.

———. "Orientalism and the October War: The Shattered Myths." In *Arabs in America: Myths and Realities,* edited by Baha Abu-Laban and Faith Zeadey, 83–112. AAUG Monograph Series, no. 5. Wilmette, IL: Medina University Press International, 1975.

———. *The Question of Palestine*. New York: Times Books, 1979.

Saliba, Najib E. *Emigration from Syria and the Syrian-Lebanese Community of Worchester, MA*. Ligonier, PA: Antakya Press, 1992.

Saliba, Therese. "Resisting Invisibility: Arab Americans in Academia and Activism." In *Arabs in America: Building a New Future,* edited by Michael Suleiman, 304–19. Philadelphia: Temple University Press, 1999.

Salibi, Kamal. *A House of Many Mansions: The History of Lebanon Reconsidered*. Berkeley: University of California Press, 1988.

Samhan, Helen Hatab. "Not Quite White: Racial Classification and the Arab-American Experience." In *Arabs in America: Building a New Future,* edited by Michael Suleiman, 209–26. Philadelphia: Temple University Press.

Sánchez, George. *Becoming Mexican American: Ethnicity, Culture and Identity in Chicano Los Angeles, 1900–1945*. New York: Oxford University Press, 1993.

al-Sarraj, Nadra Jamil. *Shuʿaraʾ al-rabita al-qalamiyya* [Poets of the Pen League]. Cairo: Dar al-maʿarif, 1989.

Sayad, Abdelmalek. *L'immigration ou les paradoxes de l'altérité*. Paris: Éditions universitaires, 1991.

Saydah, Jurj. *Adabuna wa udabaʾuna fil-mahajir al-amirkiyya* [Our Literature and Writers in the American Diaspora]. 3rd ed. Beirut: Dar al-ʿilm lil-malayin, 1964.

Scarpaci, Vincenza. "Walking the Color Line: Italian Immigrants in Rural Louisiana, 1880–1910." In *Are Italians White? How Race Is Made in America*, ed. Jennifer Guglielmo and Salvatore Salerno, 60–76. New York: Routledge, 2003.

Schilcher, Linda Schatkowski. "The Famine of 1915–1918 in Greater Syria." In *Problems of the Modern Middle East in Historical Perspective*, edited by John Spagnolo, 229–58. Reading, MA: Ithaca Press, 1992.

———. "The Hauran Conflicts of the 1860s: A Chapter in the Rural History of Modern Syria." *International Journal of Middle East Studies* 13 (1981): 159–79.

Scott, Joan. " 'L'ouvrière! Mot impie, sordide . . .': Women Workers in the Discourse of French Political Economy, 1840–1860." Chapter 7 in *Gender and the Politics of History*. New York: Columbia University Press, 1988.

Seikaly, Samir. "Shukri al-ʿAsali: A Case Study of a Political Activist." In *The Origins of Arab Nationalism*, edited by Rashid Khalidi, Lisa Anderson, Muhammad Muslih, and Reeva S. Simon, 73–96. New York: Columbia University Press, 1991.

Senechal de la Roche, Roberta. "The Sociogenesis of Lynching." In *Under Sentence of Death: Lynching in the South*, ed. W. Fitzhugh Brundage, 48–76. Durham: University of North Carolina Press, 1997.

Shah, Nayan. *Contagious Divides: Epidemics and Race in San Francisco's Chinatown*. Berkeley: University of California Press, 2001.

Shaheen, Jack. *Reel Bad Arabs: How Hollywood Vilifies a People*. New York: Olive Branch Press, 2001.

———. *The TV Arab*. Bowling Green: Bowling Green State University Popular Press, 1984.

Shakir, Evelyn. *Bint Arab: Arab and Arab American Women in the United States*. Westport, CT: Praeger, 1997.

Shaw, Stanford. "Ottoman Census System, 1831–1914." *International Journal of Middle East Studies* 9 (1978): 325–38.

Shenton, James P., and Kevin Kenny. *Ethnicity and Immigration*. Rev. ed. Washington, DC: American Historical Association, 1997.

Shepherd, Naomi. *The Zealous Intruders: The Western Rediscovery of Palestine*. San Francisco: Harper and Row, 1987.

Sherman, William. *Prairie Peddlers: The Syrian-Lebanese in North Dakota*. Bismarck: University of Mary Press, 2002.

Simons, G. L. *Imposing Sanctions: Legal Remedy or Genocidal Tool?* London: Pluto Press, 1999.

Singh, Nikhil Pal. *Black Is a Country: Race and the Unfinished Struggle for Democracy.* Cambridge, MA: Harvard University Press, 2004.

Stathakis, Paula Maria. "Almost White: Greek and Lebanese-Syrian Immigrants in North and South Carolina, 1900–1940." PhD diss., University of South Carolina, 1996.

Stein, Kenneth. *The Land Question in Palestine, 1917–1939.* Chapel Hill: University of North Carolina Press, 1984.

Stockton, Ronald. "Ethnic Archetypes and the Arab Image." In *The Development of Arab-American Identity,* edited by Ernest McCarus, 119–54. Ann Arbor: University of Michigan Press, 1994.

Suleiman, Michael W. "The Arab American Left." In *The Immigrant Left in the United States,* edited by Paul Buhle and Dan Georgakas, 233–55. Albany: State University of New York Press, 1996.

———. "Arab-Americans and the Political Process." In *The Development of Arab-American Identity,* edited by Ernest McCarus, 37–60. Ann Arbor: University of Michigan Press, 1997.

———. "The Arab Community in the United States: A Comparison of Lebanese and Non-Lebanese," in *The Lebanese in the World,* edited by Albert Hourani and Nadim Shehadi, 189–207. London: Centre for Lebanese Studies, 1992.

———, ed. *Arabs in America: Building a New Future.* Philadelphia: Temple University Press, 1999.

———. *The Arabs in the Mind of America.* Brattleboro, VT: Amana Press, 1988.

———. "Early Arab-Americans: The Search for Identity." In *Crossing the Waters: Arabic-Speaking Immigrants to the United States before 1940,* edited by Eric J. Hooglund, 37–54. Washington, DC: Smithsonian Institution Press, 1987.

———. "Impressions of New York City by Early Arab Immigrants." Unpublished manuscript, n.d.

———. Introduction to *Arabs in America: Building a New Future.* Philadelphia: Temple University Press, 1999.

———. "The Mokarzels' Contributions to the Arabic-Speaking Community in the United States." *Arab Studies Quarterly* 21 (Spring 1999): 71–88.

———. "The New Arab-American Community." In *The Arab-Americans: Studies in Assimilation,* edited by Elaine C. Hagopian and Ann Paden, 37–49. AAUG Monograph Series, no. 1. Wilmette, IL: Medina University Press International, 1969.

———. "Perceptions of the Middle East in American Newsmagazines." In *Arabs in America: Myths and Realities,* edited by Baha Abu-Laban and Faith Zeadey, 28–44. AAUG Monograph Series, no. 5. Wilmette, IL: Medina University Press International, 1975.

Takaki, Ronald. *A Different Mirror: A History of Multicultural America.* Boston: Little, Brown, 1993.

Tamari, Steve. "The Arabs of Haiti: Arab Roots in a Caribbean Society." Published in Arabic in *al-Hayat,* March 30, 1996, 22.

Tannous, Afif I. "Emigration, a Force of Social Change in an Arab Village." *Rural Sociology* 7, no. 1 (1942): 62–74.

———. "Social Change in an Arab Village." *American Sociological Review* 6, no. 5 (1941): 650–62.

Tarabein, Ahmed. "'Abd al-Hamid Al-Zahrawi: The Career and Thought of an Arab Nationalist." In *The Origins of Arab Nationalism,* edited by Rashid Khalidi, Lisa Anderson, Muhammad Muslih, and Reeva S. Simon, 97–119. New York: Columbia University Press, 1991.

Tarazi, Philip de. *Tarikh al-sihafa al-'arabiyya* [History of the Arab Press]. 2 vols. Beirut: Dar Sadr, [1913].

al-Tahir, Jalil. "The Arab Community in the Chicago Area: A Comparative Study of the Christian-Syrians and the Muslim-Palestinians." PhD diss., University of Chicago, 1952.

Tashjian, James H. *The Armenians of the United States and Canada.* Boston: Hairenik Press, 1947.

Tauber, Eliezer. *The Arab Movements in World War I.* London: Frank Cass, 1993.

———. *The Emergence of the Arab Movements.* London: Frank Cass, 1993.

Tebeau, Charlton W. *A History of Florida.* Coral Gables: University of Miami Press, 1971.

Tehranian, John. "Performing Whiteness: Naturalization Litigation and the Construction of Racial Identity in America." *Yale Law Journal* 109 (January 2000): 817–48.

Terry, Janice J. "Community and Political Activism among Arab Americans in Detroit." In *Arabs in America: Building a New Future,* edited by Michael Suleiman, 241–54. Philadelphia: Temple University Press, 1999.

———. *Mistaken Identity: Arab Stereotypes in Popular Writing.* Washington, DC: American-Arab Affairs Council, 1985.

Thernstrom, Stephen, ed. *Harvard Encyclopedia of American Ethnic Groups.* Cambridge, MA: Belknap Press, 1980.

Thompson, Elizabeth. *Colonial Citizens: Republican Rights, Paternal Privilege, and Gender in French Syria and Lebanon.* New York: Columbia University Press, 2000.

Tibawi, A. L. *American Interests in Syria, 1800–1901: A Study of Educational, Literary and Religious Work.* Oxford: Clarendon Press, 1966.

———. *A Modern History of Syria.* London: Macmillan, 1969.

Tibi, Bassam. *Arab Nationalism: A Critical Enquiry.* Translated by Marion Farouk Sluglett and Peter Sluglett. New York: St. Martin's Press, 1971.

Tignor, Robert L. Introduction to *Napoleon in Egypt: Al-Jabarti's Chronicle of the First Seven Months of the French Occupation of Egypt, 1798.* Translated by Shmuel Moreh. Princeton, NJ: Markus Wiener, 1993.

Toledano, Ehud. *The Ottoman Slave Trade and Its Suppression, 1840–1890.* Princeton: Princeton University Press, 1982.

Truzzi, Oswaldo. *Patrícios: Sírios e libaneses em São Paulo.* São Paulo: Editora Hucitec, 1997.

———. "The Right Place at the Right Time: Syrians and Lebanese in Brazil and the United States, a Comparative Approach." *Journal of American Ethnic History* 16, no. 2 (1997): 1–34.

Tu'ama, Jurj. *Al-Mughtaribun al-'arab fi amrika al-shamaliyya* [Arab Emigrants in North America]. Damascus: Wizarat al-thaqafa wal-irshad al-qawmi, 1965.

Ueda, Reed. "Naturalization and Citizenship." In *Harvard Encyclopedia of American Ethnic Groups,* edited by Stephen Thernstrom. Cambridge, MA: Belknap Press, 1980.

van der Veer, Peter. Introduction to *Nation and Migration: The Politics of Space in the South Asian Diaspora.* Philadelphia: University of Pennsylvania Press, 1995.

Vecoli, Rudolph. "Problems in Comparative Studies of International Emigrant Communities." In *The Lebanese in the World: A Century of Immigration,* edited by Albert Hourani and Nadim Shehadi, 717–24. London: Centre for Lebanese Studies, 1992.

Velcamp, Theresa Alfaro. *So Far from Allah, So Close to Mexico: Middle Eastern Immigrants in Modern Mexico.* Austin: University of Texas Press, 2008.

Waldrep, Christopher. "Word and Deed: The Language of Lynching, 1820–1953." In *Lethal Imagination: Violence and Brutality in American History,* edited by Michael A. Bellesiles, 229–60. New York: New York University Press, 1999.

Watenpaugh, Keith David. *Being Modern in the Middle East: Revolution, Nationalism, Colonialism, and the Arab Middle Class.* Princeton: Princeton University Press, 2006.

Weisbord, Robert G., and Richard Kazarian Jr. *Israel in the Black American Perspective.* Westport, CT: Greenwood Press, 1985.

Wikan, Unni. *Behind the Veil in Arabia: Women in Oman.* Chicago: University of Chicago Press, 1991.

Winant, Howard. *Racial Conditions: Politics, Theory, Comparisons.* Minneapolis: University of Minnesota Press, 1994.

Yans-McLaughlin, Virginia. *Family and Community: Italian Immigrants in Buffalo, 1880–1930.* Ithaca: Cornell University Press, 1971.

———, ed. *Immigration Reconsidered: History, Sociology, and Politics.* New York: Oxford University Press, 1990.

Younis, Adele. *The Coming of the Arabic-Speaking People to the United States.* Edited by Philip M. Kayal. Staten Island, NY: Center for Migration Studies, 1995.

Zakariya, Ahmad Wasfi. *Al-Rif al-suriy* [The Syrian Countryside]. Damascus: Matbaʿ dar al-bayan, 1955.

Zangrando, Robert L. *The NAACP Crusade against Lynching, 1909–1950.* Philadelphia: Temple University Press, 1980.

Zeine, Zeine N. *Arab-Turkish Relations and the Emergence of Arab Nationalism.* Beirut: Khayat's, 1958.

Ziadeh, Ferhat. "Winds Blow Where Ships Do Not Wish to Go." Chapter 10 in *Paths to the Middle East: Ten Scholars Look Back,* edited by Thomas Naff. Albany: State University of New York Press, 1993.

al-Zirikli, Khayr al-Din. *Al-Aʿlam* [Eminent Personalities: A Biographical Dictionary]. Beirut: Dar al-ʿilm lil-malayin, 1995.

Zogby, James, ed. *Taking Root, Bearing Fruit: The Arab-American Experience.* Washington, DC: American-Arab Anti-Discrimination Committee, 1984.

Zolberg, Aristide R. *A Nation by Design: Immigration Policy in the Fashioning of America.* Cambridge, MA: Harvard University Press, 2006.

Index

Italicized page numbers refer to illustrations.

Text:	10/13 Sabon
Display:	Sabon
Compositor:	Binghamton Valley Composition, LLC
Indexer:	Sharon Sweeney
Printer and Binder:	Maple-Vail Book Manufacturing Group

AMERICAN CROSSROADS

Edited by Earl Lewis, George Lipsitz, Peggy Pascoe, George Sánchez, and Dana Takagi